Patrick Connor's War

THE 1865 POWDER RIVER INDIAN EXPEDITION

by
DAVID E. WAGNER

Brevet Maj. Gen. Patrick Edward Connor.
Courtesy of the Wyoming State Archives,
Department of State Parks and Cultural Resources.

Patrick Connor's War

THE 1865 POWDER RIVER INDIAN EXPEDITION

by
DAVID E. WAGNER

University of Oklahoma Press : Norman

Also by David E. Wagner

Powder River Odyssey: Nelson Cole's Western Campaign of 1865—The Journals of Lyman G. Bennett and Other Eyewitness Accounts (Norman, Oklahoma, 2009)

Library of Congress Cataloging-in-Publication Data

Wagner, David E., 1939–2009
Patrick Connor's war : the 1865 Powder River Indian Expedition /
by David E. Wagner.
p. cm.
Includes bibliographical references and index.
ISBN 978-0-8061-9217-8 (paper)
1. Powder River Expedition, 1865.
2. Connor, P.E. (Patrick Edward), 1820–1891.
3. Powder River Expedition, 1865—Personal narratives. I. Title.
E83.86.W33   2010
973.8' I—dc22

Copyright ©2010 by the University of Oklahoma Press, Norman, Publishing Division of the University. Originally published in hardcover in the Frontier Military Series by the Arthur H. Clark Company, Spokane, Washington. Paperback published 2023 by the University of Oklahoma Press, Norman, Publishing Division of the University. Manufactured in the U.S.A.

The paper in this book meets the guidelines for permanence and durability of the Committee on Production Guidelines for Book Longevity of the Council on Library Resources, Inc. ∞

Dedicated to Bob McCurdy
Powder River historian

CONTENTS

Illustrations

MAPS

Acknowledgments

I would like to thank the following individuals for their assistance and support in assembling and writing *Patrick Connor's War*: Bob Snelson of Canon City, Colorado, for his help in gathering B. F. Rockafellow material; Sandra Lowry of Fort Laramie National Historic Site, who is always helpful in providing information; Randy Brown of Douglas, Wyoming, for his expertise on the Oregon Trail; John McDermott of Rapid City, South Dakota, for suggesting additional sources; and Ron Tillotson of Hardin, Illinois, for information on his great-great-grandfather, Charles L. Thomas. In an undertaking of this size, many people helped, and I apologize in advance for any names omitted.

Others assisted me during the various stages of researching. The staffs at the Bentley Library at the University of Michigan; the K. Ross Toole Archives at the University of Montana; the Nebraska State Historical Society; the Iowa State Historical Society; the Bienecke Rare Book and Manuscript Library at Yale University; the Stephen H. Hart Library at the Colorado Historical Society; the Denver Public Library; the Pearl Street Research Center at the Sioux City Public Museum; the Wyoming State Archives; and the Harold B. Lee Library, L. Tom Perry Special Collections, at Brigham Young University were all especially helpful and prompt in providing material.

My exploring partners and sounding boards were John Billow of Crest Hill, Illinois; Mike Charnota of Chicago, Illinois; and Phil Parthamer of Vancouver, Washington.

The members of Bearlodge Writers of Sundance, Wyoming—a writing and critique group—were extremely helpful and supportive as they listened to my chapters over the past several years. My narratives always came out stronger after their assessment. Any errors in the text are mine and mine alone.

Introduction

The Indian war on the northern plains of 1865 is often overshadowed by other events of the time—the climactic end of the War between the States, the assassination of President Abraham Lincoln, the jubilation of volunteers returning from a long war, and the beginning of the healing process in reconstructing the South. During this period the first major campaign of what would become known as the post–Civil War Indian wars took place in near invisibility.

Gen. George Armstrong Custer, a national wartime hero, had yet to set foot on the western plains and earn his reputation as a premier Indian fighter. An obscure Californian, Brig. Gen. Patrick Edward Connor, had gained a regional reputation as a man to be reckoned with in Indian warfare. While in command of the Military District of Utah in 1863, he led his men in a ruthless attack on a Shoshone village in retaliation for depredations committed by the tribesmen along the Overland Trail in his district. His section of the commercial road then remained quiet, and his accomplishment was duly noted by fellow westerners along the route to the east.

The story of Patrick Connor's war—better recognized as the Powder River Indian Expedition—is not well known and has not been written of in any detail to date. In 1961 LeRoy Hafen and Ann Hafen's *Powder River Campaigns and Sawyers Expedition of 1865* was published. This fine book contains military reports, diary accounts, and reminiscences of the campaign and is a mandatory reference when studying this operation. Other than this work, a chapter or two here, a page or a paragraph there, is all the coverage that this fascinating campaign has garnered over the years. Several biographies of Connor have been written, with Brigham D. Madsen's *Glory Hunter,* James F. Varley's *Brigham and the Briga-*

dier, and Fred B. Roger's *Soldiers of the Overland* standing out. But the campaign itself is covered only minimally in one or two chapters. John McDermott's fine work *Circle of Fire* is an overview of the 1865 Indian war that focuses a larger scope of events.

The author's intent is to bring the Powder River Indian Expedition to life by using eyewitness accounts of men who participated in the events of the summer of 1865. The expedition itself is covered in a day-by-day chronology of events, telling the story by using quotes from those who were there.

Three separate columns of this expedition marched on the northern plains in 1865. *Patrick Connor's War* focuses on the western column, led personally by Connor, and integrates the other two columns into the story when necessary. For full details of the eastern and center commands, the reader should refer to the author's earlier work, *Powder River Odyssey.*

Also included in the story is a detailed account of the civilian road-building expedition of James Alexander Sawyers, whose fate became interwoven with the Powder River Indian Expedition that summer. Usually treated as separate events, the two were inseparable by autumn of 1865.

The planners of the Powder River Indian Expedition of 1865 had high expectations of taming the northern plains with an organized campaign to subdue and punish the warring tribes quickly, and to pave the way for an orderly post–Civil War settlement of the West. But, alas, things do not always turn out as planned.

THE MAJOR PLAYERS

Original Planners of the Powder River Indian Expedition

Maj. Gen. John Pope,
Commander of the Military Division of the Missouri

A career military man, twenty-year-old John Pope graduated from West Point in 1842. A decorated veteran of the Mexican War, Pope held various duty assignments in the West during the 1850s. He entered the Civil War as a brigadier general in command of the District of Northern Missouri. Promoted to major general after several successful conflicts in the West, Pope transferred to the eastern theatre. His Army of Virginia fought a battle that became known as the Second Manassas, or Second Bull Run, against Robert E. Lee's army. Soundly defeated, Pope's army withdrew to Washington. He requested reassignment and moved on to command the Department of the Northwest. He proved to be successful in containing the Minnesota Sioux uprising of 1862. In early 1865 Pope transferred to the Division of the Missouri command.[1]

Maj. Gen. Grenville Mellen Dodge,
Commander of the Military Department of the Missouri

At nineteen years of age Dodge graduated from the Partridge Military Academy in Vermont in 1850. He moved to Iowa in the early 1850s and worked as a civil engineer in railroad construction. When the Civil War broke out, he accepted a commission as colonel of an Iowa regiment. Promoted to brigadier general of the volunteers in March 1862, Dodge distinguished himself during the battles for Vicksburg, and Gen. Ulysses S. Grant recommended him for promotion. In the Atlanta campaign, as a major general, he led the Sixteenth Corps under Gen. William T. Sherman. He was seriously wounded in August 1864 and, after a lengthy recuperation, Dodge took over command of the Department of the Missouri in December 1864.[2]

Military Officers and Men with Connor's Western Column

Brig. Gen. Patrick Edward Connor,
Commander of the Military District of the Plains

Connor, an Irish immigrant and a veteran of the Mexican War, moved to California in 1850. He settled in Stockton, California, successfully engaging in the road-building and construction business. In 1854 he married Johanna Connor (same last name, but unrelated) of Redwood City.

Prior to the outbreak of the Civil War, Connor had actively involved himself in the local and state militias. The forty-one-year-old volunteered for service in the Union Army in August 1861 and accepted a commission as colonel of the Third California Volunteer Infantry. Assigned to serve as commander of the District of Utah, Connor's respon-

---

[1] *American Civil War Research Database.*
[2] Ibid.

sibilities included keeping transportation and communications open on the Overland Road from California to Fort Laramie. He gained a promotion to the rank of brigadier general in 1863 after a successful attack on a Shoshone village at Bear River in Idaho Territory.[3]

Col. James Harvey Kidd,
Regimental Commander of the Sixth Michigan Volunteer Cavalry

From Ionia, Michigan, Kidd enlisted in 1862 as a captain in the Sixth Michigan Cavalry. The Sixth fought in Custer's famed Michigan Brigade in the East, gaining many honors and much recognition. By May 1864 Kidd, at twenty-four years of age, had risen to the rank of colonel and commanded the regiment.[4]

Capt. Benjamin Franklin Rockafellow,
Commander of M Company, Sixth Michigan Volunteer Cavalry

Born in New York State in 1835, Rockafellow moved with his family to Lyons, Michigan, in 1855. Rockafellow joined the Sixth Michigan Cavalry in October 1863 at Grand Rapids. Originally entering the service as a second lieutenant, he gained promotion to captain in March 1864.[5] Rockafellow was seriously wounded at the Battle of the Wilderness but recovered and rejoined his regiment before the war's end.[6]

Capt. Henry Emerson Palmer,
Commander of A Company, Eleventh Kansas Volunteer Cavalry

When the Civil War broke out, Palmer was toiling in Colorado as one of a company of twenty-four gold seekers. Twenty-three of the group left to join the Confederate Army, leaving Palmer as the lone Union man.[7] Twenty-one years old at the time, he enlisted at Fort Leavenworth, joining the Eleventh Kansas in March 1861. His regiment fought against William Clarke Quantrill's raiders in Missouri prior to his assignment at the Platte Bridge Station in early 1865.[8]

---

[3]Madsen, *Glory Hunter*, 175–77.
[4]Wittenberg, *One of Custer's Wolverines.* 8–9, 75–76.
[5]Hafen and Hafen, *Powder River Campaigns*, 152n1.
[6]*A Walk into the Past: A Tour of the Greenwood Cemetery*, 27.
[7]*Omaha Daily News*, 3 April 1911.
[8]Hafen and Hafen, *Powder River Campaigns*, 103n1.

Cpl. Charles Lawrence Thomas,
E Company, Eleventh Ohio Volunteer Cavalry
Thomas left his home at Boudes Ferry Landing, Ohio, to enlist in the Eleventh Ohio Cavalry in June 1863. Then a twenty-year-old private, he served in the West along the Overland Road for the duration of the war. Thomas earned a promotion to corporal in February 1864.[9]

Sgt. Lewis Byram Hull,
K Company, Eleventh Ohio Volunteer Cavalry
At nineteen years of age Hull left college and enlisted in the Sixtieth Ohio Infantry in November 1861. His regiment surrendered to Thomas Jonathan "Stonewall" Jackson at Harpers Ferry, Virginia, in September 1862. Paroled back to the Union Army with the agreement not to take part again in the war against Confederate troops, Hull subsequently reenlisted in the Eleventh Ohio in February 1864. Hull served in the West with that regiment for the remainder of his enlistment, earning a promotion to sergeant.[10]

Pvt. Charles W. Adams,
K Company, Eleventh Ohio Volunteer Cavalry
Adams joined the Union Army as a twenty-four-year-old private in February 1864. He spent his enlistment serving in the West with the Eleventh Ohio.[11]

Pvt. Adoniram J. Shotwell,
K Company, Eleventh Ohio Volunteer Cavalry
The twenty-eight-year-old Shotwell joined the Eleventh Ohio a few weeks after Charles Adams and spent his military time guarding the Overland Road prior to the Powder River Expedition.[12]

Pvt. Sheldon L. Wight,
F Company, Sixth Michigan Cavalry
Sheldon and his older brother, Francis, left their father's farm in Benton Township, Eaton County, Michigan, to enlist in the Union Army on

[9]Tillotson, "Prominent Events in the Life of Charles Lawrence Thomas."
[10]Hull, "Soldiering on the High Plains," 41n1.
[11]American Civil War Research Database.
[12]Ibid.

22 December 1863. Only sixteen years old at the time, Sheldon's induction papers listed his age as eighteen. Wight served with honor in the Sixth Michigan through the end of the war and traveled west with his regiment at the war's conclusion.[13]

Civilians with Connor

Miller,
name used to identify an anonymous civilian diarist

A diary describing events of the Powder River Indian Expedition of 1865 turned up in the papers of Lyman Gibson Bennett after his 1904 death in Springfield, Missouri. Bennett had served as a civilian engineer with Col. Nelson D. Cole in the Eastern Division of that expedition. For many years Bennett's descendants presumed it to be a diary kept by Lyman Bennett. The discovery in 1988 of Bennett's real diary covering the same time frame made it clear that the first diary belonged to a person who had traveled a different route and had different experiences. How long Bennett had this diary in his hands is a matter of speculation. He may have been handed the diary at the end of the campaign to enable him to map the route of the diarist as part of his official duties, or he may have acquired the diary later for unspecified reasons.

In Bennett's real diary entries of 3 and 6 July, he wrote of Mr. Miller, whom he expected to join him en route as his assistant on the expedition. No mention is made of Miller again until 25 September, at the end of the expedition at Fort Connor, when he wrote of meeting Miller, who had arrived with Connor's western command: "Saw Miller and had a good time. Learned that he had been most shabbily treated by Stonebruner. He expressed many regrets that he did not go with me."[14]

Although only speculation, the author believes that Miller may have written the anonymous diary. Chosen to be Bennett's assistant, the mysterious Mr. Miller most likely had a mapmaking or engineering background similar to Bennett's, and his style of describing the landscape traveled and recording mileage also bears a resemblance to Bennett's. The anonymous diarist wrote descriptions of getting the train through difficult geography, much like someone who worked with the pioneers

---

[13] Geyer, *Sheldon L. Wight*, 45–50.
[14] Lyman G. Bennett diary, 4 July 1865 entry.

assigned to road building and bridging rough terrain. For the sake of simplicity in this manuscript, all entries from the anonymous diary will be credited to "Miller."

A. C. Leighton,
sutler with the Powder River Indian Expedition
A well-to-do storekeeper from Ottumwa, Iowa, Leighton received the appointment from General Connor as sutler for the upcoming expedition.[15]

Finn Burnett,
assistant to A. C. Leighton
In October 1864 the then-twenty-year-old Burnett left his Missouri home to avoid conscription into the Union Army. Hired by Leighton several months later in Omaha, Burnett went to work for him as a muleskinner.[16]

Men with the Eastern Column

Col. Nelson D. Cole,
Regimental Commander of the Second Missouri
Volunteer Light Artillery
Cole, a St. Louis businessman, recruited a volunteer company in early 1861 and entered the Union Army in April as a captain. Twenty-eight years old at the time, he saw considerable action in Missouri and suffered a wound at the Battle of Wilson's Creek. He rose in rank to command an artillery regiment and took part in the Vicksburg campaign of 1863. At the end of the war, Cole and his Second Missouri Light Artillery were converted to cavalry and sent to Omaha to be part of Connor's upcoming expedition to the plains.[17]

Lyman Gibson Bennett,
civilian chief engineer of the Eastern Division of the expedition
Bennett enlisted at Oswego, Illinois, in August 1861, joining E Company of the Thirty-sixth Illinois Infantry. The twenty-nine-year-old had

---

[15] David, *Finn Burnett,* 30–31.
[16] Ibid., 20–21.
[17] Hyde and Conrad, *Encyclopedia of the History of St. Louis,* 420.

a background in surveying and mapmaking, those talents that kept him on detached duty. He rejoined his regiment to fight in the Battle of Pea Ridge in March 1862. In 1863 Bennett accepted a commission as a major in the Fourth Arkansas Cavalry (U.S.). He resigned and left the service in August 1864. Bennett then went to work for the army as a civilian engineer, primarily in the West along the Overland Trail. In late June he accepted an assignment to proceed to Omaha to be the chief engineer of Cole's upcoming expedition.[18]

Men with the Sawyers Expedition

James Alexander Sawyers,
superintendent of the government-funded road-building expedition
originating in Sioux City, Iowa
A veteran of the Mexican War, Sawyers moved to Sioux City, Iowa, in 1857 and gained success as a merchant. In 1861 he helped raise a cavalry regiment. Sawyers then enlisted in the Northern Border Brigade of the Iowa Militia and supervised the building of a chain of forts in the state in 1862. Promoted to lieutenant colonel in 1862, he subsequently resigned from the military in 1864, returning to civilian business pursuits in Sioux City.[19]

Lewis H. Smith,
chief engineer for the Sawyers Expedition
Smith came to Iowa in 1854 with a background in civil engineering. With his brother, he started a mercantile business the following year. In 1857 Smith served as a county judge. He enlisted in the Iowa Border Brigade as quartermaster in 1862. The thirty-year-old Smith joined James Sawyers's road-building and surveying expedition in 1865 as chief engineer.[20]

Corwin M. Lee,
teamster or bull-whacker with Sawyers
In 1860 Lee was living in Sioux City, working as a gunsmith. He enlisted in the Sioux City Cavalry in 1861, then transferred to the Seventh

---

[18]John F. Bradbury, "L.G. Bennett Information Sheet" (unpublished), File R274, Western History Manuscript Collection, University of Missouri–Rolla.
[19]Doyle, *Journeys to the Land of Gold*, 355–56.
[20]Ibid., 371–72.

Iowa Cavalry in 1863. At the end of his enlistment in November 1864 Lee mustered out of the service at Sioux City. The twenty-one-year-old then joined Sawyers for the expedition to Virginia City, Montana Territory, in the spring of 1865.[21]

Albert M. Holman,
teamster

In the early 1860s Holman worked at the *Western Independent,* a newspaper published in his hometown of Sergeant Bluff, Iowa. When the paper moved to Sioux City and became the *Sioux City Register,* Holman went with it. Twenty years old in the spring of 1865, Albert Holman decided to visit the goldfields of Montana and signed up with Sawyers's expedition.[22]

Edward H. Edwards,
emigrant from Iowa traveling with Sawyers to Montana

Edwards lived in Sioux City, Iowa, and in the spring of 1865 set out to seek his fortune in the Montana goldfields, along with his close friend, Samuel H. Cassady. The two bachelors joined Sawyers's train for the journey.[23]

Pvt. John Colby Griggs,
D Company, Fifth United States Volunteers,
on escort duty with the Sawyers Expedition

Originally from Missouri, Griggs joined the Confederate Army in May 1861. Wounded and taken prisoner in October 1864, Griggs made his recovery in a Union hospital and agreed to join the Union Army rather than spend time in a prison camp. Assigned to the Fifth U.S. Volunteers, the twenty-eight-year-old "galvanized Yankee" headed west with his company to escort the Sawyers Expedition.[24]

---

[21] Ibid., 383.
[22] Biographical material on A. M. Holman, including copies of his 4 March 1933 obituary, Pearl Research Center, Sioux City Public Museum.
[23] Lee diary, 13 June 1865 entry.
[24] Paul, "A Galvanized Yankee," 147. "Galvanized Yankee" was a term applied to former Confederate soldiers who had taken an oath of allegiance to the Union.

CHAPTER ONE

CONNOR TAKES OVER

Brig. Gen. Patrick Edward Connor faced a demanding challenge on 28 March 1865. The red-headed Irishman, then forty-four years old, had been named commander of the District of the Plains.[1] This newly organized military region encompassed the Overland Trail from Omaha to Salt Lake City, including portions of the present-day states of Utah, Colorado, Wyoming, and Nebraska. His immediate superiors, division commander Maj. Gen. John Pope and Department of the Missouri commander Maj. Gen. Grenville Dodge, recommended Connor for this important position because of his reputation as an Indian fighter, with Dodge writing, "You are a stranger to me, but I have placed you in command, believing that you will bend all your energies to the common objective and infuse life, discipline, and give the Indians no rest."[2]

The Civil War in the East was almost over at that time, but in the West a war with the warriors of Plains tribes—primarily Cheyenne, Sioux, and Arapaho—was in its second year with no end in sight. A conflict had been building between the army and the tribes who traditionally occupied the central Great Plains of Nebraska, Colorado, and Kansas as white settlement pushed westward. The Pikes Peak gold rush of the late 1850s had intensified the flow of immigrants and fortune seekers into the region, with towns such as Denver, Black Hawk, and Colorado City springing up on Indian lands. The tribes reacted to this encroachment by stealing stock, disrupting transportation on the main east-west arteries, and harassing military outposts. The discovery of gold in western Montana

---

[1]General Order #80 from J. F. Barnes, Assistant Adjutant General, by command of Major General Dodge, Hafen and Hafen, *Powder River Campaigns*, 27.
[2]Dodge to Connor, 29 March 1865, ibid., 30.

Territory in the early 1860s further increased the immigrant traffic, as men rushed toward this new El Dorado.

Prior to Connor receiving his new command, events on the plains went almost unnoticed, as the bloody conflict in the East attracted the focus of the nation. The year 1864 began with minor confrontations between the military and the warriors. While trying to recover stolen stock, the First Colorado Cavalry clashed with Cheyenne warriors on 12 April at Fremont Orchards in Colorado.[3] On 16 May troopers from the First Colorado approached a Cheyenne village near the Smokey Hill River in western Kansas. Peace advocate Lean Bear rode out to meet the soldiers with several other men and was promptly gunned down. Fighting broke out and the outnumbered soldiers were probably saved from annihilation by the actions of another peace advocate, Chief Black Kettle.[4]

In June, Arapaho warriors killed four members of the Hungate family at a ranch near Denver. Local officials displayed the mutilated bodies in Denver, and the outraged citizens howled for revenge.[5]

On the Oregon Trail in Nebraska and Kansas, Cheyenne and Sioux warriors spread terror between 7 and 9 August. The Plum Creek massacre and the Little Blue River raid accounted for over fifty civilian deaths, at least nine wounded, and seven white captives taken by the warriors.[6] This virtually shut down commerce on the Oregon Trail and cut off Denver and the Front Range settlements from the outside world.

Near-hysteria reigned in Denver, as citizens clamored for retaliation and protection. Colorado governor John Evans received authorization to raise a 100-day volunteer cavalry regiment. Col. John Chivington, then district commander, was charged with forming this regiment, designated the Third Colorado Volunteer Cavalry.

In late September a conference was arranged at Camp Weld near Denver for a meeting between the governor and a group of Cheyenne chiefs. Led by Black Kettle, the Indian delegates met with Governor Evans and Colonel Chivington.[7] The results of this conference were inconclusive, as Evans and Chivington remained vague about any peace propositions or guarantees. The chiefs left the conference unsure of where their so-called

---

[3]Michno, *Encyclopedia of Indian Wars*, 134–35.
[4]Ibid., 137–38.
[5]Ibid., 141–42.
[6]Becher, *Massacre along the Medicine Road*, 149–217, 251–63.
[7]Michno, *Battle at Sand Creek*, 164–67.

Brig. Gen. Patrick Edward Connor, commander of the District of the Plains. *Courtesy of the Library of Congress, LC-DIG-cwpb-06320.*

friendly tribes stood with the military. Black Kettle's Cheyenne and a few Arapaho eventually went into winter camp on Sand Creek in south-eastern Colorado, forty miles from Fort Lyon.

On 29 November, Colonel Chivington led an early-morning attack of 550 men against the Cheyenne village. Chivington's force consisted of the 100-day volunteers, the Third Colorado (then nicknamed the "Bloodless Third" for their lack of any action), and three companies of the First Colorado Cavalry. Around 150 Indians were slain, many of them women and children, in what became known as the Sand Creek massacre.[8]

In the aftermath of Sand Creek, Plains tribes banded together and intensified their hostilities. Their first act of revenge was an attack by about one thousand warriors on the small settlement of Julesburg, Colorado Territory, on 7 January 1865.[9] They sacked the town, and the badly outnumbered soldiers of the Seventh Iowa Cavalry, from nearby Fort Rankin, lost fourteen men.

The warriors then harassed stage stations and military outposts in the

----

[8] Utley, *Frontiersmen in Blue,* 294–97.
[9] McDermott, *Circle of Fire,* 14–34.

area and attacked Julesburg for a second time on 2 February.[10] The Indians looted and burned the town as the small garrison of soldiers and civilians watched from the nearby fort.

The warriors next targeted a telegraph station at Mud Springs in southwest Nebraska Territory on 4 February, running off the horse herd. A small party of soldiers and civilians defended the station until relief parties from Forts Mitchell and Laramie arrived over the next two days. After several hours of long-range fighting on 6 February, the warriors left the scene.[11] The same opposing forces had a minor fight about a mile from the confluence of Rush Creek and the North Platte River two days later.[12]

Raids along the Platte again shut down commerce as military outposts, stage stations, and ranches were attacked and miles of telegraph line destroyed. The large village that supported the Sand Creek–avenging warriors crossed the North Platte River and moved north toward the Powder River country of today's northeastern Wyoming and eastern Montana.

Gen. Patrick Connor arrived in Denver to take command of this chaotic situation in late March. Connor had previously commanded the District of Utah at Salt Lake City as colonel of the Third California Volunteer Infantry. His reputation as an Indian fighter came from leading a successful January 1864 attack on a Bear River Shoshone village whose warriors had been committing depredations on the overland road in his district.[13] A promotion to brigadier general followed this success. Connor's portion of the route had remained relatively calm after the chastisement of the Shoshone, hence his acclaim. The Denver *Rocky Mountain Daily News* reported on 21 March, "The Indians have a wholesome fear of him [Connor], and his appointment is a guarantee to all emigrants over the plains that they will be protected. It will be remembered that there were no difficulties in his district last summer."[14]

Connor's reputation was well known throughout the West. On 15 October 1864 Ben Holliday, the Overland Mail contractor, wrote to

[10]Ibid.
[11]Jones, *Guarding the Overland Trails*, 197–98.
[12]Michno, *Encyclopedia of Indian Wars,* 166, 67.
[13]Madsen, *Glory Hunter,* 65–87.
[14]*Rocky Mountain Daily News (Denver),* 30 June 1865.

secretary of war Edwin M. Stanton in Washington, D.C.: "Indians are attacking mail-coaches every few days forty to sixty miles west of Fort Kearny. Unless immediate measures are taken to stop depredations the great overland mails must again be stopped. I most respectfully urge that General Connor be assigned to this duty at once. His familiarity with Indian warfare, prompt and efficient protection to the western line, and wholesome dread of the savages of his name, point to him above all others as the man for the work of punishing these marauders."[15]

Secretary Stanton approved Holliday's request. On the next day, chief of staff Maj. Gen. Henry W. Halleck sent a message to Connor in Salt Lake City: "Give all the protection in your power to the overland route between you and Fort Kearny, without regards to departmental lines."[16]

Connor showed his aggressive nature in his telegraph to Colonel Chivington, then in Denver, on 22 October: "I am ordered by Secretary of War to give all protection in my power to overland stage between here and Fort Kearny. I contemplate going down with two companies of my cavalry. Can we get a fight out of Indians this winter? How many troops can you spare for a campaign? Answer."[17] This message caused Chivington, who was still district commander and not subject to orders from Connor, to protest to the Department of Kansas, which included Colorado Territory: "Have department lines changed?"[18]

The winter campaign was never organized, as the weather made any troop movement unrealistic at that time. Connor wrote of the inclement weather, as well the difficulties with local commanders and the department lines: "Possessing no authority to move any of these troops, which, in my judgment, could be spared for such purpose, and it being impossible to transport hither my own men [because of the weather], I am unable to even attempt an expedition against the savages, who, I am credibly informed, are now in winter quarters."[19] Connor wrote this in a report to General Halleck on 21 November, just eight days before Chivington led his troops against the Cheyenne village at Sand Creek.

---

[15] Holliday to Stanton, 15 October 1864, *The War of Rebellion*, O.R., Series 1, Volume 41/3 [S#85].

[16] Halleck to Connor, 17 October 1864, ibid, O.R., Series 1, Volume 41/4 [S#86].

[17] Connor to Chivington, 22 October 1864, ibid.

[18] Chivington to Maj. C. S. Charlot, 26 October 1865, ibid.

[19] Connor to Halleck, 21 November 1864, ibid., O.R., Series 1, Volume 41/1 [S#83].

Chivington obviously had his own agenda and was not about to share the glory with Connor.

However, Connor's 21 November report included his assessment of the situation, with the suggestion that he be given the broad authority to control troop movements in the region. He gave his plans for protecting the Overland Mail route, claiming that he could do it successfully with two additional regiments of cavalry and little additional expense to the government. His report was well received in the War Department and eventually led to the formation of the District of the Plains and his appointment as its commander. Major General Dodge wired Connor on 27 February 1865, "Go to Denver, leaving [the] District of Utah in charge of a good officer. If you have any spare troops take them with you. I am moving to strike the Indians before grass grows. Orders will meet you at Denver."[20]

Generals Pope and Dodge envisioned a broad military campaign into Powder River country early in 1865. The purpose would be to punish the warring tribes, thus keeping them on the defensive and away from the transportation routes to the south. Initially, the plan called for two columns converging on the Indians' stronghold as early in the spring as the weather and conditions would allow. In the initial planning, one of these columns would be led by Brig. Gen. Alfred Sully out of Sioux City, Iowa, on the Missouri River. Sully was arguably the most experienced Indian fighter in the army at that time. Prior to the Civil War he had campaigned against the Seminoles in Florida and the Cheyenne on the plains. In the aftermath of the Sioux uprising in Minnesota in 1862, Sully had scored major victories over the Sioux at Whitestone Hill in 1863 and Killdeer Mountain in 1864, both in northern Dakota Territory.[21] In addition to leading the expedition westward, he would have the responsibility of building a military post in the heart of the Powder River country.

The campaign called for Connor to lead the other column out of Fort Laramie on the North Platte River. Sully's command, designated as the eastern or right column, was to travel on the east side of the Black Hills and then northwest into the Powder River country of eastern Montana Territory. Connor's western or left column was to follow the Bozeman

---

[20] Dodge to Connor, 27 February 1865, ibid., O.R., Series 1, Volume 48/1 [S#101].
[21] Clodfelter, *The Dakota War*, 119–77.

Trail route along the eastern slopes of the Bighorn Mountains, then northeast to a rendezvous with the other command.

Maj. Gen. Dodge sent an urgent message to Connor on 29 March: "Troops en route to Laramie and Julesburg, with those on the route will give you 2,000 or over mounted men. I want this force pushed right on after the Indians. . . . About May 1 General Sully will leave Sioux City with a column and push west to Powder River and establish a post there. We will have to supply that column from Laramie."[22]

Connor's priorities as he assumed command of his new district included providing adequate protection for travelers, commerce, the mail, and telegraph lines on the overland road, as well as hurriedly preparing the campaign against those tribes currently in the Powder River country to the north. He telegraphed Dodge on 4 April, "I fear expedition will be detained longer than you anticipated for want of forage and supplies. Corn thus far at Julesburg and Laramie is consumed as fast as received."[23] This, of course, was not what Dodge wanted to hear at this time.

Thus the agonizingly slow preparation for the Powder River Expedition began. On 5 April Connor wrote, "I will do everything in my power to expedite the expedition north, but supplies are coming in very slowly from the [Missouri] river, and it will take a longer time than you probably anticipate to get it in motion. . . . I trust that supplies will be forwarded as rapidly as possible, particularly so as I am expected to supply General Sully's command."[24]

Connor had been instructed by General Dodge to not purchase or enter into contracts for supplies without Dodge's or his department's chief quartermaster's approval.[25] Connor wrote that, while in command in Utah, he had "deemed it necessary to purchase in open market fuel, forage, and other articles required and of which we were short." He brought up a critical point about the government bureaucracy, in that supply contracts for the coming fiscal year (1 July 1865 to 30 June 1866) had not yet been awarded to civilian suppliers, and requested "authority to continue said system in Utah until contracts are let for the ensuing

[22] Dodge to Connor, 29 March 1865, *The War of Rebellion*, O.R., Series 1, Volume 48/1 [S#101].

[23] Connor to Dodge, 4 April 1865, ibid., O.R., Series 1, Volume 48/2 [S#102].

[24] Connor to Maj. J. W. Barnes, A.A.G., Department of the Missouri, 5 April 1865, ibid.

[25] Col. J. A. Potter, Quartermaster for the Department of the Missouri, at Fort Leavenworth, Kansas, ibid.

fiscal year, also to make from time to time purchases of such small articles as may be required for immediate use."[26] Connor's methods of supplying the Powder River Expedition would become controversial in the coming months, bringing severe criticism from Gen. John Pope, division commander and Dodge's immediate superior.

The war in the East came to a close in early April as General Lee surrendered at Appomattox Courthouse. Troops who had signed up to defeat the Southern Confederacy—not to fight Indians on the plains—now clamored to be discharged. Connor's task of assembling the expedition was now made more formidable in light of the new development affecting the morale of troops over his widespread district.

On 15 April General Dodge sent a telegram to General Connor: "President Lincoln and Secretary Seward were assassinated last night; Mr. Lincoln while attending the theater; said to be done by J. Wilkes Booth; Mr. Seward at his home. Mr. Lincoln died this A.M., at 7:30; Mr. Seward at 9:30. A general gloom overspreads the community."[27]

Cpl. Charles L. Thomas was serving at Deer Creek Station at that time.[28] On hearing the terrible news of the presidential assassination, Thomas wrote to his brother on the following day:

> C.T.
> Deer Creek
> April 16th 1865
> Dear Brother
> Your welcome letter of the 11th Jan came to hand few days back. I am well and hearty. yesterday we herd by telegraph that Pres. Lincoln and Sect. Seward had been assassinated and were both dead. it was the greatest shock that ever befell the American people. it was a day of lamentation for the Soldier. I saw men that did not fear danger in eny form weap like infants. They are brave men. we drew up a petition to send to the governor of Ohio to have us relieved from here and sent to the front. our company and G co. all sined [signed] it. I don't know if it

---

[26]Connor to Maj. J. W. Barnes, A.A.G., Department of the Missouri, 5 April 1865, ibid.

[27]Dodge to Connor, 15 April 1865, ibid. Although an assassination attempt was made on secretary of state William Seward where he was severely wounded, he did survive and recover.

[28]Deer Creek Station was a telegraph station located twenty-five miles to the east of the Platte Bridge near the mouth of Deer Creek. Today's Glenrock, Wyoming, is near the site.

will do eny good or not. I hope it will. to day 900 more men got here
they belong to the 11th Kansas regiment. 200 more will be here next
week. this morning we resieved a dispatch from Gen Carner [Connor]
saying arrest and place in irons eny person or persons who express their
satisfaction at the death of our beloved President. Show them know
[no] merces [mercies]. it is just with me. you bet that the order will be
inforsed. death to all rebels and sympathizers. Thornt Dugan voted for
Lincoln. I get 18 dollars per month. none of the boys go scoting [scout-
ing] out here. they have not got eny scotes [scouts]. I will close. Give my
love to all the familie.

Yours truly,
Brother Charlie[29]

    While the country rejoiced at the end of the bloody conflict that had
torn the country apart for the last four years and grieved the death of
their beloved leader, Generals Pope, Dodge, and Connor went full steam
ahead with their plans for a major punitive campaign against the Plains
Indians. Their sense of urgency would not be matched by the bureaucracy of the government or by the men destined to carry out these grandiose plans.

---

[29] Thomas to brother, 16 April 1865. Thomas wrote "C.T.," obviously meaning Colorado Terri-
tory, when, in fact, Deer Creek Station was in Dakota Territory, later to be Wyoming
Territory. Pvt. Thornton Dugan was in Company E, Eleventh Ohio Cavalry. *American Civil
War Research Database.*

CHAPTER TWO

A Trip to St. Louis

Preparation for the Powder River Expedition started off slowly, with Generals Dodge and Connor telegraphing each other about the flow of supplies to Fort Laramie. Because of shortages and the inadequacies in the supply system, it had been standard practice for post commanders along the route to seize government supply trains intended for Julesburg, Fort Laramie, and beyond. However, Dodge wrote to Connor that "This must be stopped or else he [Col. J. A. Potter, divisional quartermaster] never can keep up the supplies."[1] Connor replied, "I have reason to believe that no trains have been seized since I assumed command. If so, it is contrary to my orders and will be seen to."[2]

Requesting more teams and wagons, Connor told Dodge, "Previous to my taking command there was plenty of transportation, because citizen's goods were thrown out on the road as their teams passed. I require 100 wagons to load with corn at Omaha or Atchison for Laramie."[3] Two days later, Colonel Potter had "at least 25,000 bushels of corn on the way to Denver, Julesburg, Laramie, and other points; starting more every day. Have just got out a train of fifty wagons complete, which will be sent at once. . . . This is all I can spare just now, but will try to send him [Connor] all he needs."[4] The army's supply system moved at a snail's pace, as Connor and Dodge pushed to ready their campaign.

General Connor organized his District of the Plains into four subdistricts. This move left him to oversee the overall district operation and

---

[1] Dodge to Connor, 21 April 1865, *The War of Rebellion*, O.R., Series 1, Volume 48/2 [S#102].
[2] Connor to Dodge, 21 April 1865, ibid.
[3] Connor to Dodge, 27 April 1865, ibid.
[4] Col. J. A. Potter to Dodge, 29 April 1865, ibid.

to prepare for the coming campaign against the Powder River Indians. The sub-district commanders had the responsibility of keeping the telegraph and mail routes open within their assigned areas. Denver was the headquarters of the South Sub-District, led by Col. Guy V. Henry.[5] Col. Robert R. Livingston of the First Nebraska Cavalry commanded the East Sub-District of Nebraska from Fort Kearny. Col. Thomas Moonlight of the Eleventh Kansas Cavalry headed the North Sub-District at Fort Laramie. Lt. Col. Milo George, of the First Battalion, Nevada Cavalry, at Camp Douglas controlled Utah Territory, designated as the West Sub-District.[6]

Indian warriors continued to harass the telegraph stations along the Oregon Trail, as Cpl. Hervy Johnson wrote to his sister on 21 April: "Two men were killed this morning on Laprelle Creek twenty miles below Deer C. [Creek] by [I]ndians."[7]

As preparations for the company proceeded, Connor used an Indian prisoner to send a message to Indian marauders. Cheyenne warrior Big Crow, who had links to the Little Blue Raid and the kidnapping of Nancy Morton of the previous August, was arrested and accused of being a murderer and a spy.[8] He had been jailed in the Fort Laramie guardhouse since February with a ball and chain attached to his leg. On 24 April Connor reported that "Indians killed one soldier and wounded another around Friday last [21 April] near Fort Laramie."[9] Connor's reaction was swift, as he wired the post commander on Saturday, 22 April: "Take Big Crow to the place where [the] soldier was killed yesterday, erect a high gallows, hang him in chains and leave the body suspended."[10] On a scaffold built a mile and a half from the fort, the execution took

[5]Jones, *Guarding the Overland Trails*, 220. Col. (Bvt. Brig. Gen.) Guy Vernor Henry was appointed as commander of the East Sub-District of the District of the Plains by General Connor on 29 March 1865. Henry was awarded the Medal of Honor for leading his troops in assaults at Cold Harbor, Virginia, on 1 June 1864. *American Civil War Research Database.*

[6]General Order Number Eight, Capt. George F. Price, A.A.A.G., District of the Plains, 8 April 1865, *The War of Rebellion*, O.R., Series 1, Volume 48/2 [S#102].

[7]Unrau, *Tending the Talking Wire*, 238. Cpl. Hervy Johnson, Company G, Eleventh Ohio Cavalry, was stationed at Sweetwater Telegraph station at this time.

[8]Jones, *Guarding the Overland Trails*, 217–18.

[9]*The War of Rebellion*, O.R., Series 1, Volume 48/2 [S#102], Connor to Dodge, 24 April 1865.

[10]McDermott, *Circle of Fire*, 57.

place the following day. Big Crow's body, left hanging and to rot, served as a warning to the tribesmen of Connor's intentions. Corporal Johnson wrote to his sister, "Last first day [Sunday] the 23rd the 'religious ceremony' of hanging an [I]ndian chief was performed at Fort Laramie."[11] For many years friendly Brule and Ogalala Sioux, generally known as the "Laramie Loafers," had camped in the vicinity of Fort Laramie.[12] One must wonder how they reacted to the spectacle.

In early May, Connor moved his headquarters to Julesburg, as he found Denver too remote for him to properly organize his expedition. He telegraphed General Dodge on 5 May, "Respectfully ask your permission to visit you at Saint Louis. It is important that I should consult with you."[13] Dodge replied, "You have permission, and I desire to see you."[14]

At Fort Leavenworth Colonel Potter received a shipment of Canadian ponies from Detroit on 1 May. He sent 316 of them toward Fort Laramie for the expedition.[15] General Connor wired Dodge from Fort Kearny on 7 May en route to St. Louis: "I most earnestly and respectfully request that no more Canadian ponies be sent me. They are utterly worthless and of no service in this district."[16] Instead of good, serviceable horses suitable for cavalry use on the plains, the Canadian ponies were mostly young colts and broken-down animals.[17]

The Indian hostilities continued, as Connor's adjutant, Capt. George F. Price, reported on 13 May from Julesburg: "Twenty or thirty Indians attempted to run off stock this morning at Dan Smith's. Troops fought them all morning. Also attacked Captain Porter's post wagon five miles below Gilman's, wounding two men. Three Indians killed."[18]

---

[11]Unrau, *Tending the Talking Wire*, 243.

[12]McDermott, *Circle of Fire*, 55.

[13]Connor to Dodge, 5 May 1865, *The War of Rebellion*, O.R., Series 1, Volume 48/2 [S#102].

[14]Dodge to Connor, 7 May 1865, ibid.

[15]Potter to Dodge, 1 May 1865, ibid.

[16]Connor to Dodge, 7 May 1865, ibid.

[17]Dodge to Meigs, 7 May 1865, ibid.

[18]Price to Connor, 13 May 1865, *The War of Rebellion*, O.R., Series 1, Volume 48/1 [S#101]; Michno, *Encyclopedia of Indian Wars*, 169. The action at Smith's ranch took place about three miles southwest of today's Gothenburg, Nebraska. Capt. Charles F. Porter was a member of Company A, First Battalion, Nebraska Cavalry. *Civil War Soldiers and Sailors System*. Gillman's ranch is approximately twenty miles northwest of Smith's ranch on the Oregon Trail. Jones, *Guarding the Overland Trails*, 28.

Maj. Gen. Grenville M. Dodge, commander of the Department of the Missouri. *Courtesy of the Library of Congress, LC-DIG-cwpb-U5485.*

As the northern tribesmen continued to terrorize outposts in the District of the Plains, Connor arrived in St. Louis on 14 May. He met with General Dodge and explained his requirements to get the long-awaited Powder River Expedition under way. Dodge responded by wiring division commander Gen. John Pope on 15 May: "I consider absolutely necessary that more cavalry be sent me. . . . General Connor also reports the Indians threatening the upper route from South Pass to Kearny. The ponies bought for him are worthless, and we will have to ship him some 800 horses, and he thinks he may need another regiment of cavalry. The order of the War Department received today will muster out about 2000 cavalry in this department, including several hundred on the plains. I should like to send about three more regiments onto the plains."[19]

On the same day, Dodge fired off a telegram to Colonel Potter, quartermaster at Fort Leavenworth: "General Connor is here. He says that there is no corn at Laramie, Julesburg, or Cottonwood, and only 1,500

---

[19]Dodge to Pope, 15 May 1865, *American Civil War Research Database,* O.R., Series 1, Volume 48/2 [S#102].

sacks at Kearny. What have you on the road?"[20] Connor had obviously communicated his message—in order to invade a vast wilderness, he needed an adequate force of men and animals, as well as the supplies to sustain them.

In March, the Third U.S. Volunteer Infantry had moved west to be assigned guard duties at many of the stage and telegraph stations along the overland route. This regiment—made up of former Confederate prisoners of war—came from the Rock Island Federal Prison in Illinois. These former Southern soldiers, labeled "galvanized Yankees," signed loyalty oaths to the Union in return for the "opportunity" to serve in the West.

In May a detachment of those volunteers departed Fort Leavenworth, bound for Julesburg and duty assignments. The party was made up of fifteen men who had been left behind for medical reasons when the regiment earlier marched west. The highest ranking soldier among them was a sergeant. Through what can only be called a tragic blunder, the party marched on the trail unarmed.

On 18 May twelve to thirty warriors, probably Cheyenne, attacked the detachment two miles east of Elm Creek Station, on the Little Blue, leaving the defenseless soldiers with two dead and six wounded. Several survivors claimed that the warriors were Pawnee, but an investigation uncovered no evidence incriminating that friendly tribe.[21] These soldiers from the South had probably never seen a Plains Indian before and therefore would have been hard pressed to tell one tribe from another.

As General Connor worked his way west from St. Louis, his adjutant, Captain Price, wired him at Atchison, Kansas, on 20 May: "Corn taken from trains on road as follows: Lieutenant Smith,[22] Alkali,[23] 50 sacks,

---

[20] Dodge to Potter, ibid.

[21] Brown, *The Galvanized Yankees*, 23–28.

[22] First Lt. James G. Smith was in Company A, Seventh Iowa Cavalry. *American Civil War Research Database.*

[23] Alkali Lake Station was located about forty miles northeast of Julesburg on the South Platte River. Jones, *Guarding the Overland Trails*, 28.

Captain Cremer,[24] Beauvais,[25] 24 sacks, Colonel Walker,[26] Alkali, 80,000 pounds. Colonel Walker says he had authority from you. No authority given in other cases."[27] Two points stand out here: first, corn for the horses and mules was still in short supply; and second, Connor's officers were still ignoring his orders about confiscating supplies en route to Fort Laramie.

Price's message continued: "Colonel Moonlight reports no Indians nearer than Big Horn and Powder Rivers. He captured Two Face and two of his band. They had Mrs. Eubanks and child. She was captured last August on Little Blue by Cheyennes."[28] Lucinda Eubanks and her daughter, rescued after nearly a year in captivity, told a story of abuse and torment by her captors to her interviewers at Fort Laramie. Two Face, an Ogalala Sioux, had purchased Mrs. Eubanks from the Cheyenne, probably with the intent of exchanging her for trade goods. From information garnered from Mrs. Eubanks, another Sioux chief, Black Foot, was arrested as a leader of other recent raids. Mrs. Eubanks's testimony of mistreatment and the two chiefs' complicity in past depredations compelled Colonel Moonlight to order Two Face and Black Foot to be put to death by hanging. Moonlight reported, "Both of the chiefs openly boasted that they had killed white men and that they would do it again if let loose."[29] The sentence was carried out on 26 May on a scaffold erected near the other gallows, where Big Crow's body still hung from his April execution. As with Big Crow, Moonlight ordered that the corpses be left hanging as a warning to those who doubted the army's resolve. To no one's surprise, the Indians camped in the vicinity of Fort Laramie were reported to be in bad humor.[30]

Also on 20 May, a band of two hundred Indians attacked Deer Creek Station on the North Platte River. The warriors were repulsed, and the

---

[24]Capt. Harrison W. Cremer was in Company C, Seventh Iowa Cavalry. *American Civil War Research Database.*

[25]Beauvais Trading Post was located approximately ten miles northeast of Julesburg on the South Platte River. Jones, *Guarding the Overland Trails,* 28.

[26]Lt. Col. Samuel Walker was in the Sixteenth Kansas Cavalry. *American Civil War Research Database.*

[27]Price to Connor, 20 May 1865, *The War of Rebellion*, O.R., Series 1, Volume 48/2 [S#102].

[28]Ibid.

[29]Moonlight's report, 27 May 1865, ibid., O.R., Series 1, Volume 48/I [S#101].

[30]McDermott, *Circle of Fire,* 62–64.

military claimed seven dead Indians and several wounded.[31] Reports of harassment by the warriors at Three Crossings Station on the Sweetwater River also came in during this time frame.[32]

Lt. Henry C. Bretney reported that on 27 May, "about 150 Indians attacked Saint Mary's Station, and in a short time succeeded in setting fire to buildings." The small garrison of five men escaped to South Pass Station.[33] At Sweetwater Station, warriors attempted to steal the herd over a five-day period at the end of May. On 1 June, after attempting to take the remainder of herd without success, the marauders cut the telegraph wire about one thousand yards east of the station and carried off about one hundred yards of wire. Small bands of Cheyenne, Sioux, and Arapaho warriors continued to harass stations all along the overland routes, while the army struggled to keep the roads open, as well as preparing to launch a major campaign into the northern tribes' heretofore-unchallenged stronghold.

Amidst all of the turmoil, good news came from General Dodge on 25 May: "Five hundred horses leave here the 26th for Kearny. Have an escort of some kind for them at the Little Blue, at such point as you may designate. . . . A regiment of cavalry is on the way here, which will be pushed right out to the Blue for you."[34] Two days later Dodge replied, "I can send you all the cavalry you wish. You must keep your mounted men active."[35] The source of this newly found abundance of cavalry regiments, the Michigan Cavalry Brigade, had been ordered to Fort Leavenworth after marching in a "Grand Review" in Washington, D.C., on 23 May. The brigade, commanded by Brig. Gen. Peter Stagg, consisted of the First, Fifth, Sixth, and Seventh Michigan Cavalry Regiments. General Connor's visit to St. Louis appeared to be paying dividends, and he now could look forward to finally getting his expedition ready to go.

---

[31] Price to Connor, 22 May 1865, *The War of Rebellion*, O.R., Series 1, Volume 48/I [S#101].
[32] Unrau, *Tending the Talking Wire*, 246.
[33] Report of 1st Lt. Henry C. Bretney, Company G, Eleventh Ohio Cavalry, to Moonlight, June — 1865, *The War of Rebellion*, O.R., Series 1, Volume 48/I [S#101]. Bretney did not date his report; only the month was listed.
[34] Dodge to Connor, 24 May 1865, *The War of Rebellion*, O.R., Series 1, Volume 48/I [S#102].
[35] Dodge to Connor, 27 May 1865, ibid.

CHAPTER THREE

COLE REPLACES SULLY

The Powder River Expedition seemed to be finally coming together—until General Pope, reacting to Indian problems elsewhere in his division, wired General Dodge on June 3: "Sully's cavalry, in consequence of stampede in Minnesota, is obliged to go to Devil's Lake. You must deal with these Indians in the Black Hills and establish the post on Powder River. I have sent up [the] Michigan brigade, and will send one and perhaps two more cavalry regiments to you. It is absolutely essential . . . that this Indian force in the Black Hills be routed as soon as possible."[1]

Connor now had the responsibility of getting the entire force in motion and building the fort on Powder River. Sully's command of twelve hundred cavalrymen, scheduled to depart Fort Pierre, Dakota Territory, in early May, now had to be replaced.[2] Juggling his resources to keep the planned campaign in motion, Dodge wired Connor on 10 June: "I shall start from here [Fort Leavenworth] by boats two regiments (Twelfth Missouri and Second Missouri) to Omaha, 1,000 strong, with sixty days' rations and transportation from the day they leave Omaha. They are ordered to march to Loup Fork as soon as both regiments reach Omaha and await instructions from you."[3] The Twelfth Missouri Volunteer Cavalry was a battle-tested regiment commanded by Col. Oliver Wells. The Second Missouri Light Artillery, while an experienced artillery regiment, had just been converted to cavalry in early June. Its commander, Col.

---

[1] Pope to Dodge, 3 June 1865, Hafen and Hafen, *Powder River Campaigns*, 30–31.
[2] Sully, report to adjutant general, Military Division of the Missouri, 22 April 1865, *The War of Rebellion*, O.R., Series 1, Volume 48/2 [S#102].
[3] Dodge to Connor, June 10, 1865, ibid.

Nelson D. Cole, a competent artillery officer, had served previously as chief of staff to Gen. Alfred Pleasanton, who commanded the cavalry in the Department of the Missouri.[4] Cole had time in grade over Wells and expected to be the commander of the Eastern Division of the Powder River Expedition.

The selection of Omaha, rather than Fort Pierre, as the jumping-off point for the eastern column would prove to be a questionable decision. The distance from Omaha to Bear Butte, one of the landmark targets, is approximately 500 miles, while Fort Pierre to Bear Butte is a mere 153 miles over a route described as "very good for a wagon road."[5] The change of starting location added at least 345 miles through a semi-mapped wilderness region to an expedition already behind schedule.

A St. Louis *Missouri Democrat* headline read, "Treachery of the Arapahoe Indians—They are on the War-Path—United States Forces Detained by Want of Supplies."[6] The Indian attacks on the Overland Road continued: "General Connor telegraphs that Indians attack some station or telegraph line daily."[7] As Connor worked his way back from Saint Louis, his adjutant, Captain Price, telegraphed him on 5 June: "Families of Cheyennes and some Sioux, principally on Powder River, 220 miles from Laramie, balance on Tongue and Big Horn, spoiling for a fight."[8] So were Generals Dodge and Connor.

"Friendly" Sioux, numbering fifteen hundred to two thousand, camped in the vicinity of Fort Laramie. Connor deemed it prudent to relocate these Indians farther east at Fort Kearny, thus keeping them away from the influence of the northern tribesmen. Connor ordered this movement with concurrence all the way to the War Department in Washington.[9] On 11 June the "friendlies," including their families, moved east under the escort of Company D and small detachments of Companies A and B of

[4]Stevens, *St. Louis*, 230–33.
[5]Lt. Carter Berkely, Sixth Iowa Cavalry, to Sully, 20 February 1865, *The War of Rebellion*, O.R., Series 1, Volume 48/I [S#101].
[6]*Missouri Democrat*, 3 July 1865.
[7]Dodge to Pope, 4 June 1865, *The War of Rebellion*, O.R., Series 1, Volume 48/2 [S#102].
[8]Price to Connor, 5 June 1865, ibid.
[9]Connor to Dodge, 15 June 1865, ibid.

the Seventh Iowa Cavalry, commanded by Capt. William D. Fouts—135 enlisted men and 4 officers. A company of Indian police under Agent Charles Elston also marched with the group. A small contingent of civilians, including the recently rescued Lucinda Eubanks and Fouts's wife, accompanied the procession. According to Capt. John Wilcox of Company B, "The Indians were all well armed with bows and arrows, and most of them with firearms also. They were ostensibly friendly, and expressed themselves as being pleased with their removal."[10] In reality, Fort Kearny's location, near the homeland of their long-time bitter enemy, the Pawnees, probably concerned many of them about the relocation. However, Captain Fouts, comfortable with this situation, refused to issue ammunition to his men.

On the afternoon of 13 June, Fouts and his command camped on the east bank of Horse Creek, about thirty-five miles east of Fort Laramie. The Sioux pitched their tepees on the west bank of the creek. The warriors had a dog feast late in the evening, and several hundred of them sat in a secret council. They probably had visitors from the warring camps, as Captain Wilcox reported, "Nothing of interest transpired during the first three days of the march except signal smokes by Indians north of the Platte by day and reputed conferences by night between them and the Indians in [the] charge of Captain Fouts."[11]

In the morning Fouts crossed the creek to hurry the Indians along and was promptly gunned down. Most of the Indians, including the Indian police, headed for the North Platte River, although they had confrontations among themselves, as not all chose to go north to join the warring tribesmen. When Captain Wilcox learned of Fouts's death, he promptly sent a messenger (who was pursued by warriors) toward Fort Mitchell, nine miles to the east. Wilcox, realizing that the soldiers were badly outnumbered, set up a defense—literally circling the wagons—and ordered ammunition issued to the troopers. With seventy mounted men, Wilcox approached the Indians, who were now crossing the North Platte River. A hot fight broke out, and the outnumbered soldiers retreated to the defensive position. A relief party arrived from Fort Mitchell, but by

---

[10]Wilcox to Price, 21 June 1865, ibid., O.R., Series 1, Volume 48/1 [S#101].
[11]Ibid.

this time the Indians had completed their crossing of the river and were headed north.[12]

Word of the fight at Horse Creek reached Fort Laramie that afternoon. Colonel Moonlight quickly put together a relief force and headed east. A messenger informed him en route of the latest developments. Moonlight then returned to Fort Laramie and put together a force of 234 men to pursue and recapture the Indians the following morning. He reported, "The whole night was consumed in crossing [the North Platte River], and at 8 o'clock next morning, 15th instant, I started down the river to where the Indians had crossed, took up the trail." Because of the poor condition of their horses, 103 men turned back to Fort Laramie over the next two days. The morning of 17 June found Moonlight and his remaining 131 men on Dead Man's Fork, 120 miles northeast of Fort Laramie. They had stopped after a twenty-mile march at 10 A.M. for breakfast and to allow their animals to graze. Approximately 200 warriors attacked the camp and promptly ran off seventy-four of the remaining horses. With the loss of the majority of their mounts, Moonlight had no choice but to burn saddles and other equipment and head back to Fort Laramie, with most of his party on foot.[13]

Connor, outraged over this turn of events, wrote to Dodge on 20 June, "Colonel Moonlight has been unfortunate in his dealings with Indians since assuming command of [the] North Sub-District. I have relieved him, and will investigate his conduct. . . . The horses lost by Colonel Moonlight day before yesterday were California horses, belonging to the California companies recently from Utah. They were the best horses I had for the present service."[14] Connor later reported, "Colonel Moonlight is on his way to Kearny, suspended from command. I have ordered him mustered out. His administration here was a series of blunders."[15]

In early June, the Michigan Cavalry Brigade arrived at Fort Leavenworth with 2,300 men and only 600 horses.[16] Dodge wired Brig. Gen. Peter

[12]Ibid.
[13]Moonlight to Price, 21 June 1865, ibid.; George E. Hyde, *Life of George Bent*, 211–12.
[14]Connor to Dodge, 20 June 1865, *The War of Rebellion*, O.R., Series 1, Volume 48/2 [S#102].
[15]Connor to Dodge, 6 July 1865, ibid.
[16]Pope to Dodge, 2 June 1865, ibid.

Stagg on 13 June, "As soon as the 900 horses now on their way from Saint Louis arrive you will move with your brigade to Julesburg, reporting there to Brig. Gen. P. E. Connor."[17] The Sixth Michigan Cavalry regiment, commanded by Col. James Harvey Kidd, set out for Julesburg on 17 June with orders to report to General Connor.[18] With the Sixth taking the majority of the available horses, the other regiments of the brigade were to follow, as soon as mounts arrived for them.

On 18 June Connor reported that troops had started to arrive in Omaha for the Eastern Division of the campaign. "I hope the remaining portion will arrive speedily, as every hour is precious. He [Cole] should arrive at Black Hills as soon as I do, but I fear will not."[19] Connor then decided to put his own man in charge of the eastern column, and a new controversy started brewing. On 22 June he notified Dodge from Julesburg that "General Heath leaves for Omaha to-day to take command of column of cavalry moving from there to Black Hills."[20] Col. Herman H. Heath of the Seventh Iowa Cavalry had recently been appointed commander of the Nebraska Sub-District, replacing Col. Robert Livingston, who mustered out of the army.[21] Paperwork had been submitted to the War Department to give Heath the honorary rank of brevet brigadier general. Connor gave Colonel Heath detailed verbal orders for the expedition before Heath left Julesburg.

Colonel Cole, while still in St. Louis, had received orders on 10 June to "proceed without delay to Omaha, Nebr., reporting through the sub-district commander to Brig. Gen. P. E. Connor, commanding District of the Plains."[22] Cole probably arrived in Omaha before Heath, around 20 June, and went to work organizing the hastily prepared expedition. With Heath leaving Julesburg on 22 June, he arrived in Omaha on perhaps the 26th or 27th. Colonel Cole objected to being put under command of Colonel Heath, as Cole outranked Heath by having an earlier promotion date. Connor had made his decision on the basis that Heath technically outranked Cole because of his brevet rank. The telegraph

---

[17]Dodge to Stagg, 13 June 1865, ibid.
[18]Stagg to Kidd, 16 June 1865, J. H. Kidd Papers.
[19]Connor to Dodge, 20 June 1865, *The War of Rebellion*, O.R., Series 1, Volume 48/2 [S#102].
[20]Connor to Dodge, 22 June 1865, ibid.
[21]Connor to Dodge, 20 June 1865, ibid.
[22]Barnes to Cole, 10 June 1865, ibid.

wires hummed on 29 June between Dodge in St. Louis, Cole and Heath in Omaha, and Connor at Fort Mitchell as the generals tried to resolve the issue and get the expedition under way.

Connor to Dodge: "Colonel Cole raises a question of rank with Heath."[23]

Connor to Cole: "You will obey General Heath, and if he is not entitled to command it will be transferred to you when I hear from department headquarters."[24]

Connor to Dodge: "General Heath telegraphs me that he is much embarrassed by Colonel Cole's conduct. Will you please telegraph to Washington to have Heath assigned, if not already so?"[25]

Dodge to Cole: "What delays you at Omaha? What are you waiting for? Has General Connor ordered you to stop there? Unless General Heath is assigned by War Department in his brevet rank you are the senior officer. You better consult General Connor, however, and make no trouble. He will, upon application decide the matter."[26]

Cole to Dodge: "I am delayed here waiting for commissary and quartermaster's stores that have not arrived."[27]

Dodge to Connor: "General Heath has not been assigned with brevet rank; until he is by the War Department we cannot assign him."[28]

Connor to Cole: "Special Orders, No. 33, relieves General Heath. You must move your column immediately. . . . General Heath will communicate the verbal instructions I gave him. I will mail instructions to Columbus [Nebraska]."[29]

Connor to Heath: "General Dodge decides that Colonel Cole is the ranking officer until you are assigned in your brevet grade. Communicate the verbal orders I gave you to Colonel Cole."[30]

Colonel Heath may have been a better choice than Colonel Cole to head the expedition simply because his regiment, the Seventh Iowa Cav-

---

[23] Connor to Dodge, 29 June 1865, ibid.
[24] Connor to Cole, 29 June 1865, ibid.
[25] Connor to Dodge, 29 June 1865, ibid.
[26] Dodge to Cole, 29 June 1865, ibid.
[27] Cole to Dodge, 29 June 1865, ibid.
[28] Dodge to Connor, 29 June 1865, ibid.
[29] Connor to Cole, 29 June 1865, ibid.
[30] Connor to Heath, 29 June 1865, ibid.

alry, had served on the frontier in Dakota and Nebraska Territories since it was organized in 1863.[31] Heath, who joined the regiment as a major that year, had experienced operating on the plains with Indian warriors as the foe, rather than Confederate rebels. Nelson Cole, with a solid wartime record, had never operated on the plains, had no experience in Indian warfare, and had never commanded an expedition of this size. However, the army's strict adherence to seniority, not common sense, dictated the decision.

With the command issue settled, the generals focused on getting the much-delayed expedition on the road. As with all of the preparation associated with the campaign, provisions intended for Cole's column were late arriving. Dodge's growing impatience at the delays was evident in his 30 June communication to Cole: "Don't wait for rations. . . . That column must get off."[32] In this message he instructed Cole to strip the local military stations of their supplies. General Connor, using his sometimes-unorthodox procurement methods, gave Cole the solution to get his command on the road: "You are authorized to purchase quartermaster's supplies and subsistence stores necessary to complete your outfit."[33]

Colonel Cole purchased the required supplies in Omaha to the tune of fifteen thousand dollars, and his command of 1,400 mounted men and 140 wagons left Omaha on 1 July, heading for the Loup River via Columbus to receive written orders from Connor regarding the campaign.[34] Dodge and Connor must have rejoiced that, at long last, one column of the Powder River Indian Expedition, as it now was officially called, was under way.

Patrick Connor had moved his headquarters to Fort Laramie in late June. In a message to General Dodge on 3 July regarding Indian depredations on the mail and telegraph lines, his temper and aggressive nature stood

---

[31]Ware, *The Indian War of 1864*, 11. Second Lt. Eugene F. Ware wrote that Herman H. Heath was a secret Southern sympathizer who had written to Jefferson Davis during the Civil War, offering his services to the Confederacy. According to Ware, one of Heath's letters had been discovered in the Confederate archives in 1866 and was read on the floor of Congress.

[32]Dodge to Cole, 30 June 1865, *The War of Rebellion*, O.R., Series 1, Volume 48/2 [S#102].

[33]Connor to Cole, 30 June 1865, ibid.

[34]Cole's official report, 10 February 1867, Hafen and Hafen, *Powder River Campaigns*, 60–61.

out: "None of them [the Indians] are to be trusted. They must be hunted like wolves. The severest punishment is necessary before we can have any peace with them. It is almost impossible to keep the telegraph line up west of here [Fort Laramie]; they cut it daily. They are getting exceedingly bold by their successes against the troops now guarding the line, which induces me to believe they may stand and fight. I sincerely hope so."[35] Connor's instructions to Col. Carroll H. Potter in Denver were equally harsh: "Treat all Indians found near mail route as hostile. . . . Show no quarter to male Indians over twelve years of age."[36] On 4 July Connor wrote his orders for Colonel Cole's eastern command, already on the trail toward the Loup River:

> In accordance with verbal instructions heretofore communicated to you through Bvt. Brig. Gen. H. H. Heath, U.S. Volunteers, you will proceed with your column by the best and most practicable route to the east base of the Black Hills, in Dakota Territory; move thence along the east base of the Black Hills to Bear's Peak [Bear Butte], situate[d] at the northeast point of the hills, and where a large force of hostile Indians are supposed to be camped. From Bear's Peak you will move around the north base of the Black Hills to the Three Peaks [Little Missouri Buttes]; from thence you will strike across the country in a north-westerly direction to the north base of Panther Mountain, where you will find a supply depot and probably part of my command.[37]

The last sentence was very critical, as Cole's column carried sixty days of rations for the men, less for their animals, and expected to be re-supplied at their rendezvous at Panther Mountain. The rest of the letter advised Cole about communications between the commands, the importance of hobbling the stock to prevent Indians from stampeding them, and pick-

---

[35] Connor to Dodge, July 3, 1865, *The War of Rebellion*, O.R., Series 1, Volume 48/2 [S#102].

[36] Connor to Potter, 3 July 1865, *The War of Rebellion*, O.R., Series 1, Volume 48/2 [S#102]. Col. Carroll H. Potter was in the Sixth United States Volunteer Infantry. Brown, *The Galvanized Yankees*, 143–44.

[37] Connor's orders to Cole, 4 July 1865, Hafen and Hafen, *Powder River Campaigns*, 35–36. Today's maps do not show "Panther Mountain," but it was listed on the G. K. Warren map of 1857, which was used by the expedition. The Panther Mountains were shown between the Tongue River and Rosebud Creek in eastern Montana. Today these mountains are generally called the Wolf Mountains. These orders were delivered to Colonel Cole at his camp at the mouth of the North Loup River on 10 July 1865.

ets and scouting parties. The most controversial instructions regarded contact with the Indians: "You will not receive overtures of peace or submission from Indians, but will attack and kill every male Indian over 12 years of age."[38] Connor would be severely chastised for this order later in the summer.

Now that the eastern, or right, column was on the march and the men and supplies needed for his part of the campaign were en route from Fort Leavenworth, Connor formulated his overall plan for the Powder River Indian Expedition. He sent a dispatch to Dodge on 5 July: "I march from here in two columns. Will send you a map showing route taken by the three columns."[39] Connor's plan called for the Sixteenth Kansas Cavalry, with six hundred men under Lt. Col. Samuel Walker, to lead the center column out of Fort Laramie north along the western edge of the Black Hills, then northwest toward the Powder and Tongue Rivers, with a rendezvous with the other columns at the Panther Mountains. Connor himself would lead the left command from Fort Laramie, following the eastern base of the Bighorn Mountains to the Tongue River, and then moving up the river northeastward to meet the other two columns. Along this route, he would construct a fort on Powder River.

On 5 July Connor reacted to rumors of a peace movement with the Indians being discussed in Washington:

> I understand by telegraphic reports that efforts will be made to make treaties with the hostile Indians. I have the honor to represent that any treaty made with hostile Indians in this district prior to their chastisement will not be observed by them [in] six months, and will only result in injury to them and the settlers and travelers in this district, and a continual expense to the government. Unacquainted as they are with the power of the Government, overtures of peace would be looked upon by them as a weakness on our part, and a treaty would only be observed so long as they received presents. They now boast that one Indian can whip five soldiers. They have certainly been successful against our troops in the last year, and until they are taught a lesson, treaties would prove unmerciful to them.[40]

---

[38] Ibid.
[39] Connor to Dodge, 5 July 1865, *The War of Rebellion*, O.R., Series 1, Volume 48/2 [S#102].
[40] Connor to Dodge, 5 July 1865, ibid.

Capt. Henry E. Palmer, Company A,
Eleventh Kansas Volunteer Cavalry.
*Courtesy of the Nebraska State Historical
Society, RG2411 PHO 4230.*

General Dodge responded, "I don't think [the] Government will interfere to make peace; they appear to [be] disposed to leave it with us."[41]

As July faded towards August, Connor and Dodge communicated
back and forth regarding supply trains, troop movements, condition of
the horses, and other topics pertaining to the preparation of the expedition. Civilian contractors became the target of Connor's ire, who commented, "I fear the rascally contractor will starve us out" and "I wish they
[the Indians] had Contractor Buckley under their scalping knives."[42]

Unrest among the troops continued: "Have five companies of the
Eleventh Kansas on that road [mail route], but they are insubordinate
and disobedient, caused by Colonel Moonlight telling them that they
were entitled to muster out and that I intended to muster them out of the
service here."[43] Dodge concurred, "All the troops are giving me great
trouble. Infantry at Fort Leavenworth mutinied; cavalry (some of it) the

[41] Dodge to Connor, 6 July 1865, ibid.
[42] Connor to Dodge, 7 July 1865, and Connor to Dodge, 15 July 1865, ibid.
[43] Connor to Dodge, 15 July 1865, ibid.

same."[44] Connor answered: "The Eleventh Kansas is still mutinous, but I cannot punish them because they are scattered and I cannot dispense with their services at present."[45]

While returning from St. Louis in June, Connor met Capt. Henry E. Palmer of the Eleventh Kansas Cavalry, who was en route to rejoin his company at Platte Bridge Station. Connor took a liking to him and had him assigned as his assistant adjutant general. In late July, Connor refused to let Palmer join his company and "issued an order announcing [Palmer] as his acting assistant quartermaster, and instructed [him] to provide transportation, forage, etc., for the expedition."[46] Captain Palmer recalled jumping into his new assignment with vigor:

> I found that there were only about seventy government wagons at Fort Laramie; that the commissary store and forage required for the expedition, and required by the command under Col. Cole, would require in the neighborhood of 200 wagons to transport the same. I was compelled to press citizens' outfits into the service.
>
> I pressed into service forty wagons belonging to Ed. Creighton, which were under charge of Thomas Alsop; captured Tom Pollock's train of thirty wagons, and other trains too numerous to mention, until I had a train of 186 wagons.[47]

Palmer's requisitioning tactics probably added to Connor's growing reputation as one who got things done, regardless of rules and regulations.

Patrick Connor's expedition was finally coming together. He had done everything within his power to get the campaign organized, including using procurement methods that were outside the strict military guidelines. This would come back to haunt him later, but for now, his two commands were almost ready to go. The Sixth Michigan Cavalry had been on the road from Fort Leavenworth since 17 June. When they arrived at Fort Laramie, the west column would be virtually complete.

---

[44]Dodge to Connor, 21 July 1865, ibid.

[45]Connor to Dodge, July 21, 1865, ibid.

[46]H. E. Palmer's account of the Connor expedition, Hafen and Hafen, *Powder River Campaigns*, 107.

[47]Ibid., 107–108. Ed Creighton was a prominent builder of the overland telegraph line in 1860–61. Tom Pollock was a pioneer of Denver, Colorado.

CHAPTER FOUR

KIDD'S DISCONTENT

Col. James Harvey Kidd was ready to go home. Commander of the Sixth Michigan Volunteer Cavalry near Julesburg, Colorado Territory, he wrote in his pocket-sized journal, "Everybody wants to go home and these plains are consigned in the curses of men and officers to a worse place than any of them care for themselves."[1]

The Sixth Michigan, one of the elite cavalry regiments of the Army of the Potomac in the East, fought at Gettysburg in July 1863 under the leadership of Brig. Gen. George Armstrong Custer. As part of the famed Michigan Brigade, the Sixth gained additional honors in many of the important encounters in the East from that point on. In early April 1865 the Sixth was at Appomattox Courthouse for the surrender of Gen. Robert E. Lee and the Confederate Army of Northern Virginia. The twenty-seven-year-old Kidd wrote to his father in Ionia, Michigan, on 31 May, "I am well and start for St. Louis today, where the regiment has already gone. I can't say whether we are to be mustered out or not. Nobody knows."[2]

Kidd then traveled by train via Columbus and Cincinnati to St. Louis, then took the riverboat *Paragon* to Fort Leavenworth, Kansas, rejoining his regiment on 9 June.[3]

On 16 June he received orders from his commander, Brig. Gen. Peter Stagg: "Col, You will march with your Regt tomorrow for Julesburg, C.T. reporting to Brig Genl P E Connor commanding Dept. of the Plains. . . .

---

[1] Kidd diary, 17 July 1865 entry.
[2] Kidd letter to father, 31 May 1865.
[3] Kidd letter to father, 12 June 1865; Kidd letter to parents, 16 June 1865; Kidd diary, 6 June 1865 entry.

Col. James Harvey Kidd, Sixth
Michigan Volunteer Cavalry, taken
at Yorktown, Virginia, in February
1864. *Courtesy of the Bentley Historical
Library, University of Michigan, James
Harvey Kidd Collection.*

You will use your own discretion about the distance you march each day,
but Genl Dodge is anxious that you get through as soon as possible."[4]

Kidd wrote to his parents that day and told them of his orders: "Julesburg is about 500 miles west of here and in the N.E. corner of Colorado T. Rec. your letter urging me to resign, but have concluded to wait
and be mustered out with the old men whose time expires October 11th
1865. We shall perhaps go through as far as Salt Lake City if not further.
You may however expect me home in the fall."[5] Kidd certainly showed a
loyalty towards his seasoned veterans, with whom he had been through
the many battles and campaigns in the East, which he clarified in a later
letter to his father: "The fact cannot be disguised that there was and is a
bitter feeling among us against the author of this wild goose chase, and
the men all not slow to say that had I refused to come with them they
would have suffered the consequences of open mutiny rather than have

---

[4]Stagg to Kidd, 11 June 1865, J. H. Kidd Papers.
[5]Kidd letter to parents, June 16, 1865.

stirred a step. I have had no trouble. My men are attached to me and if we are allowed to go home when our time expires, there will be no trouble, otherwise anticipate it."[6] He apparently had no idea of what plans Gen. Patrick Connor had for the Sixth Michigan.

Colonel Kidd led his regiment northwest out of Fort Leavenworth on the morning of 17 June. Eleven companies of the Sixth Michigan—more than five hundred men—and a wagon train of supplies made up the command. Capt. Benjamin F. Rockafellow's Company M, with sixty-five men, would start later and join him en route to Julesburg, approximately 425 miles west of Leavenworth.

Heavy rains in eastern Kansas made the going slow as the colonel wrote in his diary on 18 June, "Reveille at 4. Ordered the train out at six. Stuck in the mud. Waited till 8, and moved out. The train not yet out. Told [Captain] Lovell to park it next time so as to get out again same day if necessary."[7]

Knowing that his enlistment was up in October, Kidd was fairly upbeat during the initial part of the journey, describing on 19 June, "Passed a splendid brick house from which waved with kerchiefs from the hands of fair ladies greeting. Gave them cheese & rations. Passed through a magnificent country—can't be beat."[8]

The weather turned exceedingly hot over the next few days. The Sixth Michigan's route took them northwest to Seneca, Kansas, intersecting with the St. Joseph Road, which they would follow west and join the Oregon Trail. The St. Joseph Road mirrored the Pony Express route of 1860–61.[9] On 21 June the company "Went into camp at 3 PM opposite Seneca. Bridge gone and can't cross till morning. Best camping ground we have yet had. A good many men & Officers over in the town. Sent patrol at 8 o'clock PM to bring them into camp."[10]

On 23 June the command arrived at Marysville, Kansas. Kidd described a busy day: "Reached M—e [Marysville] at 2 o'clock. Went into

---

[6] Kidd letter to father, 21 July 1865.
[7] Kidd diary, 18 June 1865 entry. Capt. Don George Lovell was a member of Company F, Sixth Michigan Cavalry. *American Civil War Research Database.*
[8] Kidd diary, 19 June 1865 entry.
[9] Benson, *The Traveler's Guide to the Pony Express Trail*, 32.
[10] Kidd diary, 21 June 1865 entry.

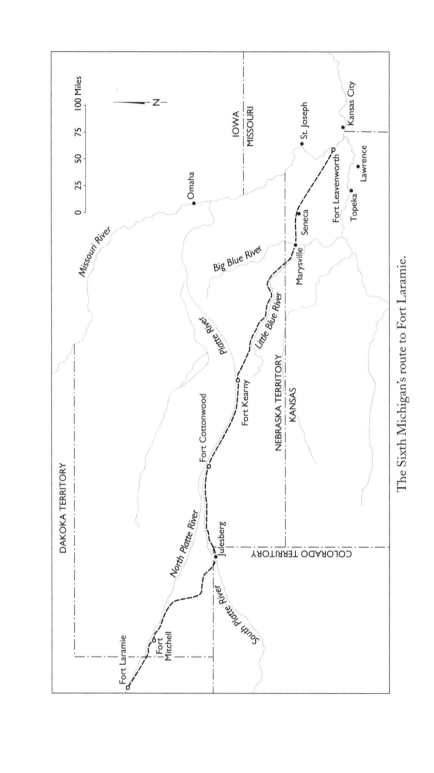

The Sixth Michigan's route to Fort Laramie.

camp. Many men soon became inebriated . . . where upon I closed the shops."[11] The local citizens of Marysville gave a ball for the officers of the regiment that evening, most of whom attended. Kidd described the town: "Marysville is situated on the 'Big Blue' [River] and is quite a 'smart place.' Several stores, a tavern-billiard saloon, Bowling alley, Whiskey shops, etc."[12]

The next morning Kidd reported, "Left Marysville at 9 o'clock, four men of Co. B deserted last night. Took horses, Capt Thomas' horses, equipt, pistols & c."[13] The regiment headed northwest and "Marched 17 miles & camped in a beautiful place. . . . Got dinner at a house. Consisted of onion & heavy biscuit."[14] The house where Kidd took dinner was probably Hollenberg Station, a road ranch and stage station located seventeen miles northwest of Marysville.[15]

There was a wind storm during the night of 26 June: "Thunder and lightning very severe. The wind amounted to some thing like a tornado."[16] Pvt. Sheldon Wight of F Company wrote, "we had a awful thunder showr [sic] joust [just about] dark."[17] The next day, the command encamped on the Little Blue River, haivng marched twenty-two miles in oppressive, suffocating heat.[18] The St. Joseph Road connected to the Oregon Trail at this point.[19] The trail continued northwest and followed the Little Blue for several days. A storm blew in again that night, which Kidd recorded in his entry for 28 June: "Heavy storm last night. Lightning struck a tree near camp."[20]

Kidd described 29 June: "Remained in camp to wash clothes and hunt.

---

[11] Kidd diary, 23 June 1865 entry.

[12] Ibid.

[13] Capt. Nelson C. Thomas was in Company B, Sixth Michigan Cavalry. *American Civil War Research Database.*

[14] Kidd diary, 24 June 1865 entry.

[15] The house is still standing today and is a Kansas State Historical Site near Hanover, Kansas. "The Hollenberg ranch house was built on Cottonwood Creek about 1857 by Gerat H. Hollenberg to capitalize on the Oregon-California emigrant trade that passed his door. . . . Emigrants were able to obtain provisions at the ranch. Three years later, it became a Pony Express home station and later a stage station." *Civil War Soldiers and Sailors System.*

[16] Kidd diary, 26 June 1865 entry.

[17] Geyer, *Sheldon L. Wight,* 92.

[18] Kidd diary, 27 June 1865 entry.

[19] Franzwa, *Maps of the Oregon Trail,* 58–59.

[20] Kidd diary, 28 June 1865 entry.

Some of our best hunters brought in several fine deer. Turkeys, squirrels, etc. were brought in in abundance. I shouldered a double-barreled fusillade [shotgun?] and assuaged the sportsman with poor success however for nary a buffalo or Antelope or Elk presented his broadside invitingly for a shot. I couldn't even hit birds and went back to camp in disgust and tired out. Heat excessive."[21]

The next day, still encamped on the Little Blue, found Kidd very relaxed as he wrote, "Splendid camping ground, this is more like a pleasure trip than anything. We start at 8 o'clock in the morning, march at a moderate gait until 1 or 2 o'clk PM, then go into camp in some 'cool grassy spot' and 'lay ourselves out' for enjoyment. We play cards, (not for money) chat, sleep, read novels, write letters, smoke, sing, etc. Boys brought a fine deer tonight. Detected Sergt Lewis Co K as the man who stole a pocket book containing $40 yesterday."[22] Kidd made no further mention of the stolen money or Sergeant Lewis, who remained with the regiment until it was mustered out of service in November.

The Sixth Michigan continued northwest following the Little Blue, making their last camp on the river on 1 July. Kidd decided to stay in camp on Sunday, 2 July, resting and feeding the stock, because the next portion of the trail, from the Little Blue to the Platte River, was thirty-five miles and barren of water or grass. Kidd ordered a dress parade that evening, but "storms intervened and stopped it."[23]

The command's most demanding day on the trail yet was 3 July, which Kidd recalled in a letter to his father:

> After leaving the Little Blue we were obliged to march 35 miles without water or rest on a hot and dusty day. Starting at 6 o'clock in the morning we pushed our way blinded by dust and choked with thirst across a barren plain until 3 o'clock in the afternoon when our eyes were gladdened with a sight of the woods fringing the banks of the Platte yet 8 miles distant and after reaching it we found our visions of comfort only half realized for the wood was across the river out of reach. The grass poor and the river water muddy and no other for the horses or ourselves.

---

[21] Kidd diary, 29 June 1865 entry.
[22] Kidd diary, 30 June 1865 entry. First Sgt. Franklin R. Lewis was a member of Company K, Sixth Michigan Cavalry. *Civil War Research Database.*
[23] Kidd diary, 2 July entry.

We camped near a dirty little burg of '*Adobe*' [Kidd's emphasis] huts (huts built of turf) dignified by the name of Dog Town. For the first time we were restricted to '*Buffalo Chips*' [Kidd's emphasis] for fuel. This novel kind of fuel answers very well in dry months there as a substitute for wood.[24]

On 4 July, the Sixth Michigan marched in to Fort Kearny, Nebraska Territory. They "went in with flying colors but met with no reception, though afterwards the officers about the fort were very hospitable."[25] In his journal Kidd wrote, "[F]ound everybody celebrating in the vino." Private Wight told of the enlisted men celebrating the Fourth, and "about one third of the boys was tipsy."[26] The Sixth's officers were invited to the local officers' Fourth of July ball that evening. Kidd wrote of a "Gay & festive time. Conviviality and hospitality are undoubtedly characteristic of the post. Had a right good time."[27]

Because of their inability to draw supplies on the holiday, the command stayed at Fort Kearny through 5 July. Kidd penned a description of Fort Kearny and the Platte River for his father:

Fort Kearney where I was July 4th is about 300 miles from Leavenworth in Nebraska Territory. It is like Fort L[eavenworth], simply a collection of barracks, answering for quarters for the troops and a depot of supplies. Here is where the two great routes from Omaha and Leavenworth converge. At this point we strike the South Fork of the Platte River along which we found plenty of grass for our stock.[28] This stream in some places yet 2 & 3 miles wide, is very shallow and were it not for the quicksand bottoms fordable at any point. It is of course not navigable. A river 2 or 3 miles wide, so shallow that a man can wade across, it is a phenomenon.[29]

Colonel Kidd, being the commander of an elite eastern regiment, may have tended to look down upon western troops as inferior. This attitude

---

[24] Kidd letter to father, 21 July 1865.

[25] Ibid.

[26] Geyer, *Sheldon L. Wight*, 94.

[27] Kidd diary, 4 July 1865 entry.

[28] Kidd is mistaken about this being the South Platte River; it is the Platte River. The river does not divide into north and south forks for another ninety miles to the west, near today's North Platte, Nebraska.

[29] Kidd letter to father, 21 July 1865.

was not uncommon in the "spit and polish" traditions of the Army of the Potomac, instilled early in the Civil War by Gen. George McClellan. With that in mind, Kidd recorded his assessment of the troops stationed at Fort Kearny: "The 1st Neb. Cav is on duty here. Do not consider this a first class regiment."[30] Kidd's evaluation of this regiment was probably accurate, for on 21 July General Connor wrote, "Part of the First Nebraska Cavalry stationed at Kearney claim, as the war is over, that they are entitled to discharge, and have mutinied. I have ordered Colonel Heath to suppress it with grape and canister, and bring the leaders to trial."[31]

The Sixth Michigan marched twenty-seven miles the next day and camped near the site of the Plum Creek massacre from the previous August. Kidd complained about the insects: "Our horses are worried by a large green-headed fly called the buffalo fly which leaves a red mark of blood when it alights. Found first symptom of knats and alkali."[32]

The march on 8 July was a miserable day on the trail: "Marched at 6 o'clock and still pestered by knats, [gnats] and blistered by heat. Our horses worried by buffalo flies, concluded to shorten up on the distance traveled per diem, since leaving Kearney. Found a very good camp for water & feed in 16 miles. Still limited to *Excremtuta* [buffalo chips, Kidd's emphasis] for wood. Found myself not well tonight. Troubled with diarrhea. Big storm of wind, thunder, lightning and rain." After all of this, Kidd's "spit and polish" nature took over, as he recorded, "Had a fine dress parade in evening."[33]

On the following day, the command marched seventeen miles and went into camp. Kidd wrote, "Took a pill of 1 gr opium 2 gr camphor, feel better this PM. Breakfasted off antelope. The rain of last night renders the air cool and no dust. This and knats have gone in out of the wet and trouble us not. Have lost 17 men by desertion thus far."[34]

The Sixth Michigan marched into Fort Cottonwood at 10 A.M. on 10 July. Located near the confluence of the North Platte and the South

[30] Kidd diary, 5 July 1865 entry.
[31] Connor to Dodge, 21 July 1865, *The War of Rebellion*, O.R., Series 1, Volume 48/2 [S#102].
[32] Kidd diary, 6 July 1865 entry.
[33] Kidd diary, 8 July 1865 entry.
[34] Kidd diary, 9 July 1865 entry.

Capt. B. F. Rockafellow, Company M,
Sixth Michigan Volunteer Cavalry,
Copyright, Colorado Historical Society
(BPF-Rockafellow, B.F., Scan
#10038728).

Platte Rivers, Fort Cottonwood sat near today's town of Maxwell, Ne-
braska.[35] Kidd described his visit: "A military post here commanded by
Brevt Brig Gen Heath, Col 7th Iowa Cav. with whom I took dinner.[36]
Found the post very quiet. An exceedingly gentlemanly set of officers.
Drew supplies of subsistence, grain and clothing."[37]

On 11 July Kidd told of meeting a colorful local character: "Reached
Jack Morrow's ranche, 12 miles from Cottonwood and camped there at
10 o'clock A.M. Found 'Jack' a gay and festive fellow. He invited myself &
Lovell to dinner and came down with a carriage and span of fast horses to
take me up to his ranche. Drove his team which can make their mile in

---

[35] The post was built in 1863, originally named Fort McKean. In May 1864 it was renamed Fort
Cottonwood. On 28 February 1866 the name changed again, this time to Fort McPherson.
Mattes, *The Great Platte River Road,* 276.

[36] Col. Herman H. Heath, Seventh Iowa Cavalry, had been in Omaha as late as 3 July, helping
organize the Eastern Division of the Powder River Indian Expedition, which left Omaha on
1 July. Wagner, *Powder River Odyssey,* 33–34, 42.

[37] Kidd diary, 10 July 1865 entry.

3 minutes. Jack is said to be worth $50,000. Indians cleaned him out last year."[38]

On 12 July, Kidd wrote, "Capt Rockafellow has been in our wake all day and overtook us with 65 men this PM."[39] Capt. Benjamin Franklin Rockafellow had left Fort Leavenworth on 24 June with Company M and the remaining regiments of the Michigan Brigade, including Brigadier General Stagg. They had arrived at Fort Kearny on 8 July, after the departure of Kidd's command. Rockafellow, who also kept a daily journal, wrote, "Genl Stagg gave me permission to go ahead and try to overtake the regiment which has three days start."[40]

The command marched to Alkali Station on the South Platte River the next day, and went into camp about noon. At the telegraph station, Kidd probably received the following order, sent on 11 July by his commander, General Stagg: "You will proceed with all dispatch to Fort Laramie reporting to Gnl Connor at that place. Draw sufficient stores at Julesburg to take you through. Gnl Connor is anxious to get you there as soon possible."[41]

A local rancher invited Colonel Kidd, Captain Rockafellow, and other officers to supper. Rockafellow described the occasion: "Had a free Champaign supper given by C. C. Mann keeper of Rising Sun Ranch 50 miles from Fort Cotton[wood] & 50 from Julesburg. . . . Oysters, cake, Strawberries."[42] True to form, Kidd "had a dress parade in the evening," which he reported was the "Finest parade we have ever had."[43] The local rancher, Mann, was quite impressed: "At dress Parade Mann who is an old trader and been on the plains many years said with oaths which can only be heard on the plains I never saw the equal of that in all my life on the plains and I have seen all the troops that crossed for many years."[44]

The insects continued to harass the column. "Weather very warm, sun shining and very dusty, gnats and mosquitoes numerous and pestiferous.

---

[38] Kidd diary, 11 July 1865 entry.

[39] Kidd diary, 12 July 1865 entry. Capt. Benjamin Franklin Rockafellow was in Company M, Sixth Michigan Cavalry. *American Civil War Research Database.*

[40] Rockafellow diary, 12 July 1865 entry, Hafen and Hafen, *Powder River Campaigns*, 159.

[41] Stagg to Kidd, 11 July 1865, J. H. Kidd Papers.

[42] Rockafellow diary, 11 July 1865 entry, Hafen and Hafen, *Powder River Campaigns*, 161.

[43] Kidd diary, 13 July 1865 entry.

[44] Rockafellow diary, 13 July 1865 entry, Hafen and Hafen, *Powder River Campaigns*, 161.

Covered my head in nets through which some of them managed to work their way, and bit fiercer than ever as though in spite for the trouble I had given them."[45]

On 15 July, Kidd reported, "Marched 21 miles and made Julesburg at 2 PM. Two or three houses and a few tents. Found the ford so bad could not cross and camped." Rockafellow added, "Near this ford was the portion of Julesburg burnt by about 1500 Indians Feby 2/65."[46] The *Rocky Mountain News* of 16 July noted, "The 6th Michigan Cavalry arrived here [Julesburg] yesterday, en route for Fort Laramie. They are a fine looking set of men and have seen some hard service in the army of the Potomac, under Phil Sheridan."[47]

The next day, Kidd received a telegram from General Connor ordering him to proceed to Fort Laramie immediately. He then described a long miserable day getting his regiment and the wagon train across the South Platte River: "Crossed the river and camped 5 miles distant on a small creak with very poor feed in a Prairie Dog village. The train, not being able to cross at the same ford went 4 miles below. They had considerable trouble and did not reach camp until long after dark finding us all drenched by a heavy rain-storm which lasted all night. Very cold all day, a drizzling rain rendering it exceedingly uncomfortable in over coats."[48]

The rain and cold weather continued all of the next day. Kidd said, "Rained hard in P.M. and much like a Mich November."[49] Rockafellow wrote, "8 mules Played out & died."[50] Pvt. Sheldon Wight of F Company described part of his day: "I fel [*sic*] out of the ranks to fix my Saddle blanket. as I was a fixing it i [I] herd [*sic*] a rattleng [*sic*] behind me. I loocked [*sic*] around and there was a rattle snake. I drew my Sabre and killed him. . . . It was Cold and windy."[51]

The storm passed and the weather grew more pleasant the next morning. The regiment only moved eight miles and went into camp where

---

[45] Kidd diary, 14 July 1865 entry.
[46] Rockafellow diary, 16 July 1865 entry, Hafen and Hafen, *Powder River Campaigns*, 162.
[47] *Rocky Mountain Daily News* (Denver), July 24, 1865.
[48] Kidd diary, 16 July 1865 entry.
[49] Kidd diary, 17 July 1865 entry.
[50] Rockafellow diary, 17 July 1865 entry, Hafen and Hafen, *Powder River Campaigns*, 163.
[51] Geyer, *Sheldon L. Wight*, 96.

Courthouse Rock on the Oregon Trail in southwestern Nebraska.
Kidd planted the regimental flag on its summit on 20 July 1865
as his troops marched by, cheering. *Author's photo.*

there was good feed and water for the animals.[52] Rockafellow wrote,
"Capt. [Jacob O.] Probasco, Lieut. [Elias B.] Stone, Sergt. [Henry A.]
Ward, Prvt [William R.] Wheeler & me went out hunting."[53] The hunt-
ing party had no success; Rockafellow only reported being harassed by
"Gnats, and Aunts [ants]." He said of their return, "Saw Rattlesnakes &
Got into camp in time for supper before dress Parade."[54]

On 19 July, after making forty miles, the Sixth Michigan camped near
one of the famous landmarks of the Oregon Trail, Courthouse Rock.

[52] Kidd diary, 18 July 1865 entry.
[53] Capt. Jacob O. Probasco was in Company E, Sixth Michigan Cavalry. First Lt. Elias B.
Stone was in Company M, Sixth Michigan Cavalry. Sgt. Henry A. Ward was in Company
K, Sixth Michigan Cavalry. Pvt. William R. Wheeler was in Company K, Sixth Michigan
Cavalry. *American Civil War Research Database.*
[54] Rockafellow diary, 18 July 1865 entry, Hafen and Hafen, *Powder River Campaigns,* 163.

They had a visitor in camp: "Met Gen [Guy V.] Henry in ambulance brought Gen Connor's compliments with directions to hurry on. Says he learned a (Mich) Colonel had been killed by his own men *En Route* [Kidd's emphasis] and was surprised to see me alive. Found him a very pleasant gentlemanly officer."[55]

The next morning, as the regiment moved out, "Col. Kidd and several officers went ahead and planted our Regt. Colors (which was presented by Ladies of Ionia) on pinnacle of Court House Rock. Were most lustily cheered by boys."[56] Private Wight carved his name in the rock.[57]

The day of 21 July found the command marching past another Oregon Trail landmark. Kidd "with several others rode over to Chimney Rock 5 miles distant. This is a still more singular freak of nature than the one we visited yesterday. A pyramid shaped mound over perhaps 300 feet, from this shoots up a perpendicular rock, a hundred feet higher resembling nothing more than a chimney. This is distinctly seen for a great distance."[58]

A rainy and cold morning greeted the command, and Colonel Kidd chose to ride in an ambulance. They passed another famous landmark, Scotts Bluff. Some portions of the trail were almost impassable. Kidd reported, "Got through and encamped at Fort Mitchell, a post 50 miles from [Fort] Laramie."[59] The fort, with walls built of sod, was named after Gen. Robert "Fighting Bob" Mitchell, district commander at the time of its construction in 1864.[60]

The weather on 23 July contrasted sharply with the previous day, as Kidd recorded the day's travel, "Took seat in ambulance again. Day hot & dry. Has been but little rain this far up and roads dusty. Passed Horse

---

[55] Kidd diary, 19 July 1865 entry. Col. Guy Vernor Henry was appointed as commander of the East Sub-District of the District of the Plains by General Connor on 30 March 1865. Henry was awarded the Medal of Honor for leading his troops in assaults at Cold Harbor, Virginia, on 1 June 1864. Jones, *Guarding the Overland Trails,* 220; *American Civil War Research Database.*

[56] Ionia was Kidd's hometown in Michigan. Rockafellow diary, 20 July 1865 entry, Hafen and Hafen, *Powder River Campaigns,* 164.

[57] Geyer, *Sheldon L. Wight,* 96.

[58] Kidd diary, 21 July 1865 entry.

[59] Ibid.

[60] Hill, *The Oregon Trail,* 99. Fort Mitchell was located near today's Mitchell, Nebraska, on the south side of the North Platte River. Built in 1864, it had a relatively short life, being abandoned in 1867. Knudsen, *An Eye For History,* 32

"Old Bedlam," officers quarters at Fort Laramie built in 1849.
Author's photo.

Creek, where were Indians signs. This is the place where Gen Moonlight prisoners made their escape." The men of the Sixth Michigan showed their displeasure at being there, as Kidd wrote, "Gen Stagg passed us today in an ambulance. Men at trains are said to have groaned him. I did not hear it."[61] Captain Rockafellow mentioned an abundance of rattle-snakes: "A great number of rattlesnakes killed on road today, and it is said a baker's dozen since we came in camp. An Adder crawled across Lt. Moore's chin while sleeping in his shelter tent."[62]

The following day was no better: "Rode in ambulance again. Hot and dusty, plenty of mosquitos & gnats. . . . Miserable barren country. Nothing but Cactus appear to grow. . . . Don't want to see any more of this god

---

[61] Kidd diary, 23 July 1865 entry.

[62] Rockafellow diary, 23 July 1865 entry, Hafen and Hafen, *Powder River Campaigns*, 166. First Lt. Malcolm M. Moore was a member of Company I, Sixth Michigan Cavalry. *American Civil War Research Database.*

forsaken vicinity. Would be satisfied to see a flood sink the whole concern."[63] Rockafellow simply noted, "Country passed through today very
poor."[64]

The Sixth Michigan finally marched into Fort Laramie on 25 July after
thirty-eight days on the trail. Kidd's description of the fort was not very
flattering: "Found a dirty ill regulated post, situated on the banks of the
Laramie, a beautiful stream, deep and rapid."[65] In contrast, Rockafellow
was fairly effusive in his description of the fort: "Fort Laramie is much
the finest station we have seen. One nice Gothic cottage, large H'd Q'rs
buildings, Bakery Shops. Quarters for men built of sun dried bricks."[66]

At Fort Laramie Kidd "Reported and received order to detach 5 companies to relieve 11 [Eleventh] Kansas on Telgph road. I am to command
a column in Powder River expedition, take two companies with me."[67]
The officers and men of the Sixth Michigan were clearly unhappy with
their new orders dispersing the regiment over a vast wilderness area (at
least to them), with less than three months to go until their enlistments
expired. Rockafellow "Got up a petition signed by officers to Genl Connor. . . . Col. [Kidd] learned of it and after seeing Genl. [Connor] said it
would not do." Kidd then held an officers meeting. "Officers at a meeting
appointed a committee consisting of Capts Rockafellow, Lovell, and
Creevy to confer with General Connor.[68] Nothing accomplished except
an assurance doubly given that we can go out when time expires. General
seems to be well disposed and I think one who fulfills his promises."[69] On
25 July General Connor telegraphed his superior, General Dodge, "Much
dissatisfaction exists in Sixth Michigan. . . . They demand their discharge. I will manage them."[70] However, on 26 July Dodge sent Connor
this message: "None of those troops can get out of service until we settle

[63] Kidd diary, 24 July 1865 entry.
[64] Rockafellow diary, 25 July 1865 entry, Hafen and Hafen, *Powder River Campaigns*, 166.
[65] Kidd diary, 25 July 1865 entry.
[66] Rockafellow diary, 25 July 1865 entry, Hafen and Hafen, *Powder River Campaigns*, 167.
[67] Kidd diary, 25 July 1865 entry.
[68] Capt. William Creevy was a member of Company C, Sixth Michigan Cavalry. *American Civil War Research Database.*
[69] Kidd diary, 26 July 1865 entry.
[70] Connor to Dodge, 25 July 1865, *The War of Rebellion*, O.R., Series 1, Volume 48/2 [S#102].

the Indian troubles. After that is done a portion will be discharged. I know that there is great dissatisfaction among them, but you must give them to understand that they must cheerfully obey the orders, and when these troubles are over their case will be considered."[71]

Captain Rockafellow noted a grim reminder of where they were, and that there still existed a condition of virtual war between the army and the Indian warriors. In his 25 July entry, he described the gallows on a bluff northeast [northwest?] of the fort where three rotting bodies were still hanging.[72]

---

[71] Dodge to Connor, 26 July 1865, ibid.

[72] Rockafellow diary, 25 July 1865, Hafen and Hafen, *Powder River Campaigns*, 167. There are no bluffs to the northeast of Fort Laramie. He must have meant northwest, where there are visible bluffs 1 to 1 1/2 miles from the fort. McDermott, *Circle of Fire*, 57, 60–62.

CHAPTER FIVE

COLLECTING LOOSE ENDS

GEN. CONNOR

Of the movements of our District Commander, the public hears and knows but very little. But enough ekes out now and then to show that movements on a very extensive scale are on foot, and although depredations are still committed by Indians, the public generally feel confident that there will be a little wholesome blood letting before fall, and that he will make this the last season when travel across the plains will not be quite as safe as over the prairies of Illinois and Iowa. We are glad to learn that the General enjoys in the highest degree, the confidence of the War Department and is receiving as promptly as can be expected, the men and materials he deems necessary for accomplishment of his work.[1]

The loose ends of the final details of outfitting the complex Powder River campaign continued to plague its planners. On 25 July Connor complained that "The Sixth Michigan arrived to-day half armed and no arms here for them."[2] Dodge responded, "What arms do the Sixth Michigan lack? Did they make requisition for them? There were plenty arms here when they left, so far as I can learn."[3] Captain Rockafellow entered in his diary, "Genl learns that some of our men have disposed of carbines and ammunition and says whoever does it shall suffer."[4] Colonel Kidd also acknowledged, "General discover[ed] that some of our men have been selling their arms," thus adding to Connor's woes.[5] Kidd's

---

[1] *Daily Rocky Mountain News*, 16 July 1865.
[2] Connor to Dodge, 25 July 1865, *The War of Rebellion*, O.R., Series 1, Volume 48/2 [S#102].
[3] Dodge to Connor, 26 July 1865, ibid.
[4] Hafen and Hafen, *Powder River Campaigns*, 172.
[5] Kidd diary, 4 August 1865 entry.

orders changed on 26 July; he was now instructed to take four companies on the Powder River Indian Expedition, instead of two as of the day before. They were undoubtedly able to re-arm the Sixth Michigan, as they were ordered to march west to meet a new challenge.

The northern tribesmen had been relatively quiet over the past several weeks, but that changed on 26 July. An attack on the Platte Bridge Station killed twenty-six men, including Lt. Caspar Collins of the Eleventh Ohio Cavalry, and wounded nine men.[6] On the morning of the 27th, Kidd was "Summoned to HQ and informed that a war-party numbering 1000 or 1500 Sioux & Cheyenne Indians had attacked Platte Bridge Station distant 128 miles. ordered to take 9 companies and proceed by forced marches to the relief of that post. Believing that they would be gone and that the order would be countermanded before I reached that place I took care to provide the command the same as though going in P.R. exped. Started at 6 P.M. and marched 8 miles and went into camp with very poor feed."[7]

There was trouble in camp that evening. "Thom Rigby and a man named Kennedy had a fight and nearly killed each other."[8] Rockafellow said, "Whiskey was the cause of the trouble." Both men were placed under arrest and returned to Fort Laramie."[9]

As Colonel Kidd unenthusiastically marched his regiment west, General Connor continued to push ahead the remaining details to get his expedition on the trail: "I respectfully ask that something be done to hurry contractors. Ammunition transferred to contractors months since, and of which I am short, has not arrived. I start on my expedition with scant supply of stores and many barefooted horses."[10] Dodge then telegraphed his superior, General Pope: "Stores that should have been at Laramie six weeks ago are stuck in the mud and the columns here started

[6]Connor to Barnes, 27 July 1865, *The War of Rebellion*, O.R., Series 1, Volume 48/2 [S#102]. Platte Bridge Station was located at the site of today's Casper, Wyoming. The city of Casper, although misspelled, is named for Lt. Caspar Collins.

[7]Kidd diary, 27 July 1865 entry.

[8]Kidd diary, 27 July 1865 entry. Pvt. Thomas S. Rigby was a member of Company D, Sixth Michigan Cavalry. Pvt. Joseph P. Kennedy was a member of Company D, Sixth Michigan Cavalry. *American Civil War Research Database*.

[9]Hafen and Hafen, *Powder River Campaigns*, 168. Rigby was mustered out of the service a short time later on 4 August 1865, no doubt, as a result of the incident. Kennedy continued in the service with the cavalry until 25 March 1866. *American Civil War Research Database*.

[10]Connor to Barnes, 27 July 1865, *The War of Rebellion*, O.R., Series 1, Volume 48/I [S#101].

out half shod and half rationed. . . . [B]ut we will overcome it all if it will only stop raining and let us have a few weeks [of] solid road."[11] The expedition would have to start short-supplied and expect to be re-fitted on the trail from Fort Laramie at a later date.

On Friday, 28 July 1865, the Sixth Michigan continued its march west toward Platte Bridge Station. Kidd's journal entry fulfilled his prediction about his present mission: "Started at 9 o'clock and marched over a rough barren country to Horseshoe Creek then learned that the war party had gone north from Platte Bridge."[12] On Saturday, they "Marched to La-bonte without discovering a spear of grass. Rain back and no grain to feed. Heavy smoke column on our right supposed to be an Indian signal having reference to movement of our column. Being no feed at Labonte, telegraphed to Gen, and went to Wagon Hound Creek, where was nothing but rushes. Rec telegram to remain here until further order."[13]

Horseshoe Creek, near today's Glendo, Wyoming, is about thirty miles northwest of Fort Laramie and flows into the North Platte River from the southwest. LaBonte Creek is eight and one-half miles southeast of present-day Douglas, Wyoming. Wagon Hound Creek enters the North Platte about a mile west of LaBonte. Kidd received his messages from telegraph stations at Horseshoe and LaBonte Creeks.

While the Sixth Michigan stayed in camp on Wagon Hound Creek resting their stock on Sunday, 30 July, other elements of the expedition began to move. Capt. Henry Palmer's "command left Fort Laramie on the 30th day of July, 1865, en route for the Powder River."[14] The civilian Miller was with a party that had left Fort Laramie the previous day and marched seven miles before going into camp. On the 30th, he wrote, "Broke camp at 6 A.M. & continued up the Platte. After passing Star Ranch . . . we halted for 2 or 3 hours, until the General [Connor] who had remained behind, caught up."[15]

General Connor listed the makeup of the expedition: "Left column commanded by Col. J. H. Kidd, Sixth Michigan Cavalry, composed of Sev-

---

[11]Dodge to Pope, 29 July 1865, ibid., O.R., Series 1, Volume 48/2 [S#102].
[12]Kidd diary, 28 July 1865 entry.
[13]Kidd diary, 29 July 1865 entry.
[14]Hafen and Hafen, *Powder River Campaigns,* 108.
[15]Miller diary, 30 July 1865 entry.

enth Iowa Cavalry, 90 officers and men; Eleventh Ohio Cavalry; 90 officers and men; Sixth Michigan Cavalry, 200 officers and men, and Pawnee Scouts, 95 officers and men, 475 officers and men." Connor also had in his plans a fourth column that would leave the main force and march west, scouting Connor's left flank, perhaps as far as the Wind River. This column would rejoin the main command again, probably on Powder River, and was designated the "West column, commanded by Capt. Albert Brown, Second California Cavalry, composed of Second California Cavalry, 116 officers and men, and Omaha Scouts, 84 officers and men; total, 200 officers and men. Each of these columns is supplied with artillery."[16]

The command also included a fifteen-man detachment, the U.S. Signal Corps, under the leadership of 1st Lt. J. Willard Brown. Capt. Frank North commanded the Pawnee scouts and Capt. Edwin R. Nash led the Omaha scouts, whose ranks were actually filled from the Winnebago tribe, who shared the Omaha Reservation in northwest Nebraska Territory. General Connor's staff consisted of five officers: Capt. J. C. Laurant, A.A.G. (assistant adjutant general); Capt. Sam Robbins, chief engineer; Capt. Henry E. Palmer, quartermaster; Capt. William H. Tubbs, A.C.S. (assistant commissary of subsistence), and 1st Lt. Oscar Jewett, A.D.C. (aide-de-camp).

The train, made up of 186 freight wagons, had 195 teamsters and wagon masters to guide them. It was controlled by Robert Wheeling, chief train master.[17] A. C. Leighton "was sutler [post trader for the expedition], and had eleven 4-mule teams, [and wagons] with goods to sell."[18] Finn Burnett, a young employee of Leighton, would gain notoriety as a participant in future events important to the history of Wyoming.[19]

---

[16]Hafen and Hafen, *Powder River Campaigns*, 40–41.

[17]Connor to Barnes, 28 July 1865, *The War of Rebellion*, O.R., Series 1, Volume 48/2 [S#102]; Hafen and Hafen, *Powder River Campaigns*, 108–109. Companies E and K of the Eleventh Ohio marched with Connor's expedition. Company K was made up partially of galvanized Yankees. Brown, *The Galvanized Yankees*, 185. The Winnebagos' chief, Little Priest, served with the rank of sergeant. McDermott, *Circle of Fire*, 100.

[18]Camp interview with Leighton, 23 February 1914, Walter Mason Camp Collection.

[19]Burnett, "History of the Western Division of the Powder River Expedition." Burnett served as an army sutler at both Fort Phil Kearny and Fort C. F. Smith. He was at Fort Phil Kearny in December 1866 when the Fetterman disaster occurred. He participated in the Hayfield fight the following August. He was one of the first white employees on the Wind River Reservation and became a close friend with Shoshone chief Washakie. David, *Finn Burnett*, 82, 125, 161–62, 226

The civilian guides included the legendary mountain man Jim Bridger, as well as Nicholas Janise, Jim Daugherty, Mitch Boyer, John Resha [Richard], Antoine LaDue [Ladeau], and James Bordeaux. This was a veritable all-star team of guides, mountain men, and traders, all of whom had been in the area for years and knew the country well.[20]

With the exception of the Sixth Michigan, which was still on Wagon Hound Creek, the expedition stopped near the location of today's Guernsey, Wyoming. Miller wrote, "Went into Camp close by a copious spring of pure water. Distance to day 7 miles. Grazing poor. Granite ledges crop out of either side of the stream formed by the spring indicating the vicinity to mountains."[21] Miller's description makes the probable location of the camp for 30 July as Cold Springs, a short distance west of Guernsey and a popular stopping place on the Oregon Trail.

Back at Fort Laramie, Lt. Col. Samuel Walker of the Sixteenth Kansas Cavalry readied his regiment of six hundred men for their march north as the center column of the Powder River Indian Expedition. Ordered to move north along the western slopes of the Black Hills, his command would eventually rendezvous with the other columns in the Powder River country. On 31 July Connor's adjutant, Captain Price, reported from Fort Laramie:

> Portion of Sixteenth Kansas mutinied last night, but weakened on the turn. Colonel Walker sent for assistance. Gave it to him, with two howitzers, double shotted, and orders to do his talking with mutineers with grape and canister. They weakened, however, before troops left the garrison, enough men of Sixteenth standing by Colonel Walker to maintain discipline. Have seven of the ringleaders now in irons. Will convene court to-day to try them. Have just returned from camp and all quiet. You need not give yourself any uneasiness concerning them; they are completely cowed.[22]

Colonel Kidd received orders the next day, 31 July, to disperse his regiment. Capt. Nelson C. Thomas, with companies B, E, and G, headed

---

[20]Hafen and Hafen, *Powder River Campaigns,* 110.
[22]Miller diary, 30 July 1865 entry.
[22]Price to Connor, 31 July 1865, *The War of Rebellion,* O.R., Series 1, Volume 48/2 [S#102].

west for Platte Bridge and Deer Creek Stations. Kidd's diary entry read, "Rec order to move to Labonte crossing 18 miles from Station on river, started at dark and went to Labonte station and camped for the night. Capt Creevy is to remain here with Companies C & D."[23] That left Colonel Kidd with Companies F, H, I, and M, the four companies assigned to the expedition. Captain Rockafellow, assigned to command the four companies, recorded, "Telegraph wire is now down between here and Deer Creek cut by Indians."[24]

Miller's journal entry for Monday, 31 July, described the travel of the rest of the command: "Struck tents early. The road now led over a range of hills which left N. Platte several miles to our right. During the forenoon we crossed 2 dry streams called Big & Little Bitter Cottonwood. At 1 o'clock P.M. we reached Horse Shoe Station, situated on a creek of the name, which affords both wood & water, but little grass. This Post is garrisoned by a company of the 3rd U.S. Vols. & a detachment of the 1st Kansas cavalry. It sports a Telegraph office. The distance from Fort Laramie is 35 miles direction NW. On leaving this post we crossed Horse Shoe Creek, & passed over a ridge to Platte River 6 miles further where we camped. Grazing good. Distance 27 miles."[25]

As the various parts of his command converged toward LaBonte Crossing on the North Platte River, Gen. Patrick Connor's long-awaited, much-anticipated Powder River Indian Expedition finally was ready to move north to challenge the warring tribes and take pressure off of the transportation routes.

---

[23] Kidd diary, 31 July 1865 entry.
[24] Hafen and Hafen, *Powder River Campaigns,* 170.
[25] Miller diary, 31 July 1865 entry.

CHAPTER SIX

1–7 August 1865

ON THE ROAD AT LAST

GEN. CONNOR'S INDIAN POLICY

. . . The General fully understands the foe he has to deal with, and says that nothing short of a defeat that shall make the red fiends believe they are to be totally annihilated will put them in the right frame of mind to bring about a lasting peace.

Every citizen of the West will rejoice to see the inauguration of this rigorous and sensible policy and will unite in the hope that no power or authority will attempt to subvert the just punishment due to our savage enemies.[1]

TUESDAY, 1 AUGUST 1865

The left column of the Powder River Indian Expedition assembled at a well-known crossing of the North Platte River. Miller described the hustle and bustle of the various elements coming together:

Broke camp at sunrise, marched 7 miles to a ford, known as La Bonte's Ford, where we went into Camp on a pleasant Bottom covered with grass. Here we found Capt. North with his Co. of Pawnees, who had arrived here about midnight previous, having gone several miles out of his way on the usual road to Platte Bridge. Shortly after we got into camp a portion of the 6th Michigan Cavalry arrived & a large train of wagons loaded with supplies destined for Powder River. They also having gone out of the way & come into Camp by the same route as Captain North. The short distance we marched to day led through a Grove of Cottonwood trees with a dense undergrowth of wild rose bushes & grease wood.[2]

---

[1] *Rocky Mountain Daily News* (Denver), 1 August 1865.
[2] Miller diary, 1 August 1865 entry.

Colonel Kidd and the four companies of the Sixth Michigan arrived at La Bonte Crossing after marching fifteen miles from the previous day's campsite. On 26 July General Connor had issued "Special Order No. 48," designating Kidd as the commander of the left column of the expedition.[3] In his diary entry for 1 August, Kidd seemed surprised as he noted Connor's presence at the crossing: "General Connor there in advance. . . . General is to go with column in person at command."[4] Captain Rock-afellow made the same observation and elaborated, "Genl seems inclined to retain command of column. Col Kidd talked very plainly to him. I expect we will have considerable hard work, receive no credit for the men we may loose and do as well as we may receive finally an unfavorable report."[5] Clearly, there were apprehensions among the officers of the Sixth Michigan as to their role.

LaBonte Crossing, later known as Bridger's Crossing and Bridger's Ferry, was located in the proximity of the railroad bridge southeast of today's Orin, Wyoming, about ten miles downstream (east) from the mouth of LaBonte Creek.[6]

Connor had planned for the expedition to move to the north bank of the river early next morning. The quartermaster, Capt. Henry Palmer, wrote:

> The spring flood that had just passed had washed away the crossing, and after ten hours' diligent searching not one of the cavalry escort could find a place to cross the river without swimming his horse and endangering his life. Coming up with the train, which had been delayed and did not reach camp until afternoon, I found the general thoroughly discouraged and more than disgusted with his guides. The river had been examined for four miles each way from LaBonta [sic] crossing, and not a place could be found where it would be possible to cross a train. The alternative was presented to march to the Platte Bridge, one hundred and thirty miles out of our regular course.[7]

---

[3]Special orders no. 48, 26 July 1865, J. H. Kidd Papers.
[4]Kidd diary, 1 August 1865 entry.
[5]Hafen and Hafen, *Powder River Campaigns*, 170.
[6]David, *Finn Burnett*, 71. David states: "The North Platte was crossed at Bridger's Crossing, which was approximately at the spot where the Colorado & Southern railroad bridge was to be built below Orin." This was confirmed to the author by recognized Oregon Trail expert Randy Brown of Douglas, Wyoming.
[7]Hafen and Hafen, *Powder River Campaigns*, 110–11.

Palmer then rode west five miles, looking for antelope. He discovered a recently used buffalo trail that crossed the river straight to the opposite bank. Curious as how the buffalo could accomplish this without swimming, he decided to investigate: "I rode my mule into the river and crossed on a good solid bottom."[8] He returned to camp:

> Soon after feasting on an antelope steak that I had captured on my expedition, and having lit my pipe, I strolled up to General Connor and asked if he proposed crossing the Platte at this point, or if he intended to go around by the bridge. The general seemed put out by my question, which under the circumstances, he considered aggravating, and answered me rather roughly that we would have to go round by the bridge. I told him if it was the train that bothered him about crossing, I would guarantee to have it on the opposite bank of the river by daybreak the next morning. The general's reply was, 'Very well, sir; have it there.' After 9 P.M. when all was still in camp, I detailed a gang of teamsters, about forty men with picks and shovels, and marched them up the river to the buffalo trail and set them to work making a road. It being a moonlight night, the work was easily prosecuted, and by break of day on the morrow the lead team of 185 wagons stood, leaders in the river, waiting the command to march.[9]

WEDNESDAY, 2 AUGUST 1865
Capt. Henry Palmer continued his story:

As soon as it was light enough to distinguish the opposite shore, I rode in ahead of the leaders and gave the command forward. There was no break or halt until the train was parked opposite the general's camp, all before sunrise. In fact, the entire train was parked, the mules turned out to graze, and the men preparing their breakfast, when the sentinels on the opposite bank of the river discovered the train beyond the Platte and gave the alarm to the general, who rushed out of his tent in his stocking feet to see what he did not believe was true. He immediately ordered "boots and saddles" to be sounded and in a short time the entire command was with us.[10]

---

[8]Ibid., 111.

[9]Ibid., 111–12. Henry Palmer wrote of this incident in a paper about the expedition in 1887, twenty-two years after the fact. Although there are several errors in his statements later in the account, it reads very true to the day-by-day chronology of events. None of the other participants wrote of this incident, so we will have to take Captain Palmer at his word.

[10]Ibid., 112.

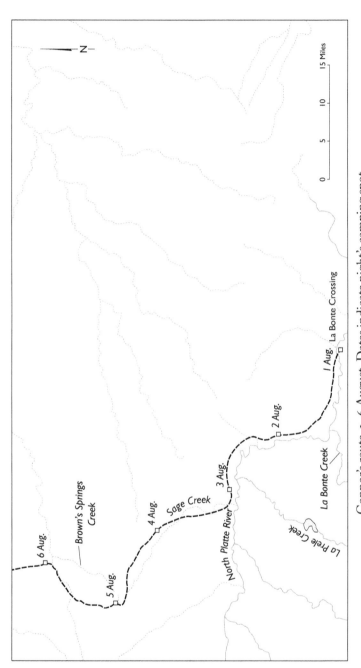

Connor's route, 1–6 August. Dates indicate night's camping spot.

Miller said of the crossing, "The supply train was on the move by day light. The entire Command crossed the River without either delay or damages. The bottom of the Ford is gravel, and perhaps the first good Ford between this & Ft. Laramie."[11]

The expedition moved west following the Council Bluffs Road, which followed the north side of the Platte and North Platte Rivers from the Council Bluffs/Omaha area to Platte Bridge Station (today's Casper, Wyoming) and beyond. Mormon pioneers had used this trail in their migration to the Great Salt Lake Valley in Utah since the late 1840s; however, many of them crossed to the south bank of the North Platte at Fort Laramie.[12]

Miller described the terrain:

> A great portion of the road was bad, as it led through the *mauvais terre de la Platte*, or bad lands of the Platte, the greater part of which are entirely destitute of vegetation. In one place the road led through a Cañon. Here we crossed a tortuous bed of a dry creek. Abrupt precipices of clay & sandstone rose on every hand, & although the attrition of the elements has formed mounds of this same material, their sides appear blistered by the action of Water & the Sun, their appearance being similar to a dusty road after a light shower of larger drops of rain. After passing through this *mauvais terre*, we went into Camp on a fine bottom, affording good grazing. Casualties, Two wagons broke down.[13]

The command marched fifteen miles and went into camp in the vicinity of today's Douglas, Wyoming. Colonel Kidd clearly did not want to be there, lamenting, "Auspices promise anything but a pleasant trip. We are all discouraged and demoralized. Have no luck in the work[s]. Our only ambition having 'worry out the time' until the 11th October."[14]

THURSDAY, 3 AUGUST 1865

Mileage reported by the various diarists was fairly accurate, since "Genl has a Roadometer attached to H'dQ'rs Ambl. [Headquarters ambulance] wheel."[15] The Roadometer, an early odometer, was designed and built

---

[11] Miller diary, 2 August 1865 entry.
[12] Hill, *The Oregon Trail*, 20.
[13] Miller diary, 2 August 1865 entry.
[14] The discharge date for much of the regiment was 11 October. Kidd diary, 2 August 1865 entry.
[15] Hafen and Hafen, *Powder River Campaigns*, 171.

by Mormon pioneer Henry Clayton in 1847. Mounted to one of the rear wheels of a wagon, the device could count up to ten miles before resetting.[16]

The country that they traveled over on this day mirrored the previous day's terrain: "The hills and country we crossed today lay in ridges & hills for miles. Is called Mauvaises Terres or bad Lands. Never shall forget their chaotic appearance. Rocks on very peak of hills looked as if worn smooth and washed under edges & sides by water. Did not make more than 12 miles march and animals in teams were nearly worn out."[17] Miller echoed this description: "Struck tents at Sunrise & passed the mouth of La Parelle [sic] Creek (which empties into the Platte from the south side) about 2 miles, where we went into Camp. The road to day led over a continuation of abrupt barren Bluffs covered with rotten sandstone."[18] Pvt. Sheldon Wight, now assigned duty as a teamster, wrote, "We Marched over the roughest Road that I ever saw. It was nothing but Rocks and hills. . . . [O]ne of my mules plaid out and I had to drive in to Camp with five mules."[19]

The command camped near a grove of large cottonwood trees close to the river and to the west of La Prele Creek. Colonel Kidd described the day as "Very dry and dusty and hot. Camped on the river and took a bath. Presented by the Indians [the scouts] with adequate nice venison. Signal officer Lieut Richards served with Gen Buford in Gettysburg Campaign. A very companionable person."[20] Kidd obviously found comfort with those who had served in the East.

FRIDAY, 4 AUGUST 1865

The expedition marched west for several miles to where the dry bed of Sage Creek crossed their path. The column then turned north, up the creek bed, with the exception of the west column: "Capt. [Albert] Brown with his Co. and another Detach' [Company A, Omaha Scouts] leave column this morning and go via Platte Bridge to pass south end of Wind

[16] Genoa, Nebraska, Historical Stars, 8.
[17] Hafen and Hafen, Powder River Campaigns, 171.
[18] Miller diary, 3 August 1865 entry.
[19] Geyer, Sheldon L. Wight, 98.
[20] Kidd diary, 3 August 1865 entry. Second Lt. A. V. Richards was in the United States Signal Corps. Hafen and Hafen, Powder River Campaigns, 108. Maj. Gen. John Buford was in command of the First Cavalry Division with the Army of the Potomac during the Battle of Gettysburg in July 1863. American Civil War Research Database.

River Mts and join us on Powder River. . . . He takes everything on pack mules."[21] Capt. Edwin R. Nash of the Omaha Scout Company gave more details:

> We left all our company wagons with the General & taking 25 days rations for two hundred men, we started at 4 o'clock A.M. and pursued our way by ourselves. The General leaves the river at this point with his command and the wagon train and strikes out due north across the country for Powder River while we go from here to Platte Bridge & then leave the road keeping a due west course, might we find a practable route across through the mountains to Tongue River & from there if circumstances will permit we are to take a due east course might we meet the General or cross their trail. When we are supposed to join him without delay by this means our column will have to travel about 200 miles more than any other column in the expedition, but being without Wagons we are expected to make better time than the rest.[22]

Miller described the route of the rest of the command: "Morning cool & pleasant with light shower. Left Platte River for a new & untraveled route. The Guide Major Bridger headed the column & led up the Bottom of a dry creek—known as Sage Creek. The direction was nearly due N[orth]. Grass abundant on the creek but, the Bottom was covered with a dense growth of sage brush. The Bluffs on either hand rose with a gentle declivity & afforded considerable Bunch grass. The soil however is barren. After marching 10 miles we went into Camp. Good grass But Bad Water."[23]

Captain Palmer, the quartermaster, told of the organization of the scouts during the march: "Flanking parties were reinforced on our line of march today, the Pawnee scouts composing same; also a party of scouts two or three miles ahead of the command. Every precaution was taken to guard against surprises. Parties were sent ahead for Indian signs, the guides reporting several strong indications of war parties having traveled the country ahead of us."[24]

An accident occurred on the march: "one Teamster run over by a Six

---

[21] Hafen and Hafen, *Powder River Campaigns*, 171. Rockafellow is referring to Connor's planned west column, which included 116 men from the Second California Cavalry and 85 men from the Company A of the Omaha scouts. The orders probably meant the south end of the Bighorn Mountains.

[22] Nash diary, 4 August 1865 entry.

[23] Miller diary, 3 August 1865 entry.

[24] Hafen and Hafen, *Powder River Campaigns*, 113.

Mule Wagon with 40 hundred pounds. The wagon passed over his right leg & striking his body at the left groin passing over his whole body. No bones broken. Boy doing well."[25]

The country through which the command marched, following the Sage Creek drainage, was treeless rolling hills covered with sagebrush. After traveling ten miles, they camped at an unnamed waterhole. Kidd wrote of a bleak campsite: "Camped in a very barren spot with no water but some brackish stuff, tasting even after boiling and made into coffee of some vile stuff."[26]

SATURDAY, 5 AUGUST 1865

Scout Jim Bridger found an Indian trail as the command continued its movement north. Rockafellow wrote that Bridger had "discovered trail of 1000 Indians which was two days old. Supposed to be bands which fought Comd at Platte Bridge."[27]

The column still followed Sage Creek. "Morning cool, clear & delightful. Broke Camp early. The general direction of our route today being nearly N.W. The Creek afforded more water & better grass than yesterday. There is a gentle grade along the route but scarcely any hill, soil somewhat improved, there being less gravel & more sand. After marching 10 miles went into Camp. This Creek heads here at Spring Bottom which affords plenty of good water, & grazing, but no wood except very large sage brush, which makes good substitute in hot weather."[28]

The expedition traveled in a northwesterly direction, crossing over the Sage Creek Divide and going into camp. They halted early, having "Moved from camp at sunrise, traveled over several little ranges of mountains and made camp at Brown's Springs at 10 o'clock A.M."[29]

Typically, the expedition would start early, such as 5 A.M., and get the traveling done before the heat of the day. Even though the command went into camp at 10 A.M., they had been traveling for five hours. The

[25] Miller diary, 4 August 1865 entry.
[26] Kidd diary, 4 August 1865 entry.
[27] Hafen and Hafen, *Powder River Campaigns*, 172.
[28] Miller diary, 5 August 1865 entry.
[29] Hafen and Hafen, *Powder River Campaigns*, 113–14. Brown's Springs and the creek that flows from it are named after 2nd Lt. John Brown of Company E, Eleventh Ohio Cavalry, who lost his life near this place in a clash with Indian warriors on 20 July 1864. *American Civil War Research Database*.

wagons could be stretched out for miles, which would delay their arrival in camp by several hours. The availability of grass, water, and firewood determined the choice of a campsite. The animals, upon which everything depended, needed the time to rest, feed, and recuperate.

General Connor remained in firm control of the operation, even though, technically, Colonel Kidd of the Sixth Michigan was in command. Palmer made an observation about who commanded: "General very vigilant and careful about being surprised; he superintends every movement himself, and is very sanguine that our expedition will be successful."[30]

SUNDAY, 6 AUGUST 1865

Connor rode out with the scouts, leaving the "column and train in my [Kidd's] charge."[31]

Miller described the morning route of the command: "Day rather hot. Broke camp early & struck a Trail called by Major Bridger Bear Lodge Trail. The general direction of our route to day being a few ° [degrees] east of north. The road led over a ridge for 3 miles, when we struck the head of a Run, called Rattlesnake Run about a mile further down."[32] The expedition left Brown's Springs, and moved over a low divide and marched northeast following the dry bed of today's Phillips Creek.

Kidd, Rockafellow, and Miller all mentioned an abundance of wild currants along the route, which Miller especially enjoyed: "Black & Yellow Currants abound here & being ripe I dismounted, slipped the Bit from the mouth of my horse. While he ate grass I ate delicious fruit. But he being sooner satisfied than I, & not content to be alone, without my consent he broke after the Command & I was left to walk or run as I choose the Balance of the way to Camp about 6 miles."[33]

The command marched twelve miles and "Made camp on the dry fork of the Cheyenne [River] at 10 o'clock A.M." Palmer continued, "Grass and water plenty. No water visible, but any quantity of it within a few feet of the surface in the sandy bed of the river. Empty cracker boxes were sunk in the sand; sand scooped out, and soon water could be dipped up by

[30]Hafen and Hafen, *Powder River Campaigns*, 114.
[31]Kidd diary, 6 August 1865 entry.
[32]Miller diary, 6 August 1865 entry.
[33]Ibid.

the bucketful, enough to water all the stock and to supply the camp. The last of the train did not reach camp until dark."[34]

The command dined on a new culinary delight: "On arriving at camp found that the advance had killed two Buffalo Bulls and for the first time dined off buffalo Beef."[35] Rockafellow told of the hunters: "The Pawnee Scouts killed two Buffaloes today and men of Signal Corps Detach' killed one. Were Three 'bulls' feeding by themselves as they do at this season of the year & often many miles from main herd."[36] Private Wight also mentioned the hunt: "Some of the Boys killed two Bufilo [*sic*] and I had some for supper."[37]

After the Sixth Michigan settled in camp, Colonel Kidd and Captains Rockafellow, Lovell, and Osmer Cole played seven games of whist, until, as Kidd related, "we discovered it was Sunday, and feel not a little ashamed of it."[38]

Also on this day, the Pumpkin Buttes, a famous landmark on the Bozeman Trail, were sighted some thirty to forty miles to the northwest, as noted by Miller and Palmer.

MONDAY, 7 AUGUST 1865

"Morning pleasant. Day rather hot," wrote Miller as the command got under way. "Struck tents early, & took up our line of march which was nearly due north. The road led over a rolling country, the elevations were of easy ascent, & descent, gradually widening out into undulating valleys, & tolerably well supplied in some places, with Bunch grass."

The terrain became increasingly difficult as the expedition moved north. "The gentle swells & valleys increased into Rugged Bluffs & deep Ravines & some labor was necessary to make it passable for the s[upply] Train, which did not get into Camp until after dark."[39] Quartermaster

---

[34]Hafen and Hafen, *Powder River Campaigns*, 114–15. The "empty cracker boxes" referred to by Palmer were large wooden crates used to carry hardtack, a hard biscuit that was a staple in the men's rations.

[35]Kidd diary, 6 August 1865 entry.

[36]Hafen and Hafen, *Powder River Campaigns*, 175.

[37]Geyer, *Sheldon L. Wight*, 98.

[38]Kidd diary, 7 August 1865 entry. Capt. Osmer Cole, Company G, Sixth Michigan Cavalry, had previously lost an arm during the Civil War. Hafen and Hafen, *Powder River Campaigns*, 260.

[39]Miller diary, 7 August 1865 entry.

Palmer recalled that "Teams gave out today, many of the mules refusing to pull."[40] Connor then ordered him to " 'Bring in the mules then.' They came in and as he knew they would with wagons and loads, though not until 8 to 10 P.M."[41] General Connor apparently knew he could count on Palmer, though not all of the wagons came in: "We dident [*sic*] get in to Camp until after dark. there was 12 Teams give out and we left the wagons."[42]

The command marched eighteen miles and camped on the "Middle Fork of the Cheyenne River," which appears on current maps as Antelope Creek.[43] Game was in abundance: "Five buffalo killed and brought in today; any quantity of buffalo and antelope in sight on both flanks."[44] Colonel Kidd recorded the Sixth Michigan's buffalo hunt, "Today Capt. Lovell & Dr [Henry Johnson] went out with Pawnees and had a buffalo hunt.[45] Had a fine time and came in full of stories of their exploits. 3 Buffaloes were killed by the party and as they fired their revolvers at them, hitting as they were several times they claim a share of the honor."[46]

So far General Connor's Powder River Indian Expedition traveled over relatively easy terrain, with little difficulty, except for the wearing down of the mules on 7 August. With good camping grounds, plentiful game, and no encounters with the Indian warriors they were seeking to punish, the atmosphere seemed to be taking on the festive air of a grand hunting trip.

---

[40] Hafen and Hafen, *Powder River Campaigns*, 115.
[41] Ibid., 175.
[42] Geyer, *Sheldon L. Wight*, 98.
[43] Both Miller and Rockafellow identified the campsite as on the Middle Fork of the Cheyenne.
[44] Hafen and Hafen, *Powder River Campaigns*, 115.
[45] Dr. Henry Johnson was an assistant surgeon with the Field and Staff Company, Sixth Michigan Cavalry. *American Civil War Research Database.*
[46] Kidd diary, 7 August 1865 entry.

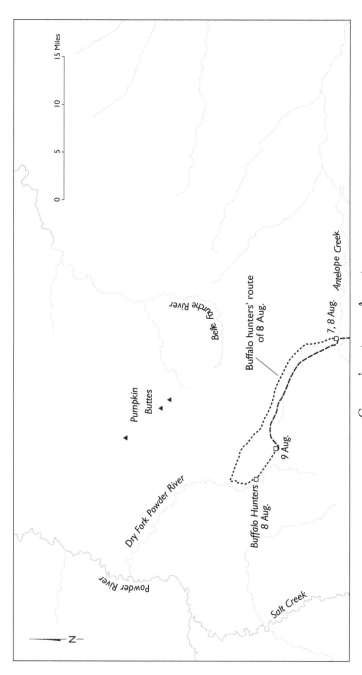

15 Miles

Belle Fourche River

Pumpkin Buttes

Dry Fork Powder River

Powder River

Salt Creek

Buffalo hunters' route of 8 Aug.

7, 8 Aug. *Antelope Creek*

9 Aug.

Buffalo Hunters 8 Aug.

N

Connor's route, 7–9 August.

CHAPTER SEVEN

8–9 August

THE BUFFALO HUNT

TUESDAY, 8 AUGUST 1865

Because the mules had been exhausted the day before, General Connor decided to rest the command for a day: "Gen Connor having concluded to keep the command in camp till tomorrow, went ahead to find a camp, ordering me to remain in command. Capt Rockafellow with some members of the Gen Staff accompanied him, the party consisting of 5 in all, and is to return today."[1] Miller saw through Connor's real intention: "In order to discover the route before us, & perhaps, indulge the desire for sport, the General in company with 2 officers 3 Guides & 1 Corpl. started out in the morning. After riding a few miles over a pleasant prairie, Game being abundant, they betook themselves to the sport."[2] Rockafellow, who rode with Connor's party, listed the hunting party: "Genl Connor, Lt. Jewett, 2nd Nevada Cav, Major Bridger, JaNise [Nicholas Janise], J. I. Brannan, guides, and we started 6:30 A.M. on a hunt after Buffalo and water."[3]

This was wild country where only a few days ago, over a thousand warriors had passed through on their way to and from the Platte Bridge fight. Had they crossed paths with a large group of warriors, Connor's hunting party would have been at their mercy and probably not survived.

---

[1] Kidd diary, 8 August 1865 entry.
[2] Miller diary, 8 August 1865 entry.
[3] Hafen and Hafen, *Powder River Campaigns*, 109. First Lt. Oscar Jewett was in Company D, First Nevada Cavalry Battalion, and Jewett served as aide-de-camp to General Connor.

The expedition would have come to an abrupt halt and the plans and preparation of the past months would have been wasted with the loss of their energetic and dynamic leader. Colonel Cole's eastern command, already on the march, had only supplies enough to get them to the proposed rendezvous at Panther Mountain. If Connor's command did not meet them to resupply, they would be in dire straits, hundreds of miles from relief. After what Connor and others had gone through to get the expedition up and running, this was a very big gamble just for a day of hunting.

Captain Rockafellow wrote an exciting account of the adventure:

We came to several fine flocks of Antelope. One flock of eight I flanked as they went around a hill. Though I dismounted and popped away at them with my Revolver, which the Genl said is like p——g against the wind, did not get one. Just as I got through came up to three Buffalo Bulls. Genl killed one and I put three shots into another which Genl afterwards gave the finishing shot. My mare Julia [was] very much frightened by them at first. After this fine sport [, we] followed down [the] dividing ridge on Maj. Bridger's old wagon trail made ten years ago. Genl decides to adopt route as his wagon road and we struck off to third ravine west of Ponkeen [Pumpkin] Buttes in search of water. Then [we] got separated, old Maj [Bridger] going up it while we went down. This was about noon and last we saw of him that day. When we found water [it] was late in [the] afternoon below forks and in main channel of Powder River which with exception of two water holes was as dry as a powder horn.[4] This forenoon [I] saw [the] first snow I ever saw in Aug. Was on peaks of Big Horn Mountain far beyond Powder River range. Pon Keen [Pumpkin] Buttes are four mountains which lay N & S [north and south], are level apparently & the same height. Made me think of telegraph letter a long mountain mark, a short one, one still longer and then one shorter still, the longest about sixty rods on top, shortest about 25 rods. Elevation above plain more than 200 feet. At [a] point below forks where we discovered water along steep bank on north side which is a ledge of coal situated much as below we discovered a herd of 11 Buffaloes 5 or 6 Bulls, 4 cows & two (2) calves which were laying off to bluff southward from us. Jonese [Janise] went off to [the] left of them and got a shot at a calf. This started herd and away we went

---

[4]The main channel of Powder River was still miles away. Rockafellow and the hunting party were on the Dry Fork of the Powder River.

after them over the bluff, my mare jumping water course after course which were such sharp courses that [I] could not see them until to them & then the only way was to jump. I believe Julia jumped one fully 16 feet wide. We followed Buffalo close along edge of high bluff. Genl Connor went so much faster than we could that he flanked them and kept them there while we popped into them. Finally they made a break down the bluff and the Genl after them went clear around point out of sight while we took after one we got detached. To escape he climbed an almost perpendicular bluff, receiving one shot from Lieut. Jewett which bled him freely. We, Lt Jewett, Guide and myself went up [a] narrow water course which under other circumstances [I] would not thought of climbing. By this time the Buffalo got about sixty rods start of us and we after him urging our horses over rather level course at height of their speed. I got the lead and leaning for'd [forward], was pressing my mare to utmost speed when she over reached and turning somer sault as quick as thought came down on my breast or chest. I thought it crushed in and was sure I could not live. Was rather pleased when found I could speak. I could not hardly move. My breast bone and right chest were badly bruised and my back seemed much jellyfied. They stopped the chase and Genl said [we] would get along to [a] spring so [he] helped me on my horse. I had to get off but trying it again got to the bottom. Unsaddled and Genl kindly furnished whisky from his flask to rub my body with and bade me take some inwardly. I could not lie down and Jonese [Janise] fixed me up well against a tree. Lt. Jewett got water and took care of Julia. We remained until moon came up when marched about three miles up channel and camped in a nice grove or rather cluster of cottonwood trees. Was about midnight before I could get in horizontal position. Buffaloes bellowing and tramping near camp and Genl ordered guard to keep them from stampeding our few horses. Were at least 25 miles from camp.[5]

The rest of the command spent a quiet day in camp. Private Wight wrote, "We toock [sic] some teems [sic] and went back after them wagons that we left the Day before."[6] Jim Bridger returned in the afternoon and updated Colonel Kidd on the hunting party's activities and whereabouts. Kidd wrote, "Gens [General's] party not making their appearance at 9 o'clock we began to feel uneasy. Bridger has come in and reports leaving them about noon 15 miles off. We send up Signal rockets and send out

[5] Rockafellow diary, 8 August 1865 entry; Hafen and Hafen, *Powder River Campaigns*, 176–78.
[6] Geyer, *Sheldon L. Wight*, 100.

scouting party of Pawnees."[7] Miller recalled, "2 signal rockets were sent up, which so terrified our Pawnee pickets, that, some of them left their posts & broke for camp."[8] Kidd and the men of the Powder River Indian Expedition were left to wonder as to the fate of their commander throughout the night.

At Fort Laramie, supplies for the expedition had finally arrived, and a wagon train carrying the goods left the fort in the morning bound for Powder River. Quartermaster Sgt. Lewis B. Hull of the Eleventh Ohio Cavalry, who would accompany the train, wrote in his diary, "Company left Laramie at 8:20. I stayed behind with the captain finished and compared muster rolls in Capt. Anderson's office. Went to old camp, saddled up, ate lunch, and came on to company's camp, below Star ranche on the Platte."[9] Pvt. Charles W. Adams, Company K, Eleventh Ohio Cavalry, also recalled, "A detachment of the 11th Ohio Cavalry, numbering about two hundred . . . left Fort Laramie August 8, 1865, on an expedition against hostile Indians then in force some three hundred miles north."[10]

WEDNESDAY, 9 AUGUST 1865

The concern for the safety of General Connor and his hunting party was, no doubt, on everyone's mind as the new day dawned. "The General not having made his appearance, our anxiety is doubled. Sound reveille at 4 o'clock and changing [his] first intention to remain in camp until he is heard from, [Kidd] got the entire command in motion, and sent flanking and scouting parties, to find him."[11] Miller described the morning march:

> Struck tents early, & proceeded on our march, under the direction of Col. Kidd who was in command. Major Bridger led the way. Our course to day was N.W. The route, although over a rolling country was easily traveled, the surface being smooth & solid. The grades gradual & easy. The view around us, almost boundless, & the landscape green, being covered with fine Buffalo grass. The few ravines, we crossed

[7]Kidd diary, 8 August 1865 entry.
[8]Miller diary, 8 August 1865 entry.
[9]Hull, *Soldiering on the High Plains*, 8 August 1865 entry.
[10]Cozzens, The *Long War for the Northern Plains*, 43–44; Adams, "Raiding a Hostile Village," *National Tribune*, 11 February 1898.
[11]Kidd diary, 9 August 1865 entry.

afforded excellent grazing. We passed by the carcasses of several Buffaloes which were killed yesterday by General's party, except the first we
saw, which was killed by the Pawnees, their choice bits tongue & testi-
cles, only being taken. We also saw herds of antelope, some of which
were killed. After marching 10 miles to the summit of the dividing ridge
between Cheyenne, we met the General & party, who Camped last
night on a dry fork of Powder River.[12]

Rockafellow recorded the Connor party's return to the main column:

Genl [General] awoke at 4 A.M. and very kindly gave me stimulant & last
he had & ordered 'to horse' and we at once resumed march sans breakfast. Saw herd of 100 Buffalos. Following up branch towards Buttes
without finding water took me to right and just left of east dividing
ridge. Started up a drove of black tailed deer. Genl and guide got a
splendid aim but both their guns snapped. They were fine sight with
such nice horns. I am extremely sore and riding up or down gives me
much pain. About 9 A.M. Jonese [Janise] discovered water and following ravine found good springs. We named them Jonese Springs. He
kept on and shortly signaled something visible, of course we supposed it
to be Indians, but proved to be column in motion. When they came up
said they considered Genl and Company gone. Had sent out Indian
scouts to hunt for us. Boys laughed at my humped up appearance. Right
ear started from its upper fastening about 1/2 inch. Right cheek somewhat bruised, hands jammed up. They found us food at once and I got
in Ambulance.[13]

Miller wrote:

After some consultation the General decided to go into camp at the
nearest watering place, which is a little out of our route, the entire
distance being 13 miles which is destitute of water. This Camp affords
only a moderate supply of Wood & Water, grazing Good. About one
mile down this Ravine, is a bed of Coal. The Pumpkin Buttes are to the
north of us, only 3 or 4 miles distant. The Snowy Range of Big Horn
Mountains is also in sight, but the atmosphere is so hazy that we cannot
distinguish their beauty.[14]

They went into camp at the newly named Janise Springs, discovered
earlier that day by guide Nicholas Janise. General Connor had success-

---

[12]Miller diary, 9 August 1865 entry.
[13]Rockafellow diary, 9 August 1865 entry, Hafen and Hafen, *Powder River Campaigns*, 178.
[14]Miller diary, 9 August 1865 entry.

fully returned from his fool-hardy hunting expedition without incident—
with the exception of the battered and bruised Captain Rockafellow—
and resumed control of the column.

The supply train continued its march northwest from Fort Laramie:
"Start early; have to wait for wagons; move very slowly. Reach camp on
Bitter Cottonwood at twelve. March 16 miles. Plenty of shade. Have
currants and cherries to eat."[15]

---

[15] Hull, *Soldiering on the High Plains*, 9 August 1865 entry.

CHAPTER EIGHT

10–14 August 1865

A LETTER TO SISTER KATE

In a letter to his sister Kate, James Harvey Kidd wrote in rather eloquent terms of his expectations for the present journey:

Dakota Territory
HQ Left Column
Powder River Ind Expedition
Wednesday Aug 9, 1865

Dear Kate
My diary says that tonight we have been constantly on the march westward and northwest fifty three (53) days since leaving Leavenworth, that we have marched 850 miles in that time. . . .[1]

We shall visit country unknown except to the hunter and trapper or Explorer and of late undisturbed by them; A country where no road marks the passage of previous parties; We are to pioneer our way through a region but imperfectly represented in the geographies, where Indians alone make their home, and where buffaloes and antelope will reward the hunter; where the hostile bands of Indians falling back before the progress of civilization still implacable and untamable. Make war upon each other, hunt and plan robbing and murdering expeditions upon the remote lines of communications between east and west. We shall see many strange, new, things, shall uncover our find of useful information, and perhaps may undergo some thing of danger and hardship, and enjoy much of adventure and sport.[2]

Col. James Harvey Kidd

---

[1] Kidd to sister Kate, 9 August 1865.
[2] Kidd to sister Kate, 9 August 1865.

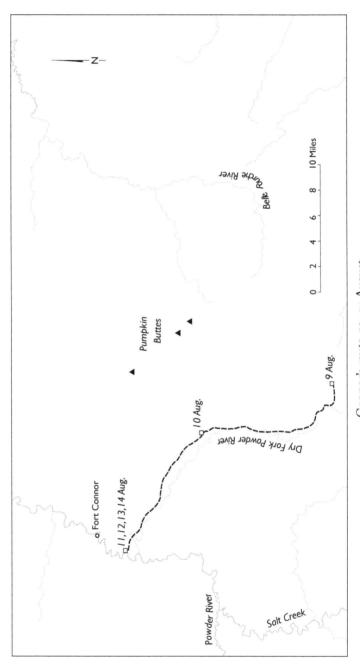

Connor's route, 10–14 August.

THURSDAY, 10 AUGUST 1865
It was an uneventful day of travel for the command:

> Morning cool & clouded. Left Camp early, & returned to the summit of the dividing ridge which we reached yesterday. After which our route along this ridge was N.W. until we reached a dry fork of Powder River which the General visited 2 days ago, which was N.W. by N. After we proceeded down the bed of the river 3 or 4 miles we found some [water?] & went into Camp. Distance 15 miles. The road to day was not so easy as yesterday. The Bluffs were big and rugged, & the Ravines were washed into deep gutters. Some water was found along the route, but in Camp it is scarce, & of bad quality. There is a continued grove of large Cottonwood all the way down the bottom of the dry steam & abundance of dry wood.[3]

The command camped on the Dry Fork of the Powder River, about twelve miles east of the main channel. Kidd attempted to duplicate the adventure of the buffalo hunting party: "Went on the flank with Lieutenant Richards and small party of Pawnees. Expecting from experience of yesterday to have a fine buffalo hunt. Traveled over a very rough country. Saw few deer and antelope and only two buffalo. Had an exciting chase after these last. Succeeded in coming upon one a bull, when an Indian killed him the first shot."[4]

The supply train from Fort Laramie continued its trek west on the Oregon Trail, as Sergeant Hull wrote, "Reveille at daybreak. Have to wait on wagons often. . . . Camp below Horseshoe station at twelve."[5]

FRIDAY, 11 AUGUST 1865
Gen. Patrick Connor had gained a reputation as one who got things done—regardless of rules and regulations. On 11 August Maj. Gen. John Pope, in his division office in Saint Louis, had had enough, and he lashed out to his subordinate and Connor's commander, Major General Dodge, with a telegram: "General Connor is ignoring the quartermaster and commissaries, and violating law and regulations in making contracts him-

---

[3]Miller diary, 10 August 1865 entry.
[4]Kidd diary, 10 August 1865 entry.
[5]Hull, "Soldiering on the High Plains," 10 August 1865 entry.

Maj. Gen. John Pope, commander
of the Military Division of the
Missouri. *Library of Congress,
LC-DIG-cwpb-06341.*

self and forcing officers to pay with public money on them. Stop all this
business at once, and order all officers to conform to law and regulations."[6] Pope's ire was raised by an incident at Camp Douglas in Utah,
where the quartermaster, Capt. E. J. Bennett, had refused to complete a
beef contract that had been privately negotiated by Connor and the sub-
district commander, Lieutenant Colonel George, without a public bid, as
required by regulations. Captain Bennett was placed under arrest.[7] When
the matter was brought to Connor's attention, he responded, "The commanding officer at Camp Douglas did not misunderstand me whether his
action and mine were legal or not. Capt. Bennett disobeyed orders."[8] All
of Connor's irregularities and cutting corners in putting the expedition
together, and now this incident, caused Pope to react.

Connor's orders to his column commanders—to kill every male Indian
over twelve years of age—next received the wrath of Pope, as he tele-

---

[6] Pope to Dodge, 11 August 1865, *The War of Rebellion*, O.R., Series 1, Volume 48/1 [S#101].
[7] Pope to Dodge, 12 August 1865, Grenville Dodge Manuscript Collection.
[8] Connor to Colonel Harris, 29 July 1865, ibid.

graphed Dodge on the same day. "These instructions are atrocious, and are in direct violation of my repeated orders. If any such orders as General Connor's are carried out it will be disgraceful to the government, and will cost him his commission, if not worse. Have it rectified without delay."[9]

Pope was so incensed that he even suggested relieving Connor for "acting with a high hand, & in violation of Law and Regulations."[10] Dodge responded, "I do not see how I can relieve him, as he is now far north of Laramie, and I know of no one I could put in command."[11]

The expedition arrived at Powder River, the first landmark on Connor's agenda:

> Our route to day was along the bottom of the dry creek we reached yesterday & was upon an average, rather heavy. Direction N.W. by N. Greasewood, Sage Brush, Artemisia, Cactus & Groves of green & dry Cottonwood abound all along this dry Creek. The dry wood is so abundant that the advance Guard had to dismount several times to clear the way & some little grading was also necessary as we crossed some of the lower Bluffs when practicable, which shortened the route. The appearance of the Crossing of Coal Beds are seen in various places all along this Creek, & some fine specimens of pure mica were picked up. Water, although scarce, & bad quality was found in several places to day. About a mile from Powder River, this Creek takes a turn to the west, where we left it, & proceeded North over the point of a high ridge, below, & between its mouth & Powder River, where we went into camp. Distance to day 13 miles. Powder River has a good current of running water, & affords good grazing, the bottom is covered with a huge Grove of Cottonwood as far as the eye can see. As I rode in advance to the River, to water my horse, I saw Six very large Wolves which crossed the River quite near me. As they showed no signs of hostility, & having nothing but a pistol, I concluded to

---

[9] Pope to Dodge, 11 August 1865, Hafen and Hafen, *Powder River Campaigns*, 43. When later confronted with these two telegrams, a chastised Patrick Connor simply said he would comply and explain his actions later. His two column commanders, Cole and Walker, however, could not be made aware of the change to their orders, as they were already beyond communication in the wilderness of Dakota Territory. Connor to Dodge, 20 August 1865, 44, ibid.

[10] Pope to Dodge, 12 August 1865, Grenville Dodge Manuscript Collection.

[11] Dodge to Pope, 11 August 1865, South Dakota Department of History *Report & Historical Collections*, Volume 31 (1962), 549.

let them go in peace. Game is very abundant. Herds of Buffalo are in the vicinity. Eight were killed to day, chiefly by the Pawnees, one fourth of which, was not used.[12]

Smoke was seen downriver. Scouts sent to investigate reported an abandoned Indian village several days old. In the evening General Connor, members of his staff, scouts, and an escort rode to the site to investigate.[13] Miller said the Pawnee scouts reported it to be a village of 150 lodges; Kidd estimated it at 500 lodges.[14] The discrepancy in the two accounts may come from the inexperienced observation of an easterner, Kidd, who had probably never seen an Indian village before. Miller reported, "Scraps of telegrams taken by them at Julesburg in Febry. Last, were scattered on the ground & the Scalp of a white man was picked up."[15] Captain Rockafellow confirmed the white scalp: "Nearby Lt. Jewett found scalp of white man dropped by them. A tuft of Sioux hair was left on top of pole with feather through it."[16]

The daily routine of camp life in the regiment was related by Colonel Kidd in his 9 August letter to his sister:

> Before I start you off on the PR Expedition let me give you an idea of our *outfit* [Kidd's emphasis] the name they give in this country to everything from a ladies wardrobe to a Brig General's Command. . . . In the first place 4 Companies of our regiment F, H, I, and M commanded by Capt Rockafellow, small companies, well worn, good companies and not ill mannered, assuming, perhaps a little of the swagger and devil-may-care air characteristic of men whose time's about out and who think they are near enough citizens to enjoy that imagination which allows a civilian to do what he has a mind to, but who submit with a quiet good grace to the order which compels them to still serve their "beloved Country" for the benefit of the Government, its Generals or Contractors or 'any other man.'. . . The Officers with us are Lovell, Rockafellow, Cole, Kellogg, Dr Johnson, Lieuts Moon, Stone, Gould, good fellows all.
>
> About *our* [Kidd's emphasis] mess four of us [Capt. Don G.] Lovell, [Capt. B. F.] Rockafellow, Dr J [Assistant Surgeon Henry Johnson]

---

[12] Miler diary, 11 August 1865 entry.

[13] Palmer's account, 11 August 1865, Hafen and Hafen, *Powder River Campaigns*, 116.

[14] Kidd diary, 11 August 1865 entry.

[15] Miller diary, 11 August 1865 entry.

[16] Rockafellow diary, 11 August 1865 entry, Hafen and Hafen, *Powder River Campaigns*, 179.

and your servant. Don, Goodfellow, Doc, and Col for short. All sleep in one tent, if not under one blanket, for I have raised myself from the ground a[t] night to spite the rattlesnakes. We all gather around the same festive bound meal times. We have provided ourselves with say 10 lbs sugar ditto coffee & dry apples, 50 lbs beans and hams 10 lbs "consecrated" (desiccated) potatoes (sort of a cross between corn-meal and saw-dust) a few cans of peaches—plenty of smoky old pipes and matches. . . . As for myself as purposeful and useless as ever, the same except that I have taken to wearing long-hair and reading novels, also eat pork and smoke (that same meerschaum you cowered comically from when I was at home on furlough) Good tobacco and cigars however I ignore entirely, like beefsteak (because they can't be had).[17]

The supply train traveled toward a rendezvous with Connor's command on Powder River. Sergeant Hull reported a day with some excitement: "Stopped at Horse Shoe; left the telegraph road and crossed the Platte. Indians seen on bluffs; go out scouting after camping. See trail but no Indians, altho some moccasin tracks were fresh. Saw bear tracks along the road. Camp on Platte at the old LaBonte camp about noon. Boys washing and swimming. Guide found where large camp of Indians had been; found scalp, boots, etc. Strong picket guard posted and arms for pillows. 16 miles."[18]

With Indians sighted in the general area, Private Adams drew the unenviable assignment of picket duty that night:

After a few days out, I was detailed on picket, and well do I remember it. I was posted a quarter of a mile from camp (alone) at dark in the sagebrush, with instructions to move fifty yards after dark, so that if Indians should be watching, they would not know just where to pounce upon me. In case I should see or hear Indians moving toward camp, I was to fire and then do the best I could. Well, I did not see any Indians, but I imagined I could hear everything. I was relieved at midnight, and it appeared to me I had been there twenty-four hours.

---

[17]Kidd to sister Kate, 9 August 1865. First Lt. Robert A. Moon was in Company I, Sixth Michigan Cavalry, and was listed as a prisoner of war from 18 October 1863 to 9 May 1865. First Lt. Elias B. Stone was in Company M, Sixth Michigan Cavalry, and 2nd Lt John T. Gould was in Company F, Sixth Michigan Cavalry. *American Civil War Research Database.*

[18]Hull, "Soldiering on the High Plains," 11 August 1865 entry.

There is no fun in sitting alone in the brush half the night, with wolves howling all around and not knowing when a grizzly or some other wild animals may be on one; to say nothing of rattlesnakes.[19]

SATURDAY, 12 AUGUST 1865

The command did not move, as scouting parties explored the Powder River:

Train remained in camp. An exploring expedition was sent up the river under the command of Lieut. Jewett with orders to proceed twenty miles to look for a better location for a military post. Twenty-five of the Sixth Michigan Cavalry went up the river with Lieut. Jewett to the crossing of the old traders' road from the Platte Bridge to the Big Horn Mountains, and past the same known as the Bozeman Trail, made in 1864 by J. M. Bozeman, of Montana. Lieut. Jewett found on both bluffs, with Indian signs all along the stream, scarcely a mile where there had not been Indian villages; some within a few weeks, some that were probably made years and years ago; some very large camps gave evidence that the Indians had very large droves of horses, as the trees were badly girdled. Numerous Indian burial trees were found, with lots of 'good Indians' tied up in them. Several bands of buffalo were seen during the day. Lieut. Jewett returned to camp the same day, having made a fifty mile march.[20]

Colonel Kidd "Rode out with General Connor several miles up the river. Found nothing new. The stream is fringed with Cottonwood groves as far as we can reach in both directions. Very little timber can however be made available for building purposes. Saw no game. Bridger accump [accompanied] us."[21]

In James Harvey Kidd's letter to his sister, he also described the Pawnee Scouts:

---

[19] Adams, "Raiding a Hostile Village."

[20] Palmer report, 11 August 1865, Hafen and Hafen, *Powder River Campaigns,* 116–17. Indian ponies would feed on cottonwood bark when grass was scarce. Palmer's use of "good Indians" probably is in reference to the frontier saying that "The only good Indian is a dead Indian." Brown, *Bury My Heart at Wounded Knee,* 170–72. Gen. Phil Sheridan is normally credited with originating the "good Indian" term in a conversation with Comanche chief Tosawi at Fort Cobb, Indian Territory (Oklahoma) in December 1868.

[21] Kidd diary, 11 August 1865 entry.

Over yonder is Company A of the "Pawnee Scouts" a Co of about 100 Pawnee Indians a tribe which is friendly and fights on our side until they can catch a white man a long way from home when they amuse themselves by scalping him and attributing the act to Sioux. We are go-ing to fight their inveterate enemies the Sioux into whose country they have never before penetrated so far. They are commanded by Capt North, a very gentleman who talks Pawnee as fluently as his own tongue. These Indians are armed with bows and arrows, guns & pistols and mounted on ponies a hardy animal which goes up and down hill with equal facility and lives on Cottonwood bark when grass can't be had. They are very much like white men *and women* [Kidd's emphasis]. Some are handsome, some are not. Some comb their hair and wash their faces, others do not. They are of fine *physique* [Kidd's emphasis], long, straight, black hair, the color of your tea kettle and have splendid teeth. They all wear the U S Uniform decorated in amenities with Crows quill-hen feathers, corn tails and other fantastic gee-gows, char-acteristic of "ye poor Indian." They are inordinate gamblers and the bravest of all the tribes of Indians.[22]

The Indian scare of the previous day lessened as the supply train crossed the North Platte. Sergeant Hull wrote, "Reveille at four. No alarm during the night. We take the advance and 6th boys the rear guard. Cross Platte at LaBonte's crossing. Travel over some very broken barren ground. See some signs of Indians. Kill large rattlesnake. Reach camp at 2, on Platte near mouth of LaPrele. Guide brought in antelope. Go seining; little good. March 22 miles."[23]

SUNDAY, 13 AUGUST 1865

The command relaxed in their camp on the banks of Powder River. "Day cool clear & delightful under the grateful shade of the low, but widespread branches of the Cottonwood, where we remained in Camp all day."[24] Colonel Kidd, not wanting to be disrespectful of the Sabbath as he had been last Sunday, recorded, "Took a bath in the morning and 'rigged out' in our best. With due respect for the day refrained from card playing and all unspoken excuses. In the utter absence of chaplains, had

---

[22]Kidd to sister Kate, 9 August 1865.
[23]Hull, "Soldiering on the High Plains," 12 August 1865 entry.
[24]Miller diary, 13 August 1865 entry.

no services. Morrison made a pudding and barring the excessive heat we rested a very luxurious & comfortable day."[25]

Miller wrote of the day's only excitement:

> Capt. Robbins returned to Camp at 12 o'clock P.M. & reported one man missing belonging to Capt. O'Brien's Company F, 7th Iowa, named Brice who came into Camp shortly afterwards. After traveling about 35 miles yesterday over a broken surface, in a West direction to the Bluffs of Old Woman's fork, a branch of Powder River, where he saw several Indians driving Stock, with other indications of Lodges in the vicinity, & not wishing to discover himself to these Indians he traveled a few miles to the North & Camped for the night. On his return to day he reports the portion of Country which he traveled as barren & quite destitute of Water.[26]

On this day Kidd also "Wrote a long letter to Kate, which will go out in the morning."[27] No doubt he referred to the letter dated 9 August that has been quoted above. A long letter of eight hand-written pages, Kidd probably started it on 9 August. In the letter he described to his sister the officers of the expedition and their troops, sometimes in unflattering terms. He seemed to have a low regard for western soldiers, while he refers to anyone who served in the East in more gentlemanly terms— probably not unusual for a college-educated man who had served under Custer and McClellan in the Army of the Potomac. At times, even Grant and Sherman were looked down upon as "westerners." Kidd wrote of Capt. Levi Marshall:

> I'll throw Capt Marshall, Company (F 11th O Cav) 'into line just here.' A Company of 80 good well-armed men commanded by a certain Marshall whose surname is Capt, a man with a great deal of whiskers, very little sense and no brains who says 'I ken jist take that air company o' mone thar un bring "em down yer an throw em inter line up yender and I ken jest lick eny number o men you ken bring agin em.' One of those meddlesome officers, self conceited, ignorant men who are always successful in making themselves ridiculous—and their neighbors uncomfortable.[28]

---

[25] Kidd diary, 12 August 1865 entry.
[26] Miller diary, 13 August 1865 entry. Capt. Nicholas J. O'Brien was a member of Company F, Seventh Iowa Cavalry. *American Civil War Research Database.*
[27] Kidd diary, 13 August 1865 entry.
[28] Kidd to sister Kate, 9 August 1865.

He also mentioned two officers of the U.S. Signal Corps who had served in the East: "With them are a small detachment of the signal corps, two officers Lieutenants Brown and Richards in charge. They like us have come down from Washington to do duty in the *wilderness* [Kidd's emphasis], nice fellows both of culture and refinement and pleasant companions '*du voyage* [Kidd's emphasis].'"

Next to receive his caustic remarks was Capt. Nicholas J. O'Brien, Company F, Seventh Iowa Cavalry, and his artillery:

> I must not omit mention of O'Brien's battery. Its Capt O'B is a good sort of a person who walks very straight, deeply impressed with his own importance and responsibility but well-meaning and brave. What shall I say of his battery? A motley assortment of pieces all sorts and calibers, a three inch rifled gun, a brass ten pounder, a howitzer, several guns designated by the euphonious appellation "Jackass." All in wretched order, drawn by poor horses badly managed. Sort of a blaspheme on the name of artillery, but good enough probably to *scar[e] Indians* [Kidd's emphasis].

Finally he described the wagons and rations: "Here comes our train 200 wagons loaded with 150000 rations to feed the Command and to supply a fort to be established somewhere in the Powder River Country: rations of mouldy dry flour petrified hard tack and bacon. The Sutlers wagons loaded with goods to swindle any of us who find it necessary or convenient to submit to the process."[29]

Sgt. Lewis B. Hull and the supply train continued on the trail of Connor's column. "Leave Platte. March north nearly all day. Roads very bad, sandy, hilly, broken; crooked turns. Move slowly; have to rest often. Company wagons, cooks, and herders reach camp at 1:30. Teams come in till four, when rear guard arrives. . . . March ten miles."[30]

MONDAY, 14 AUGUST 1865

Miller described a busy day: "2nd Lt. James Muri, Pawnee Scouts, with squad of 11 men, & a Guide, left Camp to [day] in charge of the

---

[29] Ibid. The guns that Kidd referred to as "jackasses" were probably the 1841 mountain howitzer, which could be broken down and carried by three mules: one mule carried the cannon barrel which weighed 220 pounds, a second mule packed the carriage, and a third mule carried the ammunition. Thomas, *Cannons*, 32.

[30] Hull, "Soldiering on the High Plains," 13 August 1865 entry.

mail, for Platte Bridge dis[tant] about 100 miles. Capt. North of same left with a party of Scouts, Major Brady [Bridger?] for Guide, crossed Powder River & pr[oceeded] in the direction of Tongue River to find [a] practicable road in that direction. The General has selected a site upon which to erect a Fort on the opposed side of the River, a mile above this Camp & a number of men & teams were detailed this morning to commence the work."[31]

Quartermaster Captain Palmer elaborated on the start of construction:

> The first timber was cut today for building a stockade, the general having decided to erect a fort on the opposite bank of the river at this point, on a large mesa rising about one hundred feet above the level of the river, and extending back as level as a floor about five miles to the bluffs. A very fine location for a fort, the only disadvantage being scarcity of hay land. Our stockade timber was cut twelve feet long and was eight to ten inches in thickness. The posts were set four feet deep in the ground in a trench. Every soldier and all the teamsters who could be urged to work were supplied with axes and the men seemed to enjoy the exercise, chopping trees and cutting stockade timber.[32]

Colonel Kidd wrote an almost unexplainable entry for 14 August, complaining about General Connor's indecisiveness. "The General does not seem to have decided definitely what to do and is waiting for something to turn up or for his sluggish mind to arrive at a conclusion. He is evidently a very slow tactician, obstinate, determined man who has been accustomed to have his own way. I am however on the best of terms with him."[33] Perhaps he wrote this entry in a slow period in the morning before General Connor had decided on the location of the fort and ordered work to commence, or the outburst could have had something to do with waiting for a decision about the Sixth Michigan being relieved and mustered out on time.

Kidd's letter to his sister concluded with his assessment of Gen. Patrick Connor and his staff. His frank, sarcastic style revealed a touch of prejudice against the Irish nationality, which was not uncommon in that time:

[31]Miller diary, 14 August 1865 entry. Second Lt. James Murie was in Company A Pawnee Scouts. *American Civil War Research Database.*

[32]Palmer report, 14 August 1865, Hafen and Hafen, *Powder River Campaigns,* 117.

[33]Kidd diary, 14 August 1865 entry.

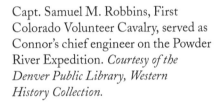

Capt. Samuel M. Robbins, First
Colorado Volunteer Cavalry, served as
Connor's chief engineer on the Powder
River Expedition. *Courtesy of the
Denver Public Library, Western
History Collection.*

Last and not least our General and his staff. Gen Connor whose real
name I suppose is Patrick O'Connor is an Irishman who in respect to
National Characteristics out-Herods Herod, a man of perhaps 40 to
45 years who has a wife and two children at Laramie. He was in the
Mexican War and was wounded at Buena Vista. Originally Col of the
2nd Cal Cav he was promoted to Brig Gen for an affair with Indians in
which his regt was engaged. Some knowing ones maliciously assert that
for what one of his subordinates (now serving on the staff) did he
himself took the credit and hence his promotion, but malice assails
everyone and this may not be true. He has for a long time been in
command of the Dist of the Plains embracing Utah Ft Kearney and the
country north and has in some way earned the sobriquet of Connor the
Indian fighter although never I believe engaged with them since the
affair alluded to. He appears to be a strict disciplinarian and not an
unpleasant man to be with although not sociable at all.

Kidd then went through most of Connor's staff:

A little modest man with black mustache who signs himself J C Laurant AAG runs the Adjutant General's offices. He came from St Louis
to take this position. He never talks and minds his own business.

The originals are Capt Robbins, Chief Engineer, and Lieut Jewett ADC standing each over six feet and well proportioned they are physically immense men. They have been to California, in the mines, have roughed it, fought Indians, and all that, carry gold watches with heavy chains, are shrewd, well educated, and thorough sharpers, and will take the spare change out of any greeny who is fool enough to bet on cards. Our Quartermaster [Capt. Henry E. Palmer] who wears a red shirt and rides a mule.[34]

Kidd ended his letter to his sister: "Give my love to all, I do not hear from you any more."[35] And so, sister Katie's letter was on its way, in the mail pouch, as the detail of Pawnee scouts headed for the Platte Bridge Station, one hundred miles to the south.

---

[34] Kidd to sister Kate, 9 August 1865.
[35] Ibid.

15–17 August 1865

SCALP DANCE

15 AUGUST 1865

Now encamped on the Powder River, construction of the fort was officially under way and caused a reshuffling of the command. Colonel Kidd was relieved of the duty of leading the left column of the expedition and was reassigned as commander of the new Fort Connor. Companies F, H, I, and M of the Sixth Michigan were assigned to build and garrison the fort.[1]

Miller described the movement of the camp and the location of the fort:

Orders were given to break Camp & cross the River, & at 2 P.M. the whole Command had crossed. The Command is divided into 2 Camps *1 1/2 miles apart on the River bottom. The troops belonging to the 6th Mi [Michigan] occupy the upper Camp. The Fort as staked out at present, will occupy a space of 500 ft. in width by 1260 ft. in length, & is intended for 12 Cos. [companies] (or more)* [Miller's emphasis] with officer Qrs. [quarters] Q.M. & C. [quartermaster and commissary] Buildings, etc. The Stockade at the N. Eastern extremity with two Bastions at the outer & opposite angles is progressing under the superintendence of Capt. Robbins Chf. Engr. The Fort is situated on an elevated piece of table land about 100 yds from the face of the bluffs on the N.W. Side of the River, & commands an extensive view, in nearly every direction, with Pumpkin Buttes a few miles to the eastward. The range of bluffs at the head of Powder River to the Southward, & Big Horn Mountains about one days ride to the Westward.[2]

---

[1]C. J. Laurant, A.A.G., 15 August 1865, Special Orders Number Five, J. H. Kidd Papers.
[2]Miller diary, 15 August 1865 entry.

Capt. Frank North, Company A,
Pawnee Scouts, Nebraska Cavalry.
*Courtesy of the Nebraska State
Historical Society, RG2320 PHO 39.*

Around noon Captain North and his Pawnee scouts returned, which
Rockafellow reported: "Capt. North of Pawnee Scouts just came in,
reports large numbers of Indians moving Northward. Says near 1000
Lodges which would be about 5000 Indians, each Lodge being one
family. Must be about 2000 warriors."[3] Miller's notes were similar: "Major Bridger says the Indians are moving in the direction of Powder River
& from the general appearance along Old Woman's Fork, thinks there
must have been at least 1500 Lodges in that vicinity lately."[4]

WEDNESDAY, 16 AUGUST 1865

General Connor's command remained in camp one and a half miles
north of the fort, waiting for the supply train from Fort Laramie to
arrive.[5] "At 2 P.M. to day, there was some little excitement in Camp,
caused by a few Indians who made their appearance on some of the bluffs

---

[3] Rockafellow diary, Hafen and Hafen, *Powder River Campaigns,* 180.
[4] Ibid.
[5] Palmer's report, ibid., 117.

a short distance from the fort. . . . Capt. North with his company of Scouts, was ordered to pursue them, Capt. Robbins, Lt. Jewett A.D.C. & several other officers accompanied Capt. North." Miller continued, "Capt. North's account states that after traveling nearly all night, during which time they crossed & recrossed Powder River several times, they halted a little before daylight to rest their horses, having traveled about 60 miles."[6]

THURSDAY, 17 AUGUST 1865

The next day Miller continued his account: "At daylight they crossed the River again, saw Camp fires, & a little further on Indians mounted on Horses, Ponies & Mules, with but one Squaw & a wounded Indian stretched on a litter & trailed along the ground, which trail the Scouts followed during the night. The Pawnees 48 in No. simultaneously gave one exultant yell, & in a few minutes more, the small warparty of Cheyennes (for such they were) ceased to exist."[7]

Captain Palmer, one of the officers who accompanied North and the Pawnees, described the action:

Capt. North followed the Indians about twelve miles without their being aware of our pursuit; then the fun began in earnest. Our war party outnumbered the enemy, and the Pawnees, desirous of getting even with their old enemy, the Sioux, rode like mad devils, dropping their blankets behind them, and all useless paraphernalia, rushed into the fight half-naked, whooping and yelling, shooting, howling—such a sight I never saw before. Some twenty-four scalps were taken, some twenty-four horses captured, and quite an amount of other plunder, such as saddles, fancy horse trappings, and Indian fixtures generally. The Pawnees were on horseback twenty-four hours, and did not leave the trail until they overtook the enemy. There was a squaw with the party; she was killed and scalped with the rest.[8]

Finn Burnett and his employer, sutler A. C. Leighton, rode with North and the Pawnees. Burnett recalled that "They were surprised and fought manfully until the last one was killed."[9]

---

[6]Miller diary, 16 August 1865 entry.
[7]Ibid., 17 August 1865 entry.
[8]Palmer's report, Hafen and Hafen, *Powder River Campaigns,* 118.
[9]Burnett, "History of the Western Division," 572, 573.

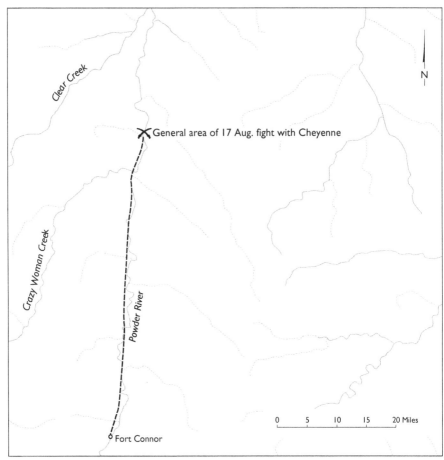

Clear Creek

General area of 17 Aug. fight with Cheyenne

N

Crazy Woman Creek

Powder River

0   5   10   15   20 Miles

Fort Connor

Pawnee fight with Cheyenne, 17 August.

George Bent, the mixed blood son of famed Colorado trader, William Bent, and Owl Woman, his Cheyenne wife, had been in the village on Sand Creek that Colonel Chivington attacked in November 1864 and rode with the raiding Cheyenne warriors in 1865. Educated in St. Louis, he wrote an account many years later of the fight on 17 August, although he was not present:

> The [Pawnee] scouts were very skillful at this kind of work and during a week or so they caught several of our small raiding parties returning from the Platte and punished them pretty severely. My step-mother

was with one of these war parties.[10] This party went up the Platte clear into the mountains, taking a great deal of plunder, and then started back for Powder River. They passed quite near to Connor's Fort without seeing any soldiers, but the next day, about fifty miles north of the fort, they ran into the Pawnee scouts. My stepmother and four men were riding some distance ahead of the others when they saw a few Pawnees on a hill to the front. The Pawnees had disguised themselves so as to appear like Cheyennes or Sioux, and they now signaled with their blankets, "We are friends; come nearer." So the Cheyennes rode forward without suspecting any danger; but when my step-mother and the four men had come quite close to the hill, a large body of Pawnees suddenly charged over the hill and attacked them, while at the same time a company of cavalry appeared off to one side and also attacked the Cheyennes. My step-mother and her four companions were overtaken and all killed, but the rest of the Cheyennes threw away their plunder and made their escape. The Pawnees claimed that they killed twenty-four Cheyennes in this fight, but that is not true.[11]

After the fight, Captain North and his command headed south and traveled back to their base camp at Fort Connor. Miller described the entry of the scouts: "At 3 P.M. one of his party who rode a mile or two in advance, entered Camp with two Scalps suspended to a pole singing the War Song & uttering shouts of savage victory as he came, he was at once surrounded by the Indians who had remained in Camp, & also the other troops, all anxious to see & learn. Shortly after Capt. North & party entered Camp with an amount of captured Stock & Groceries."[12] Palmer added a colorful description: "On their return to camp they exhibited the most savage signs of delight and if they felt fatigued did not show it—

---

[10]Hyde, *Life of George Bent*, 227. Yellow Woman was the younger sister of Owl Woman, mother of George Bent. H. L. Luebers, "William Bent's Family," *Colorado Magazine* (January 1936).

[11]Hyde, *Life of George Bent*, 227. Although Bent claims that only four Cheyenne were killed, the military reports and diaries are very consistent in stating that twenty-four Cheyenne were killed and scalped. One explanation that comes to mind is that Bent's correspondence with his biographer, George E. Hyde, did not begin until 1905, forty years after the fact. They communicated until Bent's death in 1918. Perhaps time clouded George Bent's memory.

The estimates of where this action happened vary from fifty to eighty miles north of Fort Connor, according to the various diaries and reports. It most likely took place somewhere between the mouth of Crazy Woman Creek and today's Arvada, Wyoming, on Powder River.

[12]Miller diary, 17 August 1865 entry.

rode with the bloody scalps tied to the end of sticks, whooping and yelling like so many devils."[13]

North's party had no men killed or wounded—only four horses were killed. Cheyenne casualties were all twenty-four members of the party. North and the Pawnees captured twenty-nine animals, including four government mules, plus six government and one Overland Stage Line horses. Also confiscated were two government saddles, a quantity of white women's and children's clothing, and two infantry coats.[14]

The Pawnee scouts, despite long hours in the saddle, were in a mood to rejoice. A decisive victory over their long-time enemy was a big event worthy of a celebration. "In the evening they had a war dance instead of retiring to rest, although they had been up more than thirty hours. The war dance was the most savage scene I had ever witnessed. They formed a circle and danced around a fire, holding up the bloody scalps, brandishing their hatchets and exhibiting the spoils of the fight. They were perfectly frantic with this, their first grand victory over their hereditary foe."[15] Miller simply said, "Big Camp fire & Scalp dance. The whole Camp, including the General looking on."[16] Colonel Kidd entered in his diary, "Tonight they are having a war dance at where we are all spectators. The author of Hiawatha never saw any of the barbarous realities pertaining to [the] Indian, that's certain."[17]

Captain Palmer described how the night of revelry came to a close: "These howling devils kept up the dance, first much to our amusement, until long after midnight, when finally the general, becoming thoroughly disgusted, insisted upon the officer of the day stopping the noise. After considerable talk, Captain North, their commander, succeeded in quieting them, and the camp laid down to rest; but this war dance was kept up every night until the next fight, limited, however, to 10 P.M."[18]

The supply train, which General Connor's command anxiously awaited, continued on its trek toward Powder River. Connor's hands were tied, as

[13]Palmer's report, Hafen and Hafen, *Powder River Campaigns,* 118.
[14]Gen. P. E. Connor letter to General Dodge, 19 August 1865, ibid., 46.
[15]Palmer's report, ibid., 118.
[16]Miller diary, 17 August 1865 entry.
[17]Kidd diary, 17 August 1865 entry.
[18]Palmer's report, Hafen and Hafen, *Powder River Campaigns,* 121.

he could not proceed farther north without the additional provisions transported by this train. Rather than follow Connor's path north in the Sage Creek drainage, the supply train continued west on the north bank of the Platte. Near where Deer Creek empties into the North Platte from the south, (today's Glenrock, Wyoming) they turned north on 15 August, following the path of John Bozeman's 1864 trail. On 17 August Sergeant Hull recorded, "Was up sometime before 4:30, carrying water. Break camp about noon. Camp on Dry creek, supposed to be a branch of the Cheyenne. Have to cook with sagebrush and a few tipa [*sic*] poles. Water stagnant. Get very thirsty before reaching camp again. Coal sticking out of banks all along the creek. Plenty of signs of buffaloes; guides saw a herd at a distance. 10 miles."[19] With the supply train still over thirty-five miles from Fort Connor, General Connor would have to wait a few more days.

––––––––––

[19] Hull, "Soldiering on the High Plains," 17 August 1865 entry.

CHAPTER TEN

18–22 August 1865

COWARDICE OR GOOD JUDGMENT?

FRIDAY, 18 AUGUST 1865

Connor's Command

While waiting for the arrival of the supply train, a fatal accident occurred in the Pawnee scouts' camp, which Miller wrote about:

> One of them [the scouts] was examining his pistol, he had the hammer partially raised & was revolving the cylinder, to see if all the barrels were loaded, when the hammer came suddenly down on a cap & discharged one of the barrels. The ball entered the forehead of one of the scouts (who was standing near by) & passed out at the back part of the head causing instantaneous death. This is the first & only serious accident that has yet occurred on this expedition, & the Pawnees regard it as a bad omen & the harbinger of evil to them, their Nation has suffered much from War Pestilence & Famine & The whole co. appears to be invested with superstitious awe, & gloomy forebodings of the evil which is soon to befall them.[1]

General Connor's main camp moved north two miles in the morning to ground with better grass for their stock. The Sixth Michigan stayed in its camp in close proximity to the uncompleted fort. Colonel Kidd grumbled in his diary, "[They] are staying around and eating up all the grass so I shall be obliged to send my stock a long distance to graze. Wish the Left Column of the Powder River Indian Expedition would begin to gravitate

---

[1] Miller diary, 18 August 1865 entry.

hence. Sooner the better." Kidd apparently wished for the solitude that only being in command of his regiment would bring. He then added that Connor "is not too healthy. General Connor down occasionally to blow off [talk]. Think his Irish Spleen is somewhat out of repair. Self contemplation alone seems to ease him."[2]

Supply Train from Fort Laramie

In the meantime, the wagon train continued north. "All the wagons start out in front. We overtake them and pass on. . . . Find water in one place and plenty of berries, cherries, and currants. Saw one large buck or some antelope in the distance. Guide kills antelope; have it stewed for supper. Reach camp on Wind river at 11:30.[3] Water scarce; plenty of fine shade under cottonwoods. Boys hunting. No signs of Indians. . . . 12 miles."[4]

SATURDAY, 19 AUGUST 1865

Connor's Command

Connor's camp spent a very uneventful day, which Miller recorded: "Had a pleasant shower of rain in the Evening. All quiet."[5] "Several of the staff officers, myself included," Captain Palmer recalled, "went on a buffalo hunt in the afternoon. We killed several buffalo."[6]

Supply Train

The train from Fort Laramie drew nearer, as Sergeant Hull wrote, "Reach camp on Powder River."[7] Hull was probably confused, as the waterway that they reached was more than likely Salt Creek, which was a main feature on the original Bozeman Trail route. If they truly had arrived at Powder River, they would only be an easy day from the new fort. They were still two days' travel south of Fort Connor.

---

[2] Kidd diary, 18 August 1865 entry.
[3] Doyle, *Journeys to the Land of Gold*, 353. Antelope Creek was called Wind River in 1865.
[4] Hull, "Soldiering on the High Plains," 18 August 1865 entry.
[5] Miller diary, 18 August 1865 entry.
[6] Palmer's report, Hafen and Hafen, *Powder River Campaigns*, 121.
[7] Hull, "Soldiering on the High Plains," 19 August 1865 entry.

Sunday, 20 August 1865

Connor's Command

This Sabbath was not a leisurely day of rest as the previous Sunday had been. "At 2 P.M. an alarm of Sioux was raised in Camp. Capt. North [and] his Pawnees started at once in pursuit, but his men having been hunting Buffalo & Blacktail deer (of which they killed several) in the forenoon, their Horses were not able to do much. This unwarrantable exercise of their Horses in the Hunt, in addition to the long & tedious run they had on the 16th and 17th inst. after the small war party which they exterminated, has for the present rendered their Horses unserviceable."[8]

North led his Pawnee scouts out of the camp on Powder River, taking up the trail. A few miles out he observed three parties of Indians traveling north. The Indian groups, which were later determined to be Cheyenne, each had forty or fifty people. North divided his small force into three squads: one to the right under 1st Lt. Charles A. Small, one to the left commanded by 2nd Lt. James Murie, and North leading the center squad. Each group then attacked their respective targets. The warriors fled and a running fight ensued for some miles. The pursuit progressed but, one by one, North's scouts began dropping out as their spent horses gave up. North, riding a fresh horse, soon found himself far out in front of his scouts. Looking back—one can only imagine his dismay—he found himself alone, facing a party of forty to fifty warriors. The roles of hound and fox quickly reversed, as a dozen Cheyenne now rode after the lone soldier.

The warriors overtook him and wounded his horse. Keeping the warriors at bay with his rifle, North moved toward camp on foot using his horse, wounded but still mobile, as a breastwork. Finally, Lieutenant Small appeared on a nearby hill and, seeing North's predicament, rode to his rescue. The Cheyenne, probably thinking that the company of Pawnees would be following, fled back to their main group. North had flirted with death but, with a little bit of luck, survived this dangerous situation by keeping a cool head. After regrouping his scattered force, North sent word back to camp for reinforcements, knowing that his

---

[8]Miller diary, 20 August 1865 entry.

horses were no match for the Cheyennes' fresh ponies. So far, the Cheyenne had suffered but one casualty; an old man identified as Red Bull. North's only casualty was his horse.[9]

Colonel Kidd of the Sixth Michigan was ordered to reinforce North. "Capt. North went out and killed one," wrote Kidd, "and sent in word he was in danger. I started out with 28 men, and soon met the Pawnees all coming in."[10] Grinnell claimed that North offered to go back and fight the Cheyenne, if Kidd would exchange horses with his men. Kidd refused the offer, stating that his men were too attached to their horses. North then offered to send some of his best men to show Kidd and his party where the Cheyenne were; to this Kidd agreed. Lieutenant Murie and a few of his best mounted men were assigned to go with Kidd's command, while North and the rest of his battalion returned to camp.

According to Grinnell, Kidd traveled to the area where the Cheyenne were last seen. Lieutenant Murie and his Pawnee scouts were sent ahead to a nearby hilltop to determine the location of the warriors. When they returned with their observations of the enemy, Colonel Kidd's command was nowhere to be found. A dust cloud, seen in the direction of the main camp, turned out to be Colonel Kidd and his Sixth Michiganders heading back to camp. Murie returned to camp and reported the incident to Captain North. Apparently furious at the abandonment of his men in the face of the enemy, North instructed Murie to report the incident directly to General Connor, which he did.[11]

Kidd, after meeting North coming in, described the same incident: "I however went on. Struck the Indian trail and followed it about 12 miles coming onto a party estimated at 500 or 1000. Concluded that discretion was the better part of valor and I was a long way from reinforcements, and returned without a fight."[12]

Was it cowardice or good judgment that caused Kidd to return to camp? Grinnell's account was published in 1928, sixty-three years after the 1865 campaign. His main source of information for the story was a biography of Frank North that was written by Omaha newspaper re-

---

[9]Grinnell, *Two Great Scouts*, 97–100.
[10]Kidd diary, 20 August 1865 entry.
[11]Grinnell, *Two Great Scouts*, 100–101.
[12]Kidd diary, 20 August 1865 entry.

porter Alfred Sorenson and compiled from interviews and letters with North in the early 1880s. North had died in 1885, and the biography was published in serial form in the *Omaha Bee* after his death. His younger brother, Luther H. North, also worked with Grinnell and may have passed on the same story. The younger North did not accompany Frank North on the Powder River Indian Expedition of 1865, so anything that he told Grinnell was second-hand information from his older brother.[13]

Miller, who seemed to be in close touch with the general, simply said of North's return to camp, "The General was not satisfied with the conduct of the Scouts, & Capt. Marshall Co. E 11th Ohio & Capt. N. J. O'Brien Co. F 7th Iowa in the detachments of their men were ordered to go in pursuit, it being by this time dark."[14]

MONDAY, 21 AUGUST 1865

George Bird Grinnell claimed that on the morning after the alleged abandonment of Lieutenant Murie, Connor assembled all of his captains and rode the two miles to Fort Connor. Once there, Connor called out Colonel Kidd and reprimanded him sharply within easy hearing of the other officers for the incident. The purpose of this public humiliation was to supposedly prevent a reoccurrence of this conduct from any of the officers in future action. Connor and his officers then, according to Grinnell, joined the command which was already on the march to Tongue River.[15]

Some problems exist with this account, which call into question its credibility. First, none of the diarists mention anything even remotely resembling this incident, nor do they question Kidd's conduct. Miller, Rockafellow, and Palmer all had close contact with General Connor, and some word of it would most likely have made one of their daily entries. Kidd, who wrote very candidly in his personal journal, would have probably written a scathing comment about the general if such a public humiliation had occurred. In Connor's limited correspondence during this period, there is no mention of Kidd. Second, Grinnell's account also has the

---

[13] Sorenson, "A Quarter Century on the Frontier"; Grinnell, *Two Great Scouts*, 9.
[14] Miller diary, 20 August 1865 entry.
[15] Grinnell, *Two Great Scouts*, 101–102.

command leaving on the wrong day, as the supply train had not yet arrived. The command left 22 August, after the train came in on the afternoon of the 21st.

A possible explanation of this story could be that Frank North, when later expressing his anger, told his interviewer, Sorenson, what he thought should have happened to Colonel Kidd. Sorenson, embellishing the account, may have grown the story from what should have happened to what actually happened.

Miller reported, "Moved Camp down the River under the Bluffs near the Fort. Met Capt. O'Brien with his Detachment returning to Camp. Saw no Indians. Shortly after going into Camp, Capt Marshall with his Detachment came in, & reported three Indians seen this morning, two of which were killed, the other escaped. Capt. Marshall's party picked up 10 Mules which were scattered over the Prairie & brought them into Camp."[16]

Kidd reported that Connor, who must have been frustrated, then went out in search of the warriors: "General went out with entire force in pursuit of the Indians seen yesterday. . . . General returned without having encountered any enemy worthy his *well-tempered* [Kidd's emphasis] steel."[17] Private Wight described the same event: "the Gen. and some of the Indians toock [*sic*] a piece of Artillery and went out to see what they could see. they dident [*sic*] find many. they only brought in one skelp [*sic*]."[18]

The supply train and "Companies A and G [Sixth Michigan Cavalry], Lieutenant M. M. Moon arrived escort of train" from Fort Laramie.[19] Private Adams, who was with the train, recalled, "On the evening of August 21, we arrived at Fort Connor, on Powder River."[20] General Connor now had the much-needed supplies and men that would enable him to resume the march northward and to an eventual rendezvous with the

---

[16] Miller diary, 21 August 1865 entry.
[17] Kidd diary, 21 August 1865 entry.
[18] Geyer, *Sheldon L. Wight*, 101.
[19] Kidd diary, 21 August 1865 entry.
[20] Adams, "Raiding a Hostile Village." Adams arrived at Fort Connor with the same supply train that Sergeant Hull traveled with.

other columns of the expedition. He readied his command for departure on the next day.

Whiskey in the hands of the enlisted men again caused a problem: "Some of the Boys on Co. F 7th Iowa got steam up on the high pressure principle, & burningly shot Peter Story, (one of their Co.) through both thighs."[21] Rockafellow put it in simpler terms: "Capt. N. J. O'Brien Co F 7th Iowa Cav had man shot through thigh by one of his own men who was drunk with stolen liquor."[22]

TUESDAY, 22 AUGUST 1865

General Connor had his expedition ready to roll. They "Broke Camp on Powder River at 6:30 A.M. Passed through Fort Connor & traveled in a North Westerly direction for Tongue River."[23]

Connor and Colonel Kidd did have a last-minute, heated conversation, but it was not about Kidd's performance on 20 August. "General Connor moved with left column PRE [Powder River Expedition] this morning. 'Adieu, Adieu, Adieu' 'and if forever then forever fare-thee-well.' Had a bit of spicy conversation respecting relieving us on time. Did not get much satisfaction and told him he would have no right to keep us over our time. Asked if I would abandon the post if not relieved."[24] Kidd pressed Connor about their 11 October discharge date, and Connor, not having replacement troops on the way to take over the garrison duties of Fort Connor, posed the question to Kidd of abandoning the fort. Kidd did not record his answer to the question, so one can only speculate as to how the conversation ended—probably unsatisfactorily to both parties.

As the left column of the Powder River Indian Expedition moved northwest, Miller described the aftermath of fighting from the previous day: "After traveling 8 miles, we passed the dead bodies of two Indians which Capt. Marshall's party killed yesterday. Saw a silver ring taken

---

[21] Miller diary, 21 August 1865 entry. Pvt. Peter C. Story was a member of Company F, Seventh Iowa Cavalry. *American Civil War Research Database*.

[22] Rockafellow diary, 21 August 1865 entry, Hafen and Hafen, *Powder River Campaigns*, 184. Capt. Nicholas J. O'Brien was a member of Company F, Seventh Iowa Cavalry. *Civil War Soldiers and Sailors System*.

[23] Miller diary, 22 August 1865 entry.

[24] Kidd diary, 22 August 1865 entry.

Crazy Woman Creek, near the Bozeman Trail crossing. *Author's photo.*

from the finger of one, with the name S. L. Matthews Co. A I. Mich. Cav. inscribed upon it."[25]

The group "Traveled twenty-three and one half miles and made camp on Crazy Woman's Fork of the Powder River, so named because of the fact that some fifteen years before, a poor demented squaw lived near the bank of the river in a 'wickiup' and finally died there. The water of this stream is not so good as that of the Powder river, more strongly impregnated with alkali; grass not very good; sage brush abundant; some timber on the stream. Saw some signs of Indians, but none very recent."[26]

---

[25] The ring probably had belonged to Pvt. Samuel M. [not L.] Mathews, Company A, First Michigan Cavalry, who was killed by Indians at Willow Springs, Colorado Territory, on 13 August 1865. *American Civil War Research Database.* Miller may have misspelled the name as Matthews. Miller diary, 22 August 1865 entry.

[26] Palmer's report, Hafen and Hafen, *Powder River Campaigns,* 122. The route that the command took probably mirrored today's Buffalo-Sussex Road. They camped in the vicinity of the current highway bridge that crosses Crazy Woman Creek on this route.

Back at Fort Connor, an unexpected dinner guest showed up, which Kidd recorded: "Capt [Albert] Brown [west column commander of the expedition] arrived tonight having crossed the mountains without encountering Indians. Represents the country as being full of Elk, Buffalo, Deer, antelope, bear, and pine grouse. Took supper with me."[27]

Either Kidd did not record the miseries that Brown's column had endured, or Brown did not elaborate to him of the hardships they had faced. On 15 August Captain Nash of the Omaha scouts had written: "Most of my men are now on foot. I have lost by death [starvation and lack of water] 46 horses, and many others just live to carry their empty saddles. From present indications I would not be surprised if before I got through the expedition this little captain would himself be on foot and worse than that, out of rations as the pantry begins to look rather empty for 90 men who do not know where they are or when they will get out to find more."[28] Contrary to Kidd's diary entry, Nash reported his disenchantment with Brown's leadership when confronted by Indian warriors during their trek: "One thing we do know & that is ten men and Capt Brown the great Indian fighter of the plains are driven into camp by five hostile living Indians. The most perfect disgust for this transaction is depicted on the features of both officers and privates in this camp."[29] Nash then wrote of their arrival at Fort Connor: "We are here out of rations nearly worn out by constant marching, most of the men on foot & the General gone on with all of our rations. He has been gone two days and there is but two alternatives left for us, 1st stay here and starve to death or take after the general & very near starve in doing that. Of the two evils we will avail ourselves of the last & will early in the morning start north for the general."[30]

Meanwhile, Connor, unaware of Captain Brown's arrival at the fort, was now back on the trail north to the warring tribes' stronghold area. With Fort Connor functional though still under construction, it seemed that the Powder River Indian Expedition would now have the opportunity to live up to the expectations of its planners.

---

[27] Kidd diary, 22 August 1865 entry.
[28] Nash diary, 15 August 1865 entry.
[29] Ibid., 20 August 1865 entry.
[30] Ibid., 22 August 1865 entry.

CHAPTER ELEVEN

13 June–2 August 1865

ENTER SAWYERS

B y 23 August the three main columns of the Powder River Indian Expedition were on the march toward their planned rendezvous at Panther Mountain. Colonel Cole's command, which had left Omaha on 1 July, marched north on the Little Missouri River in southeastern Montana Territory. Lieutenant Colonel Walker's Sixteenth Kansas Cavalry had departed Fort Laramie on 5 August and was moving northwest in Montana toward Box Elder Creek, en route to Powder River. General Connor marched out of Fort Connor on Powder River after delaying for the arrival of supplies and headed north toward the Tongue River.

A fourth expedition would enter the picture by late August. On 13 June a surveying and exploring party headed by James A. Sawyers departed west from the mouth of the Niobrara River in northeastern Nebraska Territory. The expedition's stated purpose was to develop an emigrant route from Sioux City, Iowa, to Virginia City, Montana Territory, and its gold fields. If this road could be developed, it would shorten the distance by hundreds of miles compared to current routes, thus making Sioux City the jumping-off and supply point for the gold seekers.[1]

The roots of Sawyers's expedition were in Iowa representative Asahel W. Hubbard's January 1865 introduction of a bill in Congress requesting federal funding for construction of a wagon road from the Missouri

---

[1] Hafen and Hafen, *Powder River Campaigns,* 219–23.

James A. Sawyers, superintendent of the Sioux City–Virginia City road-building and surveying expedition. *Courtesy of the Sioux City Public Museum, Sioux City, Iowa.*

River, via the Niobrara River, to Virginia City. This proposition was enthusiastically supported by the Sioux City business community. The measure passed in early March, and fifty thousand dollars was appropriated for the project.

Acting on the advice of Congressman Hubbard, John P. Usher, Lincoln's secretary of the interior, appointed James A. Sawyers of Sioux City, Iowa, as superintendent of the expedition. The forty-year-old Sawyers had worked with Hubbard on business and political activities in the recent past. Because of his previous military rank as a lieutenant colonel in the Northern Border Brigade of the Iowa Militia, the now-civilian Sawyers was often referred to as Colonel Sawyers.

Hubbard requested a military escort of at least two hundred cavalrymen from General Pope. Sawyers, in an effort to get his expedition on the trail quickly, traveled first to Chicago, then to Washington, to speed up the bureaucracy, and get his line of credit to the government funding established. "After considerable delay in the treasury department, on the 27th of April, funds were placed to my [Sawyers's] credit in Chicago, and I immediately commenced the purchase of the outfit."

"After purchasing such supplies as I thought proper in Chicago," Sawyers continued, "I proceeded to Sioux City and found to my surprise that, instead of any cavalry escort, two companies of the Fifth United States Volunteer Infantry, consisting of only about 118 men in all, had been sent to the mouth of the Niobrara, with rations for only three months (including May), and with scanty transportation." Companies C and D of the Fifth United States Volunteer Infantry—commanded by Capt. George W. Williford—were made up mostly of galvanized Yankees. An unhappy Sawyers protested by telegraph to General Pope, who then ordered Gen. Alfred Sully, sub-district commander, to furnish what he could. Sully sent an additional twenty-five cavalrymen from Company A, First Battalion, Dakota Cavalry, under the command of Lt. John R. Wood. Sawyers would be at odds with the military escort and Captain Williford for much of the journey ahead.[2]

From the mouth of the Niobrara River the expedition started west on 13 June after six weeks because of "Unavoidable delays in the transportation of subsistence and fitting out of teams, wagons, tents, camp equipage, etc." The expedition consisted of fifty-three men, including chief engineer Lewis H. Smith and expedition clerk Charles W. Sears. Chief guide Ben Estes was assisted by a mixed-blood Yankton Sioux, Baptiste Defond. Dr. Daniel W. Tingley accompanied the expedition as its physician. Newell M. Sawyers, younger brother of James Sawyers, served as wagon master. Also included were scouts, pioneers (road builders), herders, and drivers. Forty-five yoke of oxen pulled fifteen freight wagons loaded with "chains, tools, tents, camp equipage; and subsistence for six months." Five saddle horses and five mules rounded out the working stock. An ambulance and a mess wagon completed the transportation.[3]

The military escort's train consisted of twenty-five wagons drawn by six mules each. Sawyers was extremely critical of the mules: "These teams were small and thin at starting, and very young, but few of them being over three years old, and, as a whole, a very inferior lot of animals, wholly inadequate for the expedition, and never should have been sent

---

[2] Sawyers's official report, ibid., 226.
[3] One must marvel that Colonel Cole put his much larger expedition together in Omaha, and had it on the trail in only ten days. Sawyers's official report, Hafen and Hafen, *Powder River Campaigns*, 227.

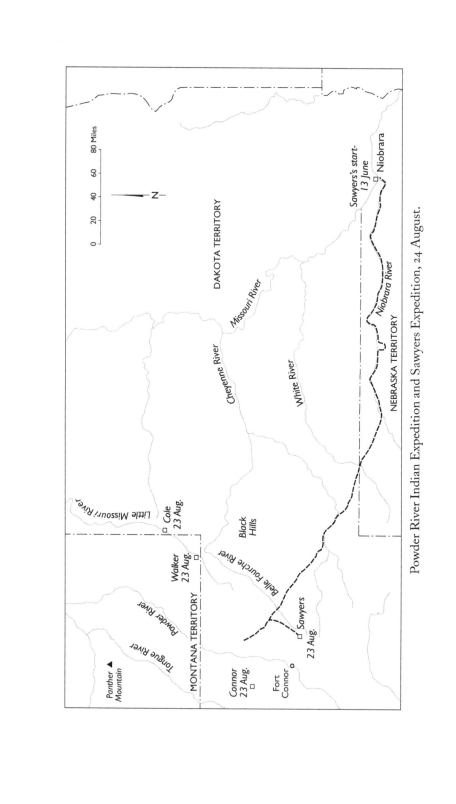

Powder River Indian Expedition and Sawyers Expedition, 24 August.

upon it."[4] Sawyers's observation—taken into consideration with similar quotes from General Connor and Colonel Cole—raise questions about the standards and/or the integrity of contractors when fulfilling government supply contracts.[5]

George W. Johnson, a galvanized Yankee serving with Company D of the Fifth U.S., gave more details: "We were ordered to Fort Leavenworth, Kansas, and shortly after, two companies of the regiment (C & D) were sent as an escort to a Wagon Road Expedition over the prairie. I was placed in charge of two pieces of artillery, which I kept throughout the march."[6] At Sawyers's request, the army furnished the expedition with forty Springfield rifles and a supply of ammunition that were distributed to the civilian employees.[7]

A commercial freight train also accompanied the party: thirty-six freight wagons were coupled together to make eighteen double wagons. Each were pulled by six yoke of oxen. They carried merchandise from a Sioux City trading firm, C. E. Hedges and Company, to open a store in Virginia City. Nineteen-year-old Nat D. Hedges, younger brother of the firm's owners, supervised this operation. John Hardin was the wagon master.[8] Sawyers had a business relationship with the Hedges brothers prior to the expedition and would be later criticized for including their commercial venture with this government-funded trek.

Four wagons of immigrants also made the trip: two families from Cedar Falls, Iowa, and two single men from Sioux City—ten people in all. Nine cows were driven by the two bachelors, Edward H. Edwards and Samuel H. Cassady, with the intent of selling fresh milk (at ten cents a quart) and butter (at forty cents a pound) to the civilians and soldiers en route.[9]

Sawyers's expedition left the town of Niobrara at 2 P.M. and proceeded upstream only four miles before going into camp. The first days of travel

---

[4] Sawyers's official report, Hafen and Hafen, *Powder River Campaigns*, 227.
[5] Ibid., 61. Cole complained about the quality of the mules supplied him at Omaha in late June with comments similar to Sawyers. Connor complained about the quality of Canadian ponies, sent to him from Detroit, on May 7. Connor to Dodge, 7 May 1865, *The War of Rebellion*, O.R., Series 1, Volume 48/2 [S#102].
[6] Letter to Mrs. Elder from George W. Johnson, 18 December 1865, Fort Phil Kearny State Historic Site.
[7] Sawyers's official report, Hafen and Hafen, *Powder River Campaigns*, 227.
[8] Doyle, *Journeys to the Land of Gold*, 346–48.
[9] Lee diary, 13 June 1865 entry.

were fairly uneventful; the party followed the Niobrara River on the south side, crossing various streams that flowed to the north. Teamster Albert M. Holman recalled, "In a few days we had all settled down to the various duties assigned each man, and were progressing slowly but surely with our oxen and their laden wagons."[10]

On 16 June teamster Corwin M. Lee described visitors to camp: "A lot of Ponca Indians around camp tonight. Their agency is only 3 or 4 miles distant on the other side of the Running Water [Niobrara River]. They are good hands to beg for something to eat and Tobuck [tobacco] as they call it. The boys persuaded one of them to mount a Mexican Mustang belonging to one of our number with the expectation of seeing him thrown, but were disappointed as he proved to be an accomplished horseman and rode him with ease. Their dress is extremely simple and primitive in style and cut consisting of either a buffalo robe or blanket and a breech cloth and sometimes with moccasins on."[11]

Emigrant Edward H. Edwards commented sarcastically on their progress on 18 June: "Since thus so far, by working hard every day, made the astonishing distance of thirty-five miles. If our future progress will be the same as the past week we will get through to Virginia City in about three years and a half." Edwards added further comment on the fresh-milk-and-butter business with partner Samuel H. Cassady, "After totaling our accounts today we found that we made about 15 dollars apiece since we left Niobrara. Last night & this morning we sold every drop of our milk."[12]

Sawyers "had determined not to travel or work on the Sabbath, except in case of necessity."[13] Pvt. John Colby Griggs wrote of the first Sunday on the trail: "Sunday, June 18. Remained in camp throughout the day for the double purpose of resting animals and men and the proper observance of the Sabbath."[14]

On 29 June Sawyers reported, "At this point, on account of his teams giving out, Captain Williford cached a load of pork and fish, and abandoned his poorest wagon, by which means he would have an occasional

---

[10]Holman account, Hafen and Hafen, *Powder River Campaigns,* 299–300.
[11]Lee diary, 16 June 1865 entry.
[12]Edwards, letter of 18 June 1865.
[13]Sawyers's official report, Hafen and Hafen, *Powder River Campaigns,* 232.
[14]Paul, "A Galvanized Yankee Along the Niobrara," 148, 18 June 1865 entry.

change [of mules], and thus better enable his teams to do their work."[15] Sawyers's concerns about the quality of the military escort's mules was obviously prophetic, as barely two weeks into the journey the animals were breaking down. With the exception of the military escort, the rest of the expedition relied on the more dependable oxen. Less expensive than mules, oxen could live off grass or sage and was the preferred beast of burden in the westward expansion to California and Oregon: "Oxen will stand the trip much better, and are not so liable to be stolen by the Indians, and are much less trouble."[16] The disadvantage to oxen was speed—about two miles per hour. Mules were faster but not as good foragers, and their disposition often proved to be problematic.

At the mouth of the Snake River the banks were high and steep, and the caravan had to travel south about ten miles to find a suitable crossing. On the morning of 1 July they crossed the river by doubling their teams and headed northwest to strike the Niobrara River again. Because of a lack of water on this trail, at 5 P.M. Sawyers decided to leave the train and drive the animals the remaining four miles to the river, reaching it at sundown. A squad of cavalrymen was sent back to guard the train.

On the following day the men and animals went back to retrieve the train. The temperature climbed to over 100 degrees. Two oxen died, and a soldier suffered from sunstroke as they traveled northwest and camped on the Niobrara River. The expedition stayed over on 4 July, where C. M. Lee described a celebration: "Lay in camp. Considerable of peach brandy drank to being as it was the fourth of July. A good deal of blowing [talking] done and some shooting at a mark for the peaches, and one or two fights among the soldiers."[17] The temperature remained in triple digits until the night of 5 July, when it rained. Much to the relief of the travelers, the weather cooled down on the following morning.

On 10 July the expedition crossed the Niobrara to the north side just above the mouth of Antelope Creek, which flows from the north.[18] The next day, Sawyers's guides advised leaving the Niobrara and moving

---

[15] Sawyers's official report, Hafen and Hafen, *Powder River Campaigns*, 237.

[16] Joel Palmer, *Journal of Travels: Over the Oregon Trail in 1845* (Portland: Oregon Historical Society Press, 1993), 197.

[17] Lee diary, 4 July 1865 entry.

[18] Col. Nelson Cole and his Eastern Division had left Omaha on 1 July and would camp near this spot on 1 August as they continued north toward the Black Hills.

northwest toward the White River. Chief scout Ben Estes had a minor confrontation with several Indian warriors on 12 July and came away with two captured ponies. On 13 July the Black Hills were sighted for the first time.[19]

The caravan reached the White River on 15 July and encamped at 4:30 P.M. after several days of difficult terrain. Three days later, they crossed the divide between the White and Cheyenne Rivers. C. M. Lee wrote, "Went 15 miles and camped on Hat Creek after four o'clock. We could see the bluffs on the Cheyenne quite plain."[20]

On 19 July Pvt. John Colby Griggs described a miserable day: "Broke camp about the usual time and proceeded over a most excellent road and about 1 o'clock when the rain commenced falling in torrents and continued for three hours; this rendered the road almost impractical in consequence of the mud sticking to the wheels and feet of the travelers; therefore we were compelled to encamp without wood or water and very poor grazing."[21] C. M. Lee gave details of their evening: "After getting to camp everybody being wet through nearly they naturally felt like having something to warm the inner man and consequently some 30 or 40 bottles of brandy . . . [were sold to the men.] The consequence was in less than half an hour 2/3 of them were tight as bricks and having a glorious time all to them selves and came near ending in a row. The drunkest of them being put to bed, order was once more restored."[22] The judgment of James Sawyers must be questioned here for allowing the free flow of liquor. As we have seen from other accounts, drunkenness usually preceded trouble in camp.

On 20 July the military escort's commander, Captain Williford, informed Sawyers that his infantrymen were in desperate need of clothing. "By this time, the soldiers accompanying us had become nearly barefoot and the officers insisted that they could travel no further without shoes."[23] Williford ordered a detachment of fifteen cavalrymen, commanded by

---

[19] Sawyers's official report, Hafen and Hafen, *Powder River Campaigns*, 241–42.
[20] Lee diary, 18 July 1865 entry.
[21] Paul, "A Galvanized Yankee Along the Niobrara," 151, 19 July 1865 entry.
[22] Lee diary, 19 July 1865 entry. Lee added his own disclaimer as to his participation in the drunken revelry: "Your humble servant in consideration of his well known temperance principles limited himself to two or three drinks."
[23] Holman account, Hafen and Hafen, *Powder River Campaigns*, 301.

2nd Lt. Daniel M. Dana, along with one wagon, to head south to Fort Laramie—about seventy-five miles—to obtain a supply of shoes. Sawyers reluctantly agreed and furnished the loan of a lighter wagon. He planned to proceed "by short stages," while waiting for the return of the party from Fort Laramie, estimated to be ten days' time.[24] Sawyers's earlier grumbling about the escort being under-supplied proved to be well founded.

Lieutenant Dana began leading his party south toward Fort Laramie at 8:30 A.M. on 21 July. Private Griggs recorded an interesting sidelight to this story: "This morning the Quartermaster, with one escort of cavalry and three Negro laundresses, proceeded to Fort Laramie on business for the command. (They left the negroes at Laramie.)"[25] During the post–Civil War period in the West, women traveling with the military on campaign were rare, if nonexistent; however, regulations during the Civil War allowed up to four laundresses per company.[26] Colonel Cole had at least one laundress, and probably more, traveling with his command. It appears that the three laundresses had had enough of life on the trail with Captain Williford's party and wanted out.

The Sawyers Expedition now had to wait for the supply detail to return from Fort Laramie and were almost "walking in place" for the next twelve days. They either stayed in camp or moved only a few miles, traveling only seventy-one miles over this period (about six miles per day). They reached the Cheyenne River on 28 July.

On the evening of 1 August at about 10 P.M., while encamped on a dry fork of the Cheyenne, gunshots broke the silence of the evening and a cry was heard from the pickets, "Indians, Indians, turn out boys, turn out." Shots were sent in that direction until someone shouted, "Hold on, Hold on, don't fire; it is the cavalry." According to C. M. Lee, Lieutenant Dana's party, returning from Fort Laramie, had attempted to "perpetrate a joke on the camp." Fortunately no one was killed or injured in what can only be described as an incredibly stupid stunt, if C. M. Lee is to be

---

[24] Sawyers's official report, ibid., 245. Second Lt. Daniel M. Dana was a member of Companies C and D, Fifth U.S. Volunteer Infantry. *Civil War Soldiers and Sailors System.*

[25] Paul, "A Galvanized Yankee Along the Niobrara," 151, 21 July 1865 entry.

[26] Kautz, *The 1865 Customs of Service,* 12–13, item 11: "Four laundresses are allowed to each company, and soldiers wives may be, and generally are, mustered in that capacity. They are then entitled to the same quarters, fuel, and rations as a soldier, and the established pay for the washing they may do for soldiers and officers."

believed.[27] Sawyers made no mention of the firing incident in his official report but did take Dana to task: "At about 10 P.M. Lieutenant Dana arrived with his command from Laramie with no supplies, having foolishly left their wagon to come up with a detachment from Laramie to the Black Hills, pass around and join General Connor, supposed to be on Powder River."[28]

The "detachment from Laramie" that Sawyers referred to was Lieutenant Colonel Walker's center column of Connor's Powder River Indian Expedition. Walker's command—still at Fort Laramie—didn't depart until 5 August and reached the Cheyenne River on 10 August, long after Sawyers had departed the area.[29] On 2 August a cavalry detachment, led by 1st Lt. Thomas G. Stull, was sent back to look for Walker's command and the wagon carrying the clothing.[30] Of course, they didn't locate it, as Connor's center column had not yet left Fort Laramie. Almost two weeks had now been lost, due to poor initial planning by the military escort and Lieutenant Dana's blunder in not returning with the wagonload of supplies. And worst of all, the foot-sore infantrymen still marched without shoes.

---

[27] Lee diary, 1 August 1865 entry, Hafen and Hafen, *Powder River Campaigns,* 302. Albert Holman also wrote of the shooting and the arrival of Lieutenant Dana's party in his reminiscent account.

[28] Sawyers's official report, ibid., 251.

[29] Walker's report, ibid., 92.

[30] Paul, "A Galvanized Yankee Along the Niobrara," 152, 2 August 1865 entry. First Lt. Thomas G. Stull was in Company C, Fifth U.S. Volunteer Infantry. *Civil War Soldiers and Sailors System.*

CHAPTER TWELVE

3–23 August 1865

THE DAMNEDEST ROUGHEST
LOOKING COUNTRY

James A. Sawyers's party traveled northwest over the next few days, moving away from the South Cheyenne River. On 4 August they crossed the divide into the Belle Fourche River drainage and camped on one of its tributaries. The expedition now was south of today's Gillette, Wyoming, in terrain described by C. M. Lee as "the damnedest roughest looking country you ever saw."[1] On 7 August they camped on the bank of the Belle Fourche River, which was nearly dry except for water in holes. They marched west, probably up Caballo Creek. Engineer Lewis H. Smith described their campsite for 9 August as "water good and permanent and grass good."[2] Lieutenant Stull and his detachment came in to camp late that evening with the bad news that they had not found the supply wagon from Fort Laramie.[3] Sawyers decided to travel northwest toward Powder River on a route to the north of the Pumpkin Buttes.[4]

A few pleasant moments occurred during the next morning's march, as they saw their first buffalo herd near the train. C. M. Lee wrote effusively, "At two o'clock we came in plain sight of the Big Horn Mountains away in the distance. They look almost like clouds. The tops of them are

---

[1] Lee diary, 5 August 1865 entry.
[2] Smith diary, 9 August 1865 entry, Doyle, *Journeys to the Land of Gold*, 373.
[3] Paul, ed., "A Galvanized Yankee Along the Niobrara," 153, 9 August 1865 entry.
[4] Sawyers's official report, Hafen and Hafen, *Powder River Campaigns,* 253.

tipped with white, which I presume is snow. They are the first mountains or hills of any great magnitude I ever saw. They look grand and majestic."[5] However, the day turned out to be a miserable experience for both men and animals as they traveled eighteen miles over a rough, waterless terrain. They spent the night in a dry camp, listening to the thirsty cattle bellowing frantically for want of water. Lee wrote bitterly that the only water available was in Sawyers's camp, and it was not shared. "The balance, as many as could, got milk. Had to put up with that and a little bread and cold meat and others had scarcely anything." According to Lee, Sawyers had brought a supply of water from the last camp, although it was generally understood among the men that this practice was forbidden, to prevent overloading the wagons.[6]

The next day, 11 August, proved to be no better than the previous one: "Traveled 14 miles over a very rough hilly country in a westerly direction. Camped a little after four o'clock near a ravine that had a little water in. With difficulty the men succeeded in getting a supply for themselves, and one half of the cattle could scarcely get a drop and nearly all near perishing for the want of water."[7] The mood of the men in camp was angry and volatile. After a heated confrontation between Sawyers and his employees that evening, Sawyers ordered that "the cavalry with 20 or 30 of the infantry mounted on mules [be] dispatched [to Powder River] in quest of water. The cattle belonging to Colonel Sawyers' outfit accompanied them."[8] Sawyers returned to camp about 3 P.M. and reported that the animals reached Powder River at 11 A.M., after fifteen miles of travel over terrain impractical for the wagon train. He expected the herd and herders to remain at the river overnight, but they came back about 12 P.M., after a large Indian village was discovered in the area.[9]

Based upon his knowledge of the rough country ahead and the presence of Indians, Sawyers decided to backtrack to their camp of 9 August and find a route to Powder River south of the Pumpkin Buttes. At noon on 13 August, after about six miles of travel, they stopped at a small spring or creek to water the stock.[10] "Before, however, the rear [of the train] had

[5] Lee diary, 10 August 1865 entry.
[6] Ibid.
[7] Ibid., 11 August 1865 entry.
[8] Paul, ed., "A Galvanized Yankee Along the Niobrara," 153, 12 August 1865 entry.
[9] Lee diary, 12 August 1865 entry.
[10] Sawyers's official report, Hafen and Hafen, *Powder River Campaigns*, 254.

reached camp, we were startled by the cry of 'Indians' 'Fallin' was the cry and the orders were obeyed as soon as said," wrote Private Griggs. "It was discovered that they [the Indians] were making a raid on the cavalry horses, which were herding close to camp. They captured and drove off seven of them."[11]

At about the time that the warriors were making their raid, Nat D. Hedges, the nineteen-year-old man in charge of the commercial train, had ridden forward to scout the trail ahead for water. After the fighting subsided, a party of twelve to fifteen mounted rescuers rode out from the train to determine his fate. After a mile or more, young Hedges's stripped and scalped body was discovered near a grove of trees bordering a ravine. According to teamster Albert Holman, "Seven arrows had penetrated his breast; a bullet hole was in his cheek, and several in his body."[12] The saddened party returned to camp with Hedges's body. It was placed in a wagon, and the caravan continued another ten miles, stopping only when darkness made further travel impractical. "Traveled till near ten o'clock then halted and corrilled [corralled] both mule and ox train together, [wagon] tongues inside. Unhitched the teams and tied them to the wagons, posted guards and lay till the break of day."[13] The military escort was on alert all night, and Private Griggs recorded, "No one allowed to sleep tonight."[14]

No Indians appeared in the morning. "Broke camp about sunrise, and made about 3 miles farther on our backward course, when we pitched camp with good water and grazing. . . . About 5 o'clock P.M. the Indians made another rush close to camp for horses, but they were driven off without booty of any kind."[15] Artillery fire and a long-range exchange of rifle shots kept the Indians at bay. After this initial rush, a large number of warriors appeared on the surrounding hilltops. Nat Hedges's body was buried in the wagon-made corral during the afternoon. The men spent another sleepless night wondering what tomorrow would bring. They camped on Bone Pile Creek, about ten miles southwest of today's Gillette, Wyoming.[16]

---

[11] Paul, ed., "A Galvanized Yankee Along the Niobrara," 154, 13 August 1865 entry.
[12] Holman account, Hafen and Hafen, *Powder River Campaigns*, 305.
[13] Lee diary, 13 August 1865 entry.
[14] Paul, ed., "A Galvanized Yankee Along the Niobrara," 154, 13 August 1865 entry.
[15] Ibid.
[16] Smith diary, 14 August 1865 entry, Doyle, *Journeys to the Land of Gold*, 374.

Early on the morning of 15 August, warriors were seen on the nearby bluffs—Sawyers estimated their numbers at five to six hundred.[17] They generally stayed out of rifle range, but Private Griggs described the exception: "Several of the brave warriors dashed past us upon their fleet ponies at full gallop, giving vent to their war whoops and brandishing scalps. Quite a number of shots were fired upon both sides of small arms; artillery was used alone by us."[18] The long-range, sporadic action continued for about three hours, with the artillery once again playing an effective role in keeping the warriors out of range. Around noon, the Indians called for a parley, and Sawyers and his two guides, Ben Estes and Baptiste Defond, went out between the lines to meet with the Indian delegates, among them George Bent.

Bent recalled, "I went forward with one of the Cheyenne chiefs to meet them. I acted as interpreter."[19] He said that Captain Williford accompanied Sawyers. It was reported that Bent told Sawyers "that there was one condition on which the Cheyennes would treat, *viz*, the hanging by the government of Colonel Chivington."[20] Obviously, Sawyers couldn't deliver the Chivington demand, but wrote, "After some parleying I decided to treat with them and for some bacon, sugar, coffee, flour and tobacco, they agreed to let us go our way."[21] Williford did not agree with this strategy, but Sawyers ordered a wagonload of supplies delivered to the warriors.

"While this was going on and for some time after," Lee wrote, "our boys were doing a brisk business in trading tobacco for moccasins. They [the Indians] were ready and anxious to trade for anything and everything that we possessed." For the footsore and barefoot infantrymen, those moccasins must have looked awfully good. Lee continued, "This trading had been going on probably for an hour after the goods had been delivered by the Colonel [Sawyers], when there was a gun discharged up on the side hill among the Indians and farther from the camp than where the trading was going. Mutually distrustful, each party of traders at the

---

[17] Sawyers's official report, Hafen and Hafen, *Powder River Campaigns,* 255.

[18] Paul, ed., "A Galvanized Yankee Along the Niobrara," 155, 15 August 1865 entry.

[19] Hyde, *Life of George Bent,* 232.

[20] Dodge to Pope, 15 September 1865, Hafen and Hafen, *Powder River Campaigns,* 50. Col. John Chivington commanded the troops at the Sand Creek massacre.

[21] Sawyers's official report, ibid., 255.

discharge broke for their friends at full speed." Two cavalrymen were found to be missing; one of them, Pvt. Anthony Nelson, was discovered dead. Lee described the scene: "He had been shot in the back with a ball, two or three arrows shot into him, and a spear run into his breast."[22] The other missing cavalryman, a Mexican named Orlando Sous, was nowhere to be found, and it was assumed that he had either been killed or deserted to the enemy, as he may have known some of the warriors.[23]

Nelson's body was brought into camp and buried in the corral. The warriors, mostly Sioux and Cheyenne, were seen no more that day. Lee summed up his feelings at day's end: "And this was the termination of all our brilliant negotiations, $500 worth of provisions, and two more men gone."[24]

The next morning dawned bright and clear, with no Indians in sight. The expedition marched southeast, following Bone Pile Creek. Private Griggs entered in his journal, "About noon we reached the camp we had on the 9th instant where we had water and tolerable good grazing. Late in the afternoon a few redskins again attempted a raid on our stock but without success. The night passed away without alarm."[25] This camp was near the junction of Bone Pile Creek and Caballo Creek, south of today's Gillette, Wyoming.

On the morning of 17 August, Sawyers wrote, "At 2 A.M. our scouts, Lieutenant Colonel [John F.] Godfrey, late of the Second Maine Cavalry, and Charles W. Sears, with Estes and Defond, our guides, started alone on a reconnaissance to Powder River, and at day-light were far away from camp."[26] The rest of the party stayed in camp on Caballo Creek for the next two days resting animals and men and waiting for the return of the scouting party.

"The reconnoitering party arrived in camp this morning at about 6 o'clock," Sawyers recorded on 19 August, "and reported that a good

[22] Lee diary, 15 August 1865 entry. Pvt. Anthony Nelson was a member of Company B, First Battalion Dakota Cavalry. *Civil War Soldiers and Sailors System.*

[23] Captain Williford's official report, 29 August 1865, Hafen and Hafen, *Powder River Campaigns,* 287. Williford wrote in parentheses, "appears on muster-rolls as John Rouse." Griggs said the man's name was Luse; Sawyers said the name was Rawze.

[24] Lee diary, 15 August 1865 entry.

[25] Paul, ed., "A Galvanized Yankee Along the Niobrara," 155, 15 August 1865 entry.

[26] Sawyers's official report, Hafen and Hafen, *Powder River Campaigns,* 256.

road may be made to Powder River, distant about fifty miles; that General Connor had passed down the Dry Fork about two days since, from appearances, with a large train."[27] With this good news in hand, Sawyers wasted little time in getting the train in motion. Chief engineer Lewis H. Smith wrote, "started train at 8 1/2 am and made 16 1/2 miles and camped on a branch of north fork of Cheyenne [Belle Fourche River] having traveled southwest toward the big buttes [Pumpkin Buttes] road fine[.]"[28] They camped about ten miles northwest of present-day Wright, Wyoming. Private Griggs wrote of the only excitement of the day: "About midnight an alarm was given by one of the sentinels shooting and killing a mule."[29]

With the following day being Sunday, the expedition stayed in camp observing the Sabbath and resting their stock. The relationship between the military and the civilians worsened to the breaking point, as teamster Lee observed:

> The military say they will not go any farther than to Connor's trail, then they will start for Laramie as they are destitute of clothing and shoes, many of them having to travel barefooted through cactus plants and sage brush while part of the mule train is already loaded with those that are so footsore they can scarcely walk at all. The officers have been threatening to leave for some time or confiscate the extra boots and shoes in the train. The surgeon repeatedly declaring his men were in no condition to travel, that he would take the responsibility of ordering them to the nearest post. And to aggravate matters, the Colonel [Sawyers] and a number of his satellites are in the habit of speaking contemptuously of their hardships and courage and their vigilance in guarding the train.[30]

Lee seemed very sympathetic towards the military escort's plight. Strangely, Sawyers made no mention of the differences with Captain Williford and his troops in his entry for this day.

Two days' travel over rough, waterless country finally brought them to the Dry Fork of Powder River and Connor's trail. Emigrant Edward H.

---

[27] Ibid., 257. Connor's command had actually traveled down the Dry Fork of Powder River on 10 and 11 August.

[28] Smith diary, 19 August 1865 entry, Doyle, *Journeys to the Land of Gold*, 374.

[29] Paul, ed., "A Galvanized Yankee Along the Niobrara," 155, 19 August 1865 entry.

[30] Lee diary, 15 August 1865 entry.

Edwards described the hardship: "Last Eve [22 August] we reached this camp more dead than alive having traveled thirty eight miles and having been for over forty Eight hours with out neither grass or a drop of water for our Stock and but very little water for the men. When we got in nearly all the men were faint and fainting with thirst such as I can not describe."[31]

On 23 August, Captain Williford "having refused to escort the train further, [Sawyers] sent Lieutenant Colonel Godfrey, with Baptiste, to discover, if possible, the whereabouts of General Connor, who was certainly on Powder River below us."[32] After several hours and thirteen miles travel, Godfrey and Baptiste Defond rode into Fort Connor and presented themselves to post commander, Col. James Harvey Kidd. "Godfrey formerly Lieutenant Col 2nd Me [Maine] sent with [a] letter from Col J A Sawyers Cmdg wagon road expedition," wrote Kidd, "stating that he struck our trail ten miles toward Laramie but his escort composed of US Inf [antry] and Dakota Cavalry has refused to go further and that he was in sad way."[33]

Recall that on the previous day, 22 August, Kidd and General Connor had a heated exchange about Kidd and his Sixth Michigan being relieved by their discharge date of 11 October. Connor, with no troops en route, went so far as to ask Kidd if he would desert if no replacements arrived. Both Kidd and Connor were unaware of the close proximity of Sawyers party and its military escort. After hearing Godfrey's story and reading Sawyers's letter, Kidd recognized that a solution to his discharge dilemma had inadvertently fallen into his lap. He immediately wrote an order to Captain Williford to report to him (Colonel Kidd) at Fort Connor, and sent it off by messenger to Sawyers's camp.[34] He then wrote a letter to General Connor, explaining the situation and presenting the idea that Captain Williford and his U.S. Volunteer Infantry be relieved of escort duty and ordered to take over garrison duties at Fort Connor. The Sixth Michigan Cavalry could then furnish a military escort for Sawyers's party

---

[31] Edwards letter of 23 August 1865.

[32] Sawyers's official report, Hafen and Hafen, *Powder River Campaigns*, 258.

[33] Kidd diary, 23 August 1865 entry.

[34] Sawyers's official report, Hafen and Hafen, *Powder River Campaigns*, 258; Paul, ed., "A Galvanized Yankee Along the Niobrara," 156, 23 August 1865 entry. Griggs wrote: "In the afternoon a dispatch was received from the fort ordering us to report there immediately."

to get them safely through to the Bighorn River. When the escort of Sawyers's expedition returned, probably in mid-September, the Sixth Michigan could travel east to be mustered out on time. Kidd then sent Capt. James H. Kellogg and an escort of three men with John Godfrey to deliver his letter to General Connor.[35]

On 23 August, General Connor's command left their camp on Crazy Woman Creek and marched northwest over a treeless, waterless, rolling country for twenty miles. They camped on Clear Creek, near the location of today's town of Buffalo, Wyoming. Captain Palmer, the quartermaster, wrote, "Made camp at 3 o'clock; grass splendid; plenty of water, clear and pure as crystal and almost as cold as ice. The stream was full of trout and the boys had a glorious time in the afternoon bathing in the ice water and fishing for trout with hooks made of willows. Several bands of buffalo had been feeding close to camp and about 5 P.M. about twenty-five cavalrymen rode out and surrounded a band and drove them into a corral formed of our wagons, and there fifteen were slaughtered and turned over to the commissary department."[36]

A new element—the Sawyers Expedition—had been added to the mix, and its story would become entwined with Connor's command for much of the rest of the adventure.

---

[35] Kidd diary, 23 August 1865 entry; Lee diary, 24 August 1865 entry. Lee stated that an escort of three men accompanied Captain Kellogg and Godfrey.

[36] Palmer's report, Hafen and Hafen, *Powder River Campaigns*, 122, 23.

CHAPTER THIRTEEN

24–27 August 1865

PAPER COLLAR SOLDIERS

THURSDAY, 24 AUGUST 1865

While the men of Connor's command rested in their plentiful camp-site, the newest addition to the campaign was up and moving early.

The Sawyers Expedition

Sawyers followed the trail down the Dry Fork of Powder River toward Fort Connor. At about noon, after traveling thirteen and a half miles, they went into camp on the east side of Powder River, across from the fort. Private Griggs reported, "The men and animals are more than jubilant at again seeing a river where they can quench their thirst and have enough left to wash human faces."[1]

Colonel Kidd met with the leaders of the civilian road-building party and the military escort, writing, "Col Sawyers and Capt Williford called, find there are two sides to this question. Mutual criminations and more criminations. Capt Williford's men are in a bad way barefooted and without clothes."[2] Probably a good amount of venting of complaints and frustrations took place, but Kidd had to wait for word from General Connor before any further action could be taken.

Connor's Command

The expedition stayed in camp on Clear Creek that day. Capt. Albert Brown and his western column, consisting of two hundred officers and

---

[1] Paul, ed., "A Galvanized Yankee Along the Niobrara," 156, 24 August 1865 entry.
[2] Kidd diary, 24 August 1865 entry.

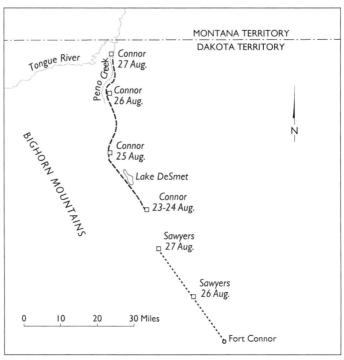

Connor's and Sawyers's movements, 24–27 August.

men, rode in and rejoined the command. Miller reported that "Capt. Kellog[g] 6th Mich Cav. arrived from Fort Connor with intelligence that the Eng'g [Engineering] party, which started from the mouth of Niobra-rah River with a view of establishing a route from that place via Bear River & Powder River to Virginia & Nevada Cities, are now in Camp on Pow-der, & the escort, 2 Co.s. U.S.V. In[fantry] Have mutinied, refused to go further."[3] Godfrey and Captain Kellogg received General Connor's reply and probably headed back to Fort Connor, about forty-two miles away.

Saint Louis, Missouri
While General Connor and his command rested contentedly in their camp on Clear Creek, decisions that would affect his immediate future were being made far to the east in Saint Louis. Maj. Gen. John Pope, in

---

[3]Miller diary, 24 August 1865 entry.

his Division of the Missouri office, wrote a letter to Connor, dated 24 August 1865, that opened with, "General: You will receive herewith the order assigning you to the command of the District of Utah and breaking up the District of the Plains. You will please proceed to your command at the earliest practicable moment and enter upon the performance of your duties." Now that the Civil War had ended, Pope was under heavy pressure from the War Department in Washington to reduce troop levels and expenses. He then proceeded to lecture Connor on the importance of following proper procurement procedures, as he was probably still seething over the incidents that had provoked Connor's 11 August rebuke. Pope further ordered that "All troops, except the regiment of infantry and the regiment of cavalry designated as the force of your district, will be put in march for Fort Leavenworth, or other proper points for muster out, without the least delay."[4]

Now here was an impossible situation: Connor had over twenty-five hundred men in three widely spread columns over a vast wilderness area who were out of communication with each other. General Dodge, Connor's immediate superior, protested, "If the Government will allow me to keep General Connor in the field with not to exceed 2,000 men of his present force, leaving the forces you have designated, to garrison posts on the plains, I will settle these Indian difficulties before spring satisfactorily to the Government, and bring about a peace that will be lasting."[5] Pope responded, "The pressure upon me about expenses on the plains is tremendous. Whether reasonable or not, the demands of the Government must be complied with."[6] Fortunately, due to logistics and Dodge's delaying tactics, Pope's letter did not reach Connor until late September, when the summer campaign was all but over.[7]

Fort Connor

Back at Fort Connor, the day ended with a moment of excitement, when "Dr Johnson and Capt Cole went hunting and on their return

---

[4]Pope to Connor, 24 August 1865, *The War of Rebellion*, O.R., Series 1, Volume 48/2 [S#102].

[5]Dodge to Pope, 31 August 1865, ibid.

[6]Pope to Dodge, 2 September 1865, ibid.

[7]The nearest telegraph station to Fort Connor was at Deer Creek, eighty-five miles to the south. During his campaign Connor moved as far as 170 miles north of Fort Connor in a wilderness area, so any communications with him would be slow and difficult.

were mistaken by the Pawnee pickets for hostile Indians."[8] Captain Rockafellow continued the story: "Indian pickets saw them come over hills when returning and came in at gallop reporting 'heap Sioux'[.] Col [Kidd] ordered Indians back to watch them and followed with comd [command] as soon as they could be got out. During this time [the] Indian [Pawnee] discovered their mistake and coming up to Col said in broken English 'White man chase Antelope, no Sioux by G——d.' This was big speech for him and he laughed as heartily as white men laughed at him."[9]

FRIDAY, 25 AUGUST 1865

Fort Connor

At noon "Capt Kellogg and Godfrey returned, bringing order written for [Kidd] to send an escort to Little Horn River with Col Sawyers, after the return of which [he] would turn over the command of this post to Capt Williford 5th U.S.V. and proceed with that portion of the regiment under [his] immediate command to Fort Laramie and report to Capt Price AAAG [Acting Assistant Adjutant General] for further orders. This gives highest satisfaction."[10]

Kidd was obviously pleased that his plan had been accepted and that he had solved the mustering-out date dilemma. It looked like a win-win situation for all parties: Captain Williford and his men were relieved from escort duty with the civilian party, Sawyers would get a new cavalry escort to guard him through the remaining unsafe Indian country, General Connor was off the hook for keeping the Sixth Michigan beyond their mustering-out date, and Kidd and his men would be mustered out on time, and probably be home by Christmas.

Connor's Command

After a pleasant day on Clear Creek, the expedition marched north, following Rock Creek and crossing it several times. "Seven miles from

---

[8] Kidd diary, 24 August 1865 entry.

[9] Rockafellow diary, 24 August 1865 entry, Hafen and Hafen, *Powder River Campaigns*, 186.

[10] Kidd diary, 25 August 1865 entry, Hafen and Hafen, *Powder River Campaigns*, 186. Rockafellow wrote that Godfrey and Kellogg returned at noon.

Clear Fork [Creek]," Palmer wrote, "we came to a pretty lake about two miles long and about three-fourths of a mile wide, which Major Bridger told us was DeSmet Lake, named for Father DeSmet."[11] Miller described the route in glowing terms: "Mountain ranges, covered with Forest trees, & Snow, long ranges of green Bluffs & Valleys, relieved by a little Lake scenery altogether peerlessly picturesque, & casting into the shade, any Landscape scenery we have yet witnessed on this route. Herds of Buffalo were surrounded to day many of them killed, some ran through the Command. The General enjoyed the sport, & hereafter, with many this day will [be] among the pleasing recollections of the past. We camped on a fine Brook which runs into the Piney Fk. [Fork] a mile below camp."[12] They camped on Little Piney Creek, near the site of where Fort Phil Kearny would be built the following year.

The Sawyers Expedition

At Sawyers's camp, across the river from Fort Connor, Lee wrote:

At noon while the most of the cattle were lying down in the shade a mile below camp, and the herders all half asleep, 10 or 12 Indians made a dash through the lower portion of the herd. Shot an arrow into one of the oxen and came very near getting three of the herders, Frank McCurdy, John Dalton, and Charley Campbell. They were all three sitting by a log when Frank got up and took off his boots and lay them down together with his gun and started across the river to turn back some of the cattle and when near across happened to look back and saw 3 or 4 of the devils slipping along the bank and gave the alarm. They fired a couple of shots at him without effect and also several at the others without doing any further damage than frightening the boys pretty badly.[13]

When rescuers from the camp arrived, the warriors were gone, as were Frank McCurdy's boots and gun and one horse. Lee also commented on Connor's order replacing their infantry escort with cavalry, saying that it "pleases our Col. [Sawyers] very much as he and the officers and men of the infantry are not very fond of each other."

---

[11] Palmer's report, Hafen and Hafen, *Powder River Campaigns*, 124.
[12] Miller diary, 25 August 1865 entry.
[13] Lee diary, 25 June 1865 entry.

SATURDAY, 26 AUGUST 1865

Connor's Command

The Connor expedition "Left Piney Fork at 6 A.M.; traveled north over a beautiful country until about 8 A.M., when our advance reached the top of the ridge dividing the waters of the Powder from those of the Tongue River."[14] The command followed the Bozeman Trail over a route that became infamous the following year. They marched north over the afore-mentioned divide, known as Lodge Trail Ridge. On the north slope, the trail followed a path down on what would later become known as Fetterman Ridge. Capt. William J. Fetterman and all eighty men with him—including two civilians—were killed there by a force of over one thousand Sioux, Cheyenne, and Arapaho warriors on 21 December 1866, only fifteen months hence.[15]

Capt. Henry E. Palmer and scout Jim Bridger rode ahead of the command to the crest of Lodge Trail Ridge. While scanning the magnificent vista before them, Bridger claimed to see a column of smoke in the vicinity of the Tongue River, about thirty miles to the northwest. Palmer said, "I again raised my glass to my eyes and took a long, earnest look, and for the life of me could not see any columns of smoke even with a strong field glass. The major [Bridger] was looking without any artificial help. . . . Yet knowing the peculiarities of my frontier friend, I agreed with him that there were columns of smoke." Palmer then suggested waiting until General Connor came up to confirm it. When Connor rode up, he looked though the field glass, and bluntly said that there was no smoke to be seen. Bridger quietly mounted his horse and rode away. Palmer asked Connor to take another look, which he did, with the same result. Palmer later overheard Jim Bridger grumbling about "these damn paper collar soldiers telling him there were no columns of smoke. The old man was very indignant at our doubting his ability to outsee us, with the aid of field glasses even."[16]

Miller described the road: "After traveling about 7 miles we came to where the Boseman road forked, one running in a northerly direction

---

[14] Palmer's report, Hafen and Hafen, *Powder River Campaigns*, 125.
[15] Brown, *Fort Phil Kearny*, 173–83.
[16] Palmer's report, Hafen and Hafen, *Powder River Campaigns*, 126–27.

Jim Bridger, famed mountain man
and one of Connor's civilian scouts.
*Courtesy of the Fort Laramie National
Historic Site, Meyers Collection.*

over a high ridge to the waters of Tongue River, the other N. Easterly
down a ravine to a Creek known as Peno's Creek."[17] The command
followed Peno Creek, which today is known as Prairie Dog Creek. The
"march down Peno Creek was uneventful, the road being very good,
much better than we had before found. This stream takes its name from
a French trapper by the name of Peno, who had been trapping for bea-
ver. . . . Our camp that night was in a valley of the Peno Creek, not far
from Tongue River, sixteen miles from Big Piney."[18]

Fort Connor/Sawyers Expedition

The Sawyers party prepared to leave the fort, as Kidd wrote, "Capt
Lovell with an escort of 20 men from Mich 6th and 25 from Dakota Cav
started for Little Horn with Sawyers Wagon Road expedition, took 20
days rations and one of the howitzers. Did not leave till 4 o'clock PM. I

---

[17]Miller diary, 26 August 1865 entry.
[18]Palmer's report, Hafen and Hafen, *Powder River Campaigns,* 127.

expect Lovell will be absent about 10 or 12 days."[19] Sawyers's original escort consisted of 118 men of the Fifth U.S. Volunteers and 25 cavalrymen of the Dakota Battalion, for a total of 143 men; now his escort was reduced to 45 cavalrymen. Capt. Osmer Cole and 1st Lt. Robert A. Moon also accompanied the detachment. After the late start from Fort Connor, they "Traveled 14 miles and camped at 11 o'clock at night without wood, water or grass, in fact the country is destitute of all vegetation."[20]

SUNDAY, 27 AUGUST 1865

Connor's Command

The expedition traveled thirteen and a half miles, following Peno Creek north. They went into camp about three miles south of the creek's confluence with the Tongue River.

Alcohol again caused problems in camp. "Shortly after camping, a dispute arose between two soldiers of a Cal. Co. who were enjoying themselves in a game of Monte; under the influence of steam [booze] one gave another the lie, which resulted in shooting at each other. The one who fired the first shot got seriously wounded in both arms."[21] Pvt. Charles Adams described the altercation: "On the afternoon of August 27, we were startled by several shots in quick succession. We were soon out in line, but we learned that two of the California boys had been playing cards and had had some disagreement and settled it with ever-ready revolvers. One had been shot through the body, the other through both arms."[22]

Fort Connor

Back at Fort Connor, Captain Rockafellow lamented, "This is a decidedly lonesome Lords day. No services, and nothing going on." Colonel Kidd and Rockafellow "entered into a solemn obligation not to drink alcoholic drinks for ten years." Kidd added the exception to their temperance pledge in his diary: "Ale excepted."[23]

---

[19] Kidd diary, 26 August 1865 entry.
[20] Lee diary, 26 June 1865 entry.
[21] Miller diary, 27 August 1865 entry.
[22] Adams, "Raiding a Hostile Village."
[23] Rockafellow diary, 27 August 1865 entry, Hafen and Hafen, *Powder River Campaigns*, 187; Kidd diary, 27 August 1865 entry.

The Sawyers Expedition

Breaking his routine of relaxing on Sunday, after a short rest in their dry camp Sawyers had his party moving again at 3 A.M. They reached Crazy Woman Creek at 10 A.M., corralled the wagons, and had breakfast. The men and animals rested in camp until 3 P.M., "then hitch up and start out again and travel until ten at night, the moon favoring us a little. The road a little rough after dark. Camp on the prairie, tie the oxen up to the wagons and have supper. The country is almost burned, occasionally a spot of grass."[24]

Connor and Sawyers now had several uneventful days of travel under their belts, and Kidd and the Sixth Michigan settled into a peaceful and probably boring routine at Fort Connor. However, a scouting party in the area of Jim Bridger's doubtful smoke sighting would complicate upcoming events for both expeditions.

------

[24]Lee diary, 27 June 1865 entry.

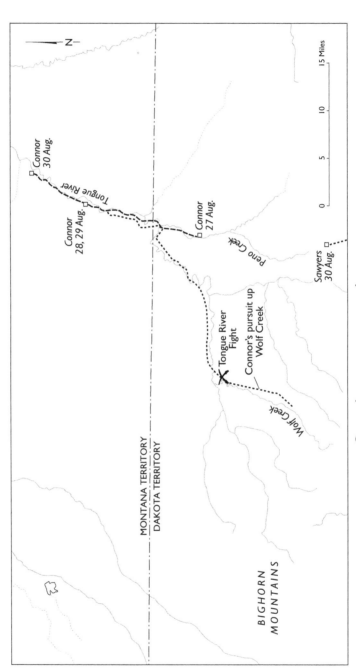

Connor's movements, 27–30 August.

CHAPTER FOURTEEN

28–30 August 1865

THE FIGHT ON TONGUE RIVER

MONDAY, 28 AUGUST 1865

After a stretch of calm days for Connor, Sawyers, and Kidd, Connor's soldiers headed down Tongue River Canyon while Sawyers's group continued on their route. Kidd remained at the fort.

Fort Connor

After receiving a large sack of mail from Deer Creek Station on the previous evening, Colonel Kidd "sent [Capt. James] Kellogg off to Gen Connor with [an] escort of fifteen men" with dispatches for the general.[1]

Connor's Command

The expedition left their camp, a few miles south of the Montana border. Miller described the march:

Struck tents at 6. A.M. & proceeded down Peno's Creek over a difficult road, to Tongue River, about 4 miles, & traveled down the bottom, crossing & recrossing the River 12 times during the day, which was not difficult, as the bed of the River is hard & not deep, after traveling a few miles down the River, the bottom became so narrow in places it is a mere cañon, the road also was more difficult. The Bluffs now on either side, assume the magnitude of Mountains, most of them are red, & covered with a growth of scrubby Pine & cedar. After traveling 16 miles we camped at a point on the River about midway in its passage through the Wolf Mountains where there is but little grass & plenty of game.[2]

---

[1] Kidd diary, 28 August 1865 entry.
[2] Miller diary, 28 August 1865 entry.

Tongue River Canyon. *Author's photo.*

Connor's command marched north, crossing the Montana border near the mouth of Peno Creek. They then followed the Tongue River into a narrow canyon near today's Decker, Montana, and camped in an area that is now under the waters of the Tongue River Reservoir. The site was probably near today's popular camping and boat-launching area known as Peewee Point.

Captain Nash "went out this morning with ten men on a scout on the left, and about noon when near 10 miles from the column I struck a fresh trail & found a few fires which were not entirely out. Agreeable to orders I immediately returned & reported the fact to the general. He has sent Capt North with 20 men to follow the trail."[3] North and his Pawnees rode out to investigate in the area where Bridger had claimed to see smoke two days earlier.

––––––––
[3] Nash diary, 28 August 1865 entry.

Genuine excitement filled the camp that evening."Capt. North of the Pawnees, who was ordered out on a scout, sent word in at night by two Scouts, that he had discovered an Indian Village about 12 miles west of last night's Camp."[4] Jim Bridger's sighting of a smoke column may have been accurate, although Palmer still doubted that the old man had actually seen it—"Bridger understood well enough that that was a favorite locality for Indians to camp, and that at most any time could be found a village there; hence his declaration that he saw columns of smoke."[5]

In language that typifies the disdain of many nineteenth-century white westerners towards the native tribesmen, Captain Palmer then wrote in melodramatic, graphic terms:

> The general immediately called me to his tent and instructed me to take command of the camp, keeping the wagons in the corral, protect the stock, and hold the position until he should return—that he was going out to fight the Indians. I had never been baptized with Indian Blood, had never taken a scalp, and now to see the glorious opportunity pass was too much. So, with tears in my eyes, I begged of the general to allow Lieut. Brewer, of the Seventh Iowa Cavalry, who I knew had just reported to me as very sick, to remain with the train, and that I be allowed to accompany him in the glorious work of annihilating savages. The general granted my request.[6]

Always a man of action, General Connor hastily put together a strike force consisting of 215 men of the Second California, Seventh Iowa, and Eleventh Ohio Cavalries, including 90 men of the Pawnee and Omaha scout companies.[7] Civilian sutler A. C. Leighton and his assistant Finn Burnett rode with them.[8] Jim Bridger, Antoine Ladeau, and probably the other civilian guides, accompanied the party.[9]

Pvt. Charles W. Adams, who rode with the attackers, wrote, "The order was to get ready to start as soon as possible. Two hundred men

---

[4]Miller diary, 28 August 1865 entry.

[5]Palmer's report, Hafen and Hafen, *Powder River Campaigns*, 127.

[6]Ibid., 128. First Lt. John S. Brewer was a member of Company F, Seventh Iowa Cavalry. *Civil War Soldiers and Sailors System*. However, Connor decided not to put the ailing Lieutenant Brewer in charge of the train, instead assigning Captain Nash of the Omaha Scouts to command the guard of the wagons. Nash diary, 28 August 1865 entry.

[7]Connor's report of 30 August 1865, Hafen and Hafen, *Powder River Campaigns*, 47.

[8]Burnett, "History of the Western Division," 574.

[9]Humfreville, *Twenty Years among Our Hostile Indians*, 355.

and two six-pounder howitzers were soon ready, and we started at dusk."[10] Pvt. Adoniram J. Shotwell of the same company recalled, "Soon Bridger was all animation, and after a hasty consultation, two hundred and fifty good mounts were in the saddle, and with General Connor at the head, set out on a night's ride to reach that band of warriors before break of day."[11]

Connor and his men rode off into the night, following the course of the Tongue River, with the intent of attacking the Indian village at dawn, approximately thirty-six miles to the southwest. He left sufficient men, under Captain Nash to guard the camp.

The Sawyers Expedition

The Sawyers Expedition "Started again at 3 P.M. [August 27] and traveled twenty-three miles over a rolling country and arrived at 9 A.M. of the 28th at the Clear Fork of the Powder River, where we remained during the balance of the day."[12] They camped in the same area where Connor's command had camped on 23 and 24 August, on Clear Creek, near the location of today's town of Buffalo, Wyoming.

Teamster Lee commented on the competency of their new military escort: "A squad of 15 or 20 cavalry [commanded by Captain Kellogg] passed through our camp last night on their way to Connor with mail. They came right into our camp without being challenged as no pickets were out. They thought we were very careless and could be very easily cut to pieces by an enemy. So much for an escort of which such great things are prophesied and who are able to whip ten times their number of Indians and of whom only one third have guns."[13]

TUESDAY, 29 AUGUST 1865

Connor's Fight on Tongue River

Connor's force rode on through the darkness. Palmer described the night's trek: "Our line of march lay up the valley of Tongue River, after

---

[10] Adams, "Raiding a Hostile Village."

[11] Rogers, *Soldiers of the Overland*, 203, reprint of a 13 May 1916 newspaper article in the *Freeport Ohio Press.*

[12] Sawyers's official report, Hafen and Hafen, *Powder River Campaigns,* 259.

[13] Lee diary, 28 June 1865 entry.

we had passed the point where our wagons had struck the stream, we found no road, but much underbrush and fallen timber; and as the night was quite dark, our march was very greatly impeded, so that at daylight we were not within many miles of the Indian village."[14]

Connor's approaching force "traveled all night, following the river, and just before daylight, the command was halted. General Connor made us a little speech, saying we were near the village, and he had no idea what force was there, but had confidence in the men and expected each to do his duty. Should we get in close quarters, the men should group in fours; under no circumstances were we to use revolvers unless there was no other chance, and then be sure and leave one charge for ourselves, rather than fall into the hands of the Indians. We were to avoid killing women and children as much as possible."[15]

The village that Connor's party rode toward was a Northern Arapaho encampment of about five hundred people. Chief Black Bear and his people had been described by an earlier traveler as "tall, noble looking men, well dressed in skins & with good buffalo robes for blankets."[16]

After Chivington's attack at Sand Creek in November 1864, many of the Arapahoes had aligned themselves with the Cheyenne and Sioux in raids on the Overland Road. Under the leadership of Chiefs Medicine Man and Black Bear, they had left the area of Camp Collins, Colorado Territory, in April 1865 and joined in the attacks, which were primarily west of Fort Laramie as far as South Pass. Black Bear's band of Northern Arapaho moved to Powder River country in August and camped on the south side of Tongue River, near the mouth of Wolf Creek close to today's Ranchester, Wyoming.[17]

At daylight—which would be around 4 to 5 A.M. on the northern plains at that time of year—the command was still several hours from the village.

[14] Palmer's report, Hafen and Hafen, *Powder River Campaigns*, 128, 129.

[15] Adams, "Raiding a Hostile Village." According to Warren White, director of the Carter County Museum in Ekalaka, Montana, the revolvers used in 1865 by the military were of the "cap and ball" design and were virtually impossible to reload on horseback once the initial six shots were fired.

[16] Trenholm, *The Arapahoes, Our People*, 146–47. Footnote 23 on page 146 attributes the quote to a soldier with the Utah Expedition of 1857. John Pulsipher, in *The Utah Expedition, Far West and the Rockies*, Leroy R. Hafen and Ann W. Hafen, eds. (Glendale, Calif.: The Arthur H. Clark Company, 1955), 8:198–99.

[17] Trenholm, *The Arapahoes, Our People*, 201–207.

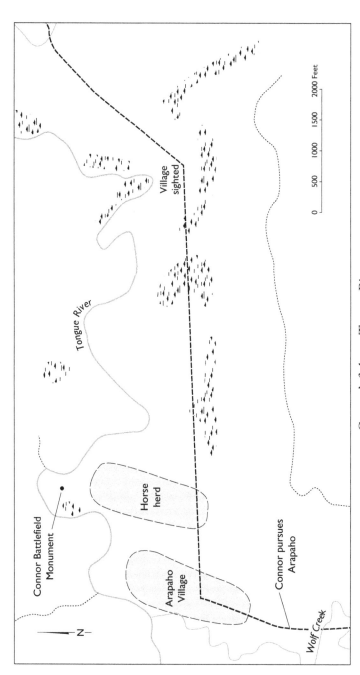

Connor's fight on Tongue River.

According to Palmer, it was he and Captain Frank North (who had joined the command en route) who led Connor's force during this portion of the march. After 7:00 A.M. Palmer and North sighted the village on the south bank of the Tongue River. "Just before me lay a large mesa or table containing five or six hundred acres of land all covered with Indians' ponies, except a portion about one-half mile to the left, which was thickly dotted with Indian tepees full of Indians."[18] Word was sent back to Connor, who quickly formed up his troops in battle formation. Private Shotwell described the scene: "Orders were whispered and the front filed right and left, and in less time than I tell it, that column of mounted men had formed a vast crescent and were charging pell mell into we knew not what."[19] Private Adams told of the first moments:

[I]t was about 8:00 A.M. when we saw an Indian on a high point riding in a circle—their sign of danger. Then the bugle sounded forward, and away we went. As we neared the village, the command divided, some turning to the right, others to the left. Then for an hour or more was an exciting time. The Indians had some of their tepees down and ponies packed, and some were so heavily loaded that when they tried to run, the packs pulled them over and they lay with their feet in the air.

The squaws, papooses, horses, and dogs were all running to save themselves. As we were armed with Spencer carbines, the firing became lively. The first Indian I saw down was an old man, shot through the body. We learned he was the "medicine man." The Indians ran to a high point and rallied, but they could not stand long before the Spencers.[20]

General Connor wrote in his official report of the fight, "I have the honor to report that at 7 1/2 A.M., on the morning of the 29th inst. after a nights march of forty miles, I surprised and attacked Black Bear's tribe or band of Arapahoe Indians, numbering over five hundred souls."[21] Connor proved that he did not command from the rear, which Finn Burnett recalled: "A. C. Leighton and I, with General Connor and his staff, General Connor leading the charge, and in the confusion we found

---

[18] Palmer's report, Hafen and Hafen, *Powder River Campaigns,* 129.

[19] Rogers, *Soldiers of the Overland,* 203.

[20] Adams, "Raiding a Hostile Village." The Spencer carbine was the primary cavalry weapon for the Union Army during the last years of the Civil War. A seven-shot repeater that fired a .52 caliber bullet, it was one of the few weapons available at that time that used a metallic cartridge.

[21] Connor's report, 30 August 1865, Hafen and Hafen, *Powder River Campaigns,* 46.

ourselves out in front and between the fire of our own troops and the Indians. General Connor ordered us to lie down on our horses, and just as we did this a shot struck the bugler [Richard Yates] just below his cartridge belt." The teenage bugler, known as "Little Dick" to his comrades, refused medical assistance and continued to carry dispatches back and forth across the battlefield during the fight.[22]

Leighton recalled a close call for the general:

Just as he [Connor] was about to charge, his horse ran away with great strength and he could not do anything with him. The horse ran straight for the Indian camp. We could see, however he was trying to pull him around to the left, pulling with all his might on the left rein. Just before reaching the camp the horse began to turn but he struck the edge of the camp. We saw an Indian run up to him with a gun and we thought Connor gone, but then we noticed him draw his pistol (he carried a 36-caliber navy pistol) and throw out his right arm and the Indian jumped up and fell forward on his gun, breaking the stock. Connor, we saw later shot him through the heart.[23]

After a hot fight that lasted perhaps an hour, the majority of the warriors and their families had succeeded in getting away from the village site, leaving their lodges and most of their possessions behind. Connor wrote, "The Indians were about moving their camp and had all their riding horses saddled, and upon my approach, they fled toward the Bighorn Mountains which were about 12 miles distant. I pursued them and had a running fight for ten miles, when the Indians entered a canyon in the mountains, where I did not consider it safe to follow them, having at this time only three officers and ten men with me."[24] Their escape route followed Wolf Creek, a stream that enters the Tongue River just west of their camp. Although one of Captain O'Brien's howitzers suffered a broken axle, they were fired at warriors fleeing from the village. The cannons apparently were not fired at the village because of the troops fighting at close range there.[25]

Connor's men and horses had been moving continuously for over thirteen hours, and as they followed the fleeing Indians, animals began

[22]Burnett, "History of the Western Division," 575.

[23]A. C. Leighton interview with W. M. Camp, 23 February 1914, Walter Mason Camp Collection.

[24]Connor's report, 30 August 1865, Hafen and Hafen, *Powder River Campaigns*, 46, 47.

[25]David, *Finn Burnett*, 85.

giving out. Like Captain North's experience on 20 August, Connor found himself chasing a foe that began to outnumber him.[26] Adams described the turn of events: "After we gave up the chase and turned back, the Indians turned on us, and as our horses were run down and theirs fresh, they might have cut us off from the rest, if they had tried. They followed us back to the village and got in the brush on the opposite side of the river, but a few shells from the howitzer scattered them."[27]

Also adding to the cause of Connor's dwindling pursuit force, many of the Pawnee and Omaha scouts and some white soldiers had begun to pillage the Arapahoe's left-behind possessions rather than join the chase up Wolf Creek. The general would show his displeasure of this lapse by his scouts later.[28]

During the pursuit, "one of North's braves picked up a little Indian boy that had been dropped by the wayside. The little fellow was crying, but when picked up by the soldier Indian, fought like a wild cat. One of our men asked the Indian what he was going to do with the papoose. He said: 'Don know; kill him mebby.' He was told to put him down and not to injure the bright little fellow. The Indian obeyed, and at least one papoose owed his life to the kind hearted soldier."[29]

Burnett and Palmer both wrote about an unfortunate soldier of the Eleventh Ohio who had an arrow lodged in his tongue. Palmer said they had to cut out the tongue to remove the arrowhead;[30] Burnett said they could not extract it until they returned to their camp.[31] Sgt. Pleasant W. Brown, Company K, Eleventh Ohio, recalled, " I remember Comrade Johnson of our company, who was shot, the arrow going through his cheek and tongue, and fastening itself in the jawbone, where it remained until we arrived back at camp, where the doctor and another man were required to get it out."[32] The poor fellow was identified as Pvt. Ed Ward, alias John Johnson, a galvanized Yankee.[33]

---

[26] Palmer's report, Hafen and Hafen, *Powder River Campaigns,* 132.
[27] Adams, "Raiding a Hostile Village."
[28] Connor's report, 30 August 1865, Hafen and Hafen, *Powder River Campaigns,* 47.
[29] Palmer's report, ibid., 136.
[30] Ibid., 131, 132.
[31] Burnett, "History of the Western Division," 575.
[32] P. W. Brown's reminiscent account, *The National Tribune,* 9 June 1910, United States Army War College and Carlisle Barracks, Carlisle, Pennsylvania.
[33] Hull, "Soldiering on the High Plains," footnote 44.

Capt. Jacob Lee Humfreville, commander of K Company, Eleventh Ohio Cavalry, told of an experience at the village site: "A guide named Antoine Ladeau, a Canadian Frenchman, was riding beside me. Pointing to a heap on the ground that looked like some buffalo skins, he said: 'Do you see that Indian lying under his robe pretending to be dead?' Whereupon Ladeau rose in his stirrups, took aim with his carbine, and sent a bullet into the lurking foe. The Indian jumped two or three feet from the ground after being shot, and fell a corpse."[34]

Finn Burnett recalled another incident during that period:

There were a number of Indians in the brush along the creek who were firing at the men who were at work destroying the village. Major [Nicholas J.] O'Brien was ordered to drive them out of the brush, and he and his men were skirmishing along the creek driving the warriors ahead of them, when two women came out of the brush, the old one with her left hand extended saying How! How! and approaching the Major. A. C. Leighton came up behind the two women and called to the Major to look out as the old one had a hatchet in her right hand behind her back. The warning came just in time to save the Major's life. The woman threw the hatchet just as Leighton called, and it grazed the Major's head. He had a pistol in his hand and shot before he thought. When he realized what he had done he was sorry and said: "Great God, boys, don't ever tell that I killed a squaw."[35]

Lt. Oscar Jewett, Connor's aide-de-camp, was wounded in the village, "shot through the thigh and through the hand. The men that were with him give him great praise for his courage and judgment on the battlefield. He stood behind his horse and was firing over the horse's rump as coolly as if he had been firing at a blackbird until he received those wounds, and then remarked he thought that was not a very safe place for Jewett and quietly led his horse away."[36]

Connor wrote in his report of the fight, "I captured five hundred horses, mules, and ponies, and took prisoners seven women and eleven children, and killed as near as I can estimate thirty-five warriors [later revised to sixty-three killed]—casualty on our side was my aide-de-camp, Lieutenant Jewett, First Bat. Nev. Cavalry, and my three orderlies, and

[34] Humfreville, *Twenty Years among Our Hostile Indians*, 355. Humfreville added: "one of the troopers facetiously remarking, 'Be quiet after this, please,' this caused a grim smile."
[35] Burnett, "History of the Western Division," 575.
[36] Alonzo Jewett, Oscar's brother, writing to their parents, 25 November 1865.

Lt. Oscar Jewett, Company D, First Nevada Volunteer Cavalry, was Connor's aide-de-camp. *Courtesy of the Denver Public Library, Western History Collection, Z-499.*

one man of the signal corps, who was near my person during the engagement, and two men of Company K, Eleventh Ohio Cav., severely but not dangerously wounded, and one Omaha Scout killed."[37]

Connor returned to the village site about 12:30 P.M. He then ordered "all their lodges, winter stores, clothing, robes, etc." to be burned.[38] At 2:30 P.M., Connor ordered his force to move out of the destroyed Arapaho village and return to their wagon train, camped in the Tongue River Canyon. Captain North and the Pawnees led the way, driving the captured stock. The cavalrymen followed and were continually harassed well into the night by angry Arapaho warriors who hoped to recapture their animals.[39]

---

[37]Connor's report, 30 August 1865, Hafen and Hafen, *Powder River Campaigns*, 46. Connor wrote: "Subsequently the Indians acknowledged a loss of sixty three (63) warriors killed and a large number wounded." Connor's Official Report of the Powder River Indian Expedition, 4 October 1865, Grenville Dodge papers.

[38]Connor's report, 30 August 1865, Hafen and Hafen, *Powder River Campaigns*, 46.

[39]Connor's report, 30 August 1865, Hafen and Hafen, *Powder River Campaigns*, 47. Connor reported: "I captured five hundred horses, mules, and ponies." Palmer said "about 1,100 head of ponies captured." Ibid., 135.

The Sawyers Expedition

The expedition moved out at 7 A.M. on 29 August after grazing their stock for several hours. They followed the trail that Connor's command had marched over on 25 August and camped on Little Piney Creek. "After getting into camp quite a wind storm came up, followed by a little shower of rain. The first we have had for a month."[40]

Fort Connor

The same windstorm hit the fort: "Had a terrific Dakota sand storm which leveled nearly every tent in camp and filled and covered everything with sand. First came a terrible wind which leveled all our tents and then as if regretful of the work it did blowed up the sand to bury the wreck."[41]

WEDNESDAY, 30 AUGUST 1865

Connor's Command

"At 11 P.M. last night some Indian Scouts arrived in camp & from that hour until daylight this morning arrivals were constant, by which time all the troops came in."[42] Connor reported, "I reached my camp at 2 A.M. of August 30th 1865 having marched over one hundred (100) miles, fought the battle and brought the captured stock back with me inside of thirty (30) hours." He then wrote of his prisoners: "I also captured four squaws and seven children taking them with me to my camp where I released them next morning not wishing to be encumbered with them. The prisoners informed me that the Arapahoes (the tribe I had attacked) under the leadership of Black Bear and Medicine Man would, they thought, gladly make peace with the whites. I accordingly sent them word that I did not desire to kill them if they would behave themselves and be good Indians. I also sent them a letter for safe conduct to Fort Laramie in the event of their desiring to make a treaty with us."[43]

Later in the morning, General Connor assembled his command in his typical no-nonsense manner. Miller described the scene: "The Genl. was enraged with the plunderers of yesterday & ordered all the plunder in

---

[40] Lee diary, 29 June 1865 entry.
[41] Rockafellow's diary, 29 August 1865 entry, Hafen and Hafen, *Powder River Campaigns,* 188.
[42] Miller diary, 30 August 1865 entry.
[43] Gen. Patrick E. Connor's official report of 4 October 1865, Grenville M. Dodge Papers.

Camp gathered up & burned, after which he told them, that hereafter when a battle was pending, there would be a detail of White troops who would remain behind with instructions to shoot every soldier Red, White, or Black who would be found plundering before the Battle ended, after which they might help themselves. A Winnebago [Omaha scouts] Chief, called Little Priest, distinguished himself for bravery, his conduct was highly commended & suitable rewarded by the Genl. 3 others of his tribe received similar marks of distinction."[44]

Captain Nash described the plunder brought back from the Arapaho village: "There was no end to the amount of Indian saddles, robes (and some of the finest I ever saw) all kinds of Indian accoutrements, clothing, camp and garrison equipment, ropes, lariats & every thing that is customary for Indian villages to be possessed of."[45]

General Connor wrote in his report of the battle, "I should have pursued the enemy farther after resting my horses, were it not that the right column of my expedition is out of supplies, and are waiting me near the Yellowstone."[46] Time had come to move the expedition north toward the rendezvous site of Panther Mountain, as there were two commands en route (Cole's and Walker's) that would soon be, if not already, in desperate need of the supplies carried by Connor's train. "Break camp after noon and move down the river," Sergeant Hull wrote in his journal, "crossing it thirteen times. Bluffs very high and rugged, all look as if they had been thrown up by volcanoes ages ago. Large masses of solid cinder to be seen. Camp at Redrock cañon. 10 miles."[47]

The Sawyers Expedition
The Sawyers party left their camp on Little Piney Creek and followed Connor's trail on the Bozeman Road north. After fording Big Piney Creek, they traveled over Lodge Trail Ridge and down Fetterman Ridge to Peno Creek.

During the afternoon there was a dispatch found stuck up on an old Elk horn along side of the road from Col. Bridger to Sawyers directing the latter to take the left hand or old Boseman [sic] trail ahead. A few miles

[44]Miller diary, 30 August 1865 entry.
[45]Nash diary, 29 August 1865 entry.
[46]Connor's report, 30 August 1865, Hafen and Hafen, *Powder River Campaigns,* 47.
[47]Hull, "Soldiering on the High Plains," 30 August 1865 entry.

from camp we met the mail party [under Captain Kellogg] coming back that passed through our camp a few nights ago. They reported Indians ahead too thick for them to pass through, that they appeared to be traveling north with their packs and squaws. And this morning about seven hundred or more of the mounted warriors attacked them, a few of them following until they nearly reached us. Fortunately no one was hurt, the balls barely missing some of them.[48]

The mail party camped with the Sawyers Expedition that night, with plans to attempt again to reach Connor on the next morning.

Thus the stage was set for the next episode, as James Sawyers planned to follow Bridger's instructions and travel northwest on the Bozeman Trail toward Tongue River. This move would take them directly into the area of the destroyed Arapaho village with the many angry and vengeful warriors who were reported on the trail ahead by the mail detail.

---

[48] Lee diary, 30 June 1865 entry. Jim Bridger was known to be illiterate, so someone else wrote the note for him. Doyle, *Journeys to the Land of Gold,* 399n40.

CHAPTER FIFTEEN

31 August–1 September 1865

RUNNING THE GAUNTLET

THURSDAY, 31 AUGUST 1865

While Connor's troops headed toward the rendezvous point at Panther Mountain, the Sawyers Expedition prepared to follow the Bozeman Trail to Tongue River.

The Sawyers Expedition

In the aftermath of the fight with the Arapaho, the wagon train, along with the mail detail from Fort Connor, started early and followed Connor's trail. In four or five miles they reached the Bozeman Trail cutoff to the northwest that was described in Bridger's note of the previous day. Sawyers followed that route, while Captain Kellogg and the mail party trailed Connor's path northeast down Peno Creek. In a move that would leave the road builders with dangerously thin protection, Kellogg took ten or fifteen of Sawyers's military escort with him, in order to strengthen his attempt to break through the warriors encountered the previous day and to reach Connor.[1]

The party crossed the divide between Peno and Goose Creeks on a path that took them through the area of today's Sheridan, Wyoming. Sawyers described the route: "Traveled twenty-two miles in a course a

---

[1] Lee diary, 31 August 1865 entry. Lee said ten or fifteen men went with Captain Kellogg, while Albert Holman said twenty of the escort left with Kellogg. Hafen and Hafen, *Powder River Campaigns,* 319, 320. The author chose to use Lee's number because he wrote his account in a "real-time" journal, while Holman's reminiscent account was published in 1924.

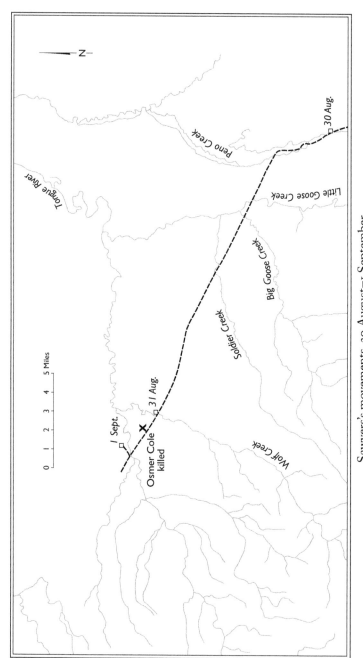

Sawyers's movements, 30 August–1 September.

little west of north, and camped at 5 P.M. on the middle branch of Tongue River; crossed two small streams and the South branch of Tongue River by good fords, which we made."[2]

The two small streams that Sawyers mentioned were Little Goose and Big Goose Creeks; the so-called south branch of Tongue River was Soldier Creek. The expedition camped on the bank of Wolf Creek, referred to by Sawyers as the middle branch of Tongue River. This stream is the same one that General Connor had followed while pursuing the fleeing Arapaho villagers southwest toward the Bighorn Mountains only two days before. Several miles to the northeast, the destroyed Arapaho village still smoldered.

The day ended on a tragic note, as teamster Corwin M. Lee described:

> Here I have to record another unfortunate event, the death of Captain [Osmer] Cole of the 6th Michigan cavalry, which happened just about sundown as the front of the train began to corrill. The Captain, with two or three men, was in advance and two or three Indians had been seen on the hills ahead. Cole passed ahead by himself to see what had become of them, when 8 or 10 of them made a rush for him from behind the hills and arrived within gunshot before he could wheel his horse and retreat, and fired a shot that brought him off his horse. Captain [Lovell] who was a short distance behind fired a shot at them and ran back to camp after help and returned to the spot with a dozen cavalry, but the red devils had disappeared taking with them the Captain's horse and equipment, revolver, and had also taken what things he had in his pockets, but strange to say had not scalped him. Probably they saw the cavalry and had no time to do it. When on a hill a mile back from camp I could see Indians running when after the captain but at such a distance could not distinguish who or what they were.[3]

Connor's Command

The expedition marched northeast at 6 A.M., following the winding course of the Tongue River. Sgt. Lewis Hull described the route: "Heavy timber on river, most I have seen since leaving Kansas (that is, the most on the level). Indian camps have been all along the river. Game plenty, but advance keeps most of it out of our sight. Sagewood and greasewood

---

[2] Sawyers's official report, Hafen and Hafen, *Powder River Campaigns,* 260.
[3] Lee diary, 31 August 1865 entry.

and prickly pears are the chief vegetation; most of the grass eaten by the
buffaloes. . . . March 15 miles."[4] The expedition went into camp near
today's Birney, Montana.

Col. Nelson Cole, commander of the eastern column now on Powder
River, had sent a search party led by Lt. Abram S. Hoagland west to
locate Connor.[5] Hoagland reached Tongue River on 31 August in the
vicinity of the area designated as the rendezvous site, approximately fifty
miles north of Connor's camp that day. Cole—desperately needing the
supplies in Connor's train—was told upon the return of the search party
that they had found no trace of Connor, and reported the terrain too
rough for their wagons to travel. Cole subsequently based his next decisions on that intelligence, first deciding to move south in the direction of
Fort Laramie, then reversing that decision and moving north toward the
Yellowstone River. After seeing smoke in that direction, Cole assumed
that it was Connor signaling him.[6]

Fort Connor

Colonel Kidd sounded bored in his journal entry: "Nothing but loung-
ing about camp."[7] Captain Rockafellow concerned himself with preda-
tors in close proximity of the fort: "Wolves came close up to stockade and
howled their best. We made arrangements so guards will not be alarmed
at shots tonight, and Capt. Tubbs is going to throw out spoiled meat and
of course we are to kill wolves."[8]

FRIDAY, 1 SEPTEMBER 1865

The Sawyers Expedition

The train moved out in the morning, passing the spot where Osmer
Cole had been killed the previous evening. They traveled several miles,

---

[4] Hull, "Soldiering on the High Plains," 31 August 1865.
[5] Col. Nelson D. Cole should not be confused with Capt. Osmer Cole, who was killed that day
while escorting the Sawyers party. They were not related. First Lt. Abram S. Hoagland was
in Battery K, Second Missouri Light Artillery. *Civil War Soldiers and Sailors System.*
[6] Nelson Cole's report, 10 February 1867, Hafen and Hafen, *Powder River Campaigns,* 72, 73.
[7] Kidd diary, 31 August 1865 entry.
[8] Hafen and Hafen, *Powder River Campaigns,* 109. Capt. William H. Tubbs was in Company
E, Fourteenth Connecticut Infantry, and served as assistant commissary of subsistence in the
Powder River Expedition. Rockafellow diary, 31 August 1865 entry, ibid., 188.

crossing the divide between Wolf Creek and the Tongue River. Teamster Lee described the Tongue River as a "mountain stream of good size, rapid current, rocky bottom, and good grass. . . . The banks lined with timber and brush." The wagons, in single file, began crossing the river. The lead wagons then continued northwest toward the foothills across the valley. By the time that the rear vehicles were crossing, the train stretched out for about a mile. Lee, who was with the third wagon from the end, observed, "As we were driving up slowly in the rear and waiting for the train in front to cross I could not help but observe what a fine chance for Indians to surprise and attack us and especially after we had discovered fresh signs of them and ashes that were still warm."[9] Albert Holman similarly recalled, "Instinctively every teamster took from the wagon his gun as an additional weapon, for we all wore revolvers buckled at our waists day and night."[10]

A herd of about forty spare oxen—some of which were footsore or crippled—followed the train. Driven by two herders on horseback, the cattle also included the nine cows of emigrants Edward H. Edwards and Samuel H. Cassady. Edwards described the next action: "[T]he whole train had crossed over. The rear guard and the herders with the loose stock which had not as yet crossed were fired upon by Indians concentrated in the thick brush that lined the bank of the stream. All the men got away safely but the Redskins got 22 head of cattle (including 3 of our cows and the Settler's Bull) and got away with them."[11]

The warriors, later identified as Arapaho, came out of the brush and rode along the sides of the train, firing long-range shots at the wagons. Lee wrote, "The guard and occasionally a driver returning fire at every opportunity, for they kept such a running around that it was almost impossible to get a shot at them."[12] The estimates of the number of warriors at this point of the fight vary significantly; Lee said twelve to fifteen warriors, and Holman recalled over one hundred. As the front of the train was alerted to the attack on the rear, the process of corralling the wagons began. They circled the wagons near the foothills, and the

---

[9] Lee diary, 1 September 1865 entry.
[10] Holman account, Hafen and Hafen, *Powder River Campaigns*, 323.
[11] Edwards papers, 18 September 1865 letter.
[12] Lee diary, 1 September 1865 entry.

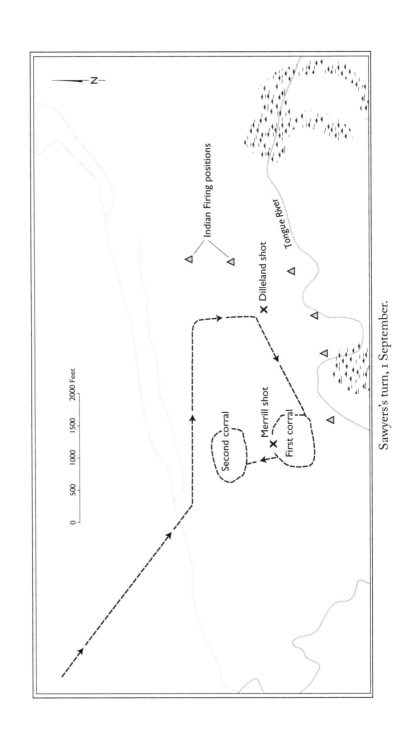

Sawyers's turn, 1 September.

warriors quickly took advantage of the high ground and fired shots into the wagon-made corral. Both Holman and Lee mentioned the Arapahos' obvious lack of gunpowder. Holman recalled, "This we knew by the slight effect the bullets had when they struck the cattle, and even those that hit the men hardly grazed the skin."[13] Lee wrote, "One of the cooks, Jack Marshall, was struck in the neck with a spent ball; did not break the skin."[14]

The warriors were observed driving the cattle into the timber on the south side of the river, where "a great fire had been built and from the bleating of the poor animals taken from us, we knew that some were being killed preparatory to a feast."[15] This angered Sawyers's men, and the cannon was brought out from the corral about two hundred yards toward the warriors, with twenty-five men to support it. Two or three shells were exploded over the warriors, and "The surprise to them must have been complete for with yells of rage and indignation they jumped up and began to scatter. Mounting their ponies, they crossed the river and rode in a circling manner around near us. Having done all the damage possible with the howitzer, we waved our caps and with cheers and yells of derision, we hauled the cannon back to the corral."[16]

"After laying still a couple of hours," Lee wrote, "it was thought we might move on by going in double column. The rear of the train had no more than fairly got started before they [the warriors] began to flock around, and as near as we could judge near 75 of them and began to fire into us from all [a]round."[17] The train proceeded north through broken, hilly terrain for about a mile, with the warriors taking advantage of the ground to continue to shoot into the wagons. Sawyers then decided that they could better protect themselves on the flat, open river bottom and reversed the train south, back toward the Tongue River.

---

[13]Holman account, Hafen and Hafen, *Powder River Campaigns,* 322. The warriors' guns of 1865 were muzzle-loaders, and the light velocity of their bullets would be due to an inadequate load of gunpowder.

[14]Lee diary, 1 September 1865 entry.

[15]Holman account, Hafen and Hafen, *Powder River Campaigns,* 323.

[16]Ibid.

[17]Lee diary, 1 September 1865 entry. Lee said "75 Indians," while Holman, writing in 1924 (fifty-nine years later), said "between five and six hundred Indians." Holman account, Hafen and Hafen, *Powder River Campaigns,* 323.

"I was on the rear of one line of wagons," Lee wrote, "and John Dalton on the other. As we passed onto the bottom we turned to the left and went down stream. The balls flying around us nicely, the rear being the special object of the attack. Two or three horses were shot clear through and several oxen struck by nearly spent balls. My nigh wheeler received one such on the right hip as we came onto the bottom."[18] The train continued downstream for about a mile, approaching a ravine that ran directly across their path and served as an Indian firing position. Sawyers turned the wagons to the right, exposing the teamsters who walked on the left side of their wagons to be fired upon from the flank, and then turned right again, and moved up river a short distance and started to corral. Lee described the chaotic scene: "While the front is corrilling the rear has to go very slowly and occasionally halt in order to allow them to get into place properly. All this time the rear being under fire from the ravine and from the bank of the stream."

Teamster Albert Holman, who was farther to the front of the train, de-scribed what happened next: "The firing had now become quite rapid. The writer [Holman] with his trailer and six yoke of cattle had now gotten fairly straightened out on the turn and looked back to see how the next driver was coming around with his 'swing around.' This young man, James Dilleland, had gotten his team about straight. His back was toward the Indians. Before I turned my eyes he threw up his hands and fell forward on his face. A bullet entering the small of his back passed through him."[19]

Dilleland, though seriously wounded, was still alive. "One of the sol-diers assisted him into another wagon. The team being left until the rest were all in, when the Colonel drove it up from off the left side."[20]

As the wagon corral formed, the men found themselves under fire from the dense underbrush along the river. Lee attributed the shooting of Dilleland to a specific warrior "who proved himself to be a good marks-man and in possession of a good rifle. . . . Moving his position up stream a little where he could command the corrill, he kept up his sharp shooting,

[18] Lee diary, 1 September 1865 entry. The nigh or near wheeler in a six-oxen or -mule team was the animal closest to the wagon on the left. Mark L. Gardner, *Wagons for the Santa Fe Trade* (Albuquerque: Univ. of New Mexico Press, 2000), 11.

[19] Holman account, Hafen and Hafen, *Powder River Campaigns*, 326.

[20] Lee diary, 1 September 1865 entry.

several of the boys narrowly escaping them, myself among the number. One of the emigrants from Cedar Falls, of the name of [E. G.] Merrill, was more unfortunate. He received a ball in the breast that lodged under his left arm. The ball came into the corrill between two wagons and crossed over to the other side to where he was standing. At the time I was lying down and distinctly heard the ball whistle and strike him. The ball coming near two hundred and fifty yards."[21]

This position proved to be too close to the river bank, and Sawyers decided to move the corral again, this time an additional two hundred yards away from the Indians' firing positions. The move came off without incident and the firing died down around four o'clock in the afternoon as the warriors' concealed firing positions on all sides were now out of range. Edward H. Edwards described the tense situation: "Rifle pits dug, breast works thrown up, and everything put in readiness to defend ourselves to the last."[22]

"Towards dusk some Indian who could talk tolerable English approached as near as prudent and called out that he did not wish to fight but wished to smoke and for someone to come out. He was told to come down that we would not hurt him, but he was evidently afraid to trust us."[23]

During the evening, they buried Osmer Cole in the west side of the corral. E. G. Merrill died from his wound around 10 P.M.[24] James Dilleland clung to life through the night.

Although in his official report Sawyers wrote little of the movement of the train on 1 September, teamsters Holman and Lee were highly critical of the leadership. Holman wrote, "The fact was we had too large and cumbersome a train for the number of men. So many were required to take care of the train that few were left for defensive purposes. Had the number of our cavalrymen been a hundred or more, we could have traveled without much danger, for the Indians could not stand before any number of us when we assumed the offensive."[25] Lee, obviously incensed,

---

[21] Ibid.
[22] Edwards papers, 18 September 1865 letter.
[23] Lee diary, 1 September 1865 entry.
[24] Ibid.
[25] Holman account, Hafen and Hafen, *Powder River Campaigns,* 325.

said, "Two men were sacrificed by a want of foresight and judgment in taking the train around the way it was. When every driver saw and felt that it was reckless and useless exposure of their lives without the opportunity of defending themselves and protected only by an escort that was barely able to defend themselves. Every man is ready and willing to fight, and fight to the last at every unavoidable necessity for it, but to be thus paraded around and made a target of by a judgment that fails to appreciate a real danger and to act judiciously and promptly under it calls forth loud and deep condemnations from all around."[26]

Holman and Lee probably echoed the sentiments of the majority, if not all, of the teamsters after running the gauntlet created by the slow, sweeping right turn made by the train on the river bottom under fire. Two men lay dead or dying, and it would have been more had it not been for the poor arms and lack of gunpowder of the warriors. Sawyers certainly should be faulted for the indecisive movement of the train after the initial attack on the rear of the wagons at the river crossing, but that would not even have been an issue, as Holman pointed out, had they had an adequate cavalry escort. Recall that they left Fort Connor with only forty-five cavalrymen—further reduced on 31 August by Kellogg's mail detail taking additional men—leaving about thirty cavalrymen to guard a train of approximately sixty wagons.

A long day ended with the Sawyers Expedition's wagons circled on the flat bottomland of Tongue River, unsure of what the next morning would bring.

Connor's Command

The same day, unaware of Sawyers's plight, General Connor "resumed my march down Tongue River sending out scouting parties to ascertain the whereabouts of the right and center Columns."[27] Connor sent Capt. Levi Marshall and fifty men of E Company, Eleventh Ohio Cavalry, north toward the Yellowstone River to locate the commands of Colonel Cole, out of Omaha, and Lieutenant Colonel Walker, out of Fort Lara-

---

[26] Lee diary, 1 September 1865 entry.
[27] Connor's official report, submitted on 4 October 1865 to Major Barnes, Grenville Dodge Manuscript Collection.

mie. Connor was becoming "seriously annoyed" that they had not yet contacted him.[28]

Capt. Henry Palmer recalled that "early in the morning a cannon shot was heard. No two persons could agree in what direction the sound came from, but as this was the day fixed for the general rendezvous of Cole and Connor's command near the mouth of the Rosebuds, some eighty miles away, it was supposed that the sound came from that direction."[29] Col. Nelson Cole's command, camped on Powder River at the mouth of Alkali Creek on 1 September, was attacked by Sioux warriors who attempted to run off their grazing stock. This action took place at 5 P.M., so the cannon shot could not have been from them. However, Sawyers's men had fired their mountain howitzer at the Arapaho in the morning. If Palmer did hear a cannon firing, it would have been from there.

"Broke camp early," Miller wrote, "& proceeded down the River in a N. Easterly direction. The road to day was not good, some labor was necessary in several places to make it passable, & 2 or 3 Wagons were damaged. The Bottom gradually widens, & timber increases, both, in size & quantity, in some places there was a dense undergrowth [of] Rose Bushes Greasewood & Sage Brush. . . . Dist. 15 miles. Crossed river 9 times."[30]

Sgt. Lewis Hull added a poignant reminder that probably mirrored many soldiers' thoughts: "This makes the end of nineteen months since leaving home, and still going further with no prospect of returning to civilization."[31]

Fort Connor

Rockafellow continued the story of his wolf hunt. "Sutler & I laid out until one o'clock but they [the wolves] were too sharp for us. We only got one shot each, though they came near enough so we could hear them snuff and snarl. Their howling was splendid. One of the party on flats near river shot one. I saw two large white ones but were too far away for

---

[28] Ibid.
[29] Palmer's paper, Hafen and Hafen, *Powder River Campaigns*, 136, 139.
[30] Miller diary, 1 September 1865 entry.
[31] Hull, "Soldiering on the High Plains," 1 September 1865 entry.

good shot. Wolf took piece of meat from wagon masters cook shanty."[32] Kidd simply wrote, "All quiet on the Powder."[33]

It may have been all quiet on the Powder, but that was certainly not the case on the Tongue River, as James Sawyers pondered the road build-er's dilemma and, farther north, Patrick Connor looked for his missing commands.

---

[32] Rockafellow diary, 1 September 1865 entry, Hafen and Hafen, *Powder River Campaigns*, 188, 189.

[33] Kidd diary, 1 September 1865 entry.

CHAPTER SIXTEEN

2–6 September 1865

STALEMATE AND MISSING COMMANDS

Connor's missing eastern and center columns were on Powder River, traveling in close proximity to each other after a chance meeting in mid-August. Col. Nelson Cole, with a force of 1,400 cavalrymen and 140 freight wagons, made up the eastern column, while Lt. Col. Samuel Walker led the center column, with 600 mounted men and a mule pack train. At this point in the campaign, both commands were nearly out of rations for their men, and their grain-fed eastern horses and mules were starving, unable to find adequate forage on the sparse prairie grass. After a scouting party sent west to locate Connor's command on Tongue River was unsuccessful, Cole, who had not had any communications from Connor since 10 July, was unsure if the general was even in the field. Walker made no attempt on his own to locate Connor, simply accepting the results of Cole's failed scouting party.

Meanwhile, on Tongue River Connor's western column of the Powder River Indian Expedition could not carry out his grandiose plans for the campaign without uniting with the other two columns. He had the smallest of the three forces in the field—400 officers and men—but carried the much-needed rations in his wagon train to re-supply the missing commands.

Into this unraveling situation came the civilian expedition of James Sawyers, now under siege on Tongue River by Arapaho warriors. At this time, none of the widespread units were in contact with each other or

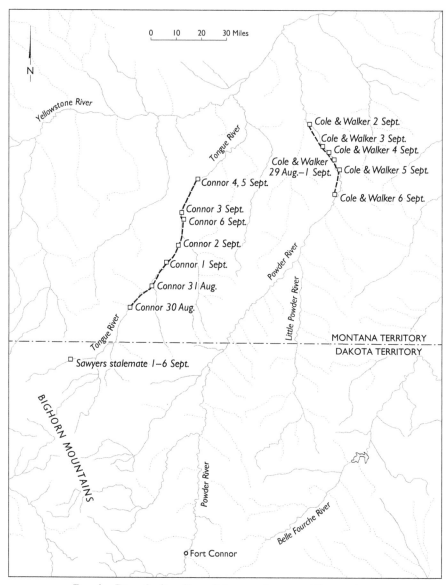

Powder River Indian Expedition, 30 August–6 September.

with Fort Connor. In fact, Cole and Walker were still unaware of the fort's existence.

SATURDAY, 2 SEPTEMBER 1865

The Sawyers Expedition

The morning turned cool after a heavy nighttime rain. The warriors, though still in sight, stayed well out of range, as the train remained circled on the Tongue River bottomland. James Sawyers estimated the number of Indians at 250 to 300.[1] Before noon, the same Indian who had spoken to them in English on the previous evening called out from cover for tobacco, saying they didn't want to fight. John Hardin, the wagon boss for the commercial portion of the train, went out with some tobacco and convinced the Indian, apparently a chief, to meet with him and come into the corral.

From the Indian—who identified the warriors as Arapaho from Black Bear's band—they learned of Connor's attack and the subsequent destruction of the Arapahos' nearby village three days ago. He told Sawyers's men that Connor had released the women and children who had been taken prisoner from the village and "given some paper talk to show that they were good Indians. It was at their camp in the mountains and would be here by noon. They were told that when the letter came and proved all right we would give them some provisions."[2]

Other Indians apparently joined the initial visitor to the wagon corral. Lee wrote: "A little after noon the letter came and proved to be from Connor, and was dated on the 30th of August, and stated . . . that they [the Arapaho] were severely punished in the fight of yesterday, that they wished for peace and ordered anybody of soldiers or white men whom they should meet to give them a safe conduct to Fort Laramie."[3]

Sawyers, realizing his precarious position, wrote: "To peace, of course, we were agreed, as they greatly outnumbered us, and were well armed and

---

[1] Sawyers's official report, Hafen and Hafen, *Powder River Campaigns*, 261.

[2] Lee diary, 2 September 1865 entry. Lee said that the chief claimed that the Indians attacking the train yesterday were Sioux and Cheyenne, but it is well documented that those tribes were on Powder River at that time, near the mouth of the Little Powder River. The Indian probably said this to defuse the situation by blaming yesterday's attack on others. Hyde, *Life of George Bent*, 237.

[3] Lee diary, 2 September 1865 entry.

Lower Tongue River, north of today's Ashland, Montana. *Author's photo.*

mounted, and our cattle began to need water and grass."[4] Sawyers and the
Indian delegates agreed to send three warriors and three cavalrymen to
Connor's camp north of them on Tongue River. The purpose for the
soldiers was to get reinforcements, and the Indians' goal was to obtain the
return of their ponies. As a show of good faith, "ten of their number [the
Arapaho] placed themselves in the hands of the military as hostages,"
wrote Lee. "Notwithstanding this apparent confidence in them there was
still a deep distrust. Although outside circumstances corroborated their
statement, every precaution was taken to guard against treachery and
surprise. . . . The men keeping their arms where they could seize them at
a moments notice."[5] Under this shaky truce, the stock was turned out to
graze without incident.

[4] Sawyers's official report, Hafen and Hafen, *Powder River Campaigns,* 262.
[5] Lee diary, 2 September 1865 entry.

The day ended on a somber note. "During the afternoon, James Dillon [Dilleland] died and in the evening he and Merrill were buried together in a trench on the south side of the corrill."[6] Albert Holman added some details to the burial: "On that night, in order that the Indians in our tent would not know what was going on, our fiddler took out his violin and in front of the tent regaled them with music. To add further to the amusements and divert the minds of our guests from the real purpose, a number of the boys danced cotillions, jigs, and reels. In the center of the corral was a much different scene, for there another group was solemnly digging a grave."[7]

Connor's Command

Captain Kellogg's mail detail came in, as Sergeant Hull described an otherwise uneventful day: "Mail arrived from Fort Connor last night under escort of 6th Michigan. Indians likely to cause trouble. Heavy rain; all well soaked. Lay up till noon, drying blankets, washing, fishing, and some writing letters. Break camp and move on. Camp on river about sunset. March 10 miles."[8] Connor's men bivouacked a few miles south of today's Ashland, Montana.

Fort Connor

Rockafellow, with his daily wolf report, wrote, "Last night wolves came near picket post and one of boys shot a large gray fellow which he presented to me and I got Indian Charley to tan for me."[9] Colonel Kidd's abbreviated entry for the day read: "Nothing to interrupt our serenity."[10]

SUNDAY, 3 SEPTEMBER 1865

The Sawyers Expedition

James Sawyers had decided to make the best of the situation and stay corralled until military reinforcements arrived from General Connor.

---

[6] Ibid. Lewis H. Smith, chief engineer, said that Dilleland died on 3 September and he and Merrill were buried on 6 September. Sawyers used the same dates in his official report, but the author chose to use 3 September because of Holman's details and because that was the only night that the Indians stayed in the camp. It made little sense to hold on to the bodies for three days. Doyle, *Journeys to the Land of Gold,* 377

[7] Holman account, Hafen and Hafen, *Powder River Campaigns,* 337.

[8] Hull, "Soldiering on the High Plains," 2 September 1865 entry.

[9] Rockafellow diary, 2 September 1865 entry, Hafen and Hafen, *Powder River Campaigns,* 189.

[10] Kidd diary, 2 September 1865 entry.

During the night one of the lightly guarded hostages "escaped," causing alarm in the camp. The men were awakened and put on the alert, but as morning dawned, their concerns proved to be unwarranted. Later in the morning, several warriors came into the camp, among them the one that had walked away.

C. M. Lee, always the critic, wrote:

> Nothing more of interest occurred until near evening when we had another fine opportunity of witnessing the results of the brilliant policy of our leaders. The ten [Arapaho] that had remained with us as pretended prisoners and hostages had been allowed to keep their arms. Six or eight came in, all allowed to keep their arms with them. Quietly collecting around the tent where the others were and wishing to have a talk, the Colonel [Sawyers] and Lt. Moon of the 6th Michigan, ever ready to negotiate, sat down among them to hear and be heard. The Indians by some excuse or reason had all drawn their bows, strung them and carried an arrow fitted ready for instant use. Our boys seeing this and anticipating trouble nearly all got hold of their guns and collected on the side next to where the Indians were just outside of the corrill, the boys staying mostly on the inside. The Indians pretended to be alarmed and insisted on our laying down our arms, as there were many of us and few of them.[11]

Sawyers called out for the men to remain calm and to keep their weapons out of sight. One of the Indians outside of the conference fired his gun in the air. "Fortunately Capt. Lovel stood close by," said Lee, "and called out that it was nothing, they only fired to see what we would do, or there would have been a volley fired into the Indians. . . . Several times the guns were cocked and leveled but the fact that two of our men [Sawyers and Moon] were completely in their power without the possibility of assisting them prevented the firing."

At dusk the Indians, including the hostages, left the camp, taking Sawyers and Moon with them. A short distance from camp, the warriors released the two men, taking their revolvers, which they promised to return the next day. Thus ended a potential bloodbath in the making— brought about by Sawyers's very questionable judgment in putting himself and Moon in such a vulnerable situation.

---

[11] Lee diary, 3 September 1865 entry.

Lee, in a surprising moment of empathy, reflected: "I am almost satisfied in my own mind that the Indians intended to act in good faith with us on their part, but guess we lacked the understanding and ability to treat with them without alarming their suspicious natures."[12]

Connor's Command

Captain Kellogg and the mail detail probably started back toward Fort Connor in the morning. The weather had turned inclement: "Has been cold, dreary day, raining most of the time, some snow. The weather very disagreeable for a mounted man who had to march sixteen miles in snow and rain."[13] Hull and Miller both wrote of a large elk shot close to camp, and an abundance of fish in the river, mainly catfish.[14] The command march downriver sixteen miles, camping about ten miles north of today's Ashland, Montana.

The Missing Commands

On 2 September, Colonel Cole's and Lieutenant Colonel Walker's commands had marched north on Powder River and camped a few miles south of the mouth of Mizpah Creek, about forty miles south of the Yellowstone River. A winter-like storm blew in that night, and the worn-down, starving livestock suffered unmercifully—this being after a hot grueling, march of twenty-four miles over barren country that day.

On the morning of 3 September, a number of horses and mules were found dead or dying as a result of the storm. Because of the desolate nature of the country ahead, both commanders decided that it would be better to head south toward Fort Laramie, rather than taking their chances on the Yellowstone. Cole reported: "During the march down the river and back to grass 225 horses and mules died from excessive heat,

---

[12] Ibid. The sequence of events is also confirmed by chief engineer Lewis H. Smith in his diary entry for 3 September 1865. Sawyers doesn't mention it in his official report. Sawyers's official report, Hafen and Hafen, *Powder River Campaigns,* 262.

[13] Palmer's account, Hafen and Hafen, *Powder River Campaigns,* 139. On Powder River, thirty-five miles south of the Yellowstone River, the storm had a devastating effect on Colonel Cole's eastern column, as "225 horses and mules died from excessive heat [of the previous day], exhaustion, starvation, and extreme cold." Nelson Cole's official report, 10 February 1867, ibid., 75.

[14] Hull, "Soldiering on the High Plains," 2 September 1865 entry; Miller diary, 3 September 1865 entry.

exhaustion, starvation, and extreme cold, and in consequence a number of wagons had to be destroyed, together with a considerable amount of no longer needed quartermaster's stores."[15]

Fort Connor

This was a quiet Sunday at the post. Col. James Harvey Kidd's journal entry simply read: "want to go home."[16]

MONDAY, 4 SEPTEMBER 1865

The Sawyers Expedition

The three Arapaho men who had accompanied the messengers to Connor returned around noon, according to C. M. Lee.[17] Lee wrote: "they did not come into camp. Dinner was taken out to them. They said some thirty men [soldiers] were coming. . . . They would not come into camp for they did not understand why their men were not here, but passed towards the mountains."[18] The three Arapaho turned back when they met Captain Kellogg's mail detail returning, as General Connor, still unaware of Sawyers's plight, had not yet dispatched reinforcements towards the road builders' position.

Lee continued: "At two or three o'clock 12 or 15 more [warriors] approached camp, part of those that escaped yesterday. The Colonel [Sawyers], Lieutenant [Moon], and Captain [Lovell] went out to meet them. The Lieut. received back his revolver; the Col.'s was not in the party but said they would bring it tomorrow. Their reason for doing as they did yesterday, they were afraid of being shot. They were anxious to trade but were put off until tomorrow; were very anxious to trade for gun caps, offering exorbitant prices for them, but this was not allowed."[19]

Connor's Command

The expedition broke camp at 7 A.M. and continued north on Tongue River. Miller described a changing terrain: "As we left Camp, the timber

---

[15] Cole's official report of 10 February 1865, Hafen and Hafen, *Powder River Campaigns,* 75–76.
[16] Kidd diary, 3 September 1865 entry.
[17] Sawyers said "towards night." Hafen and Hafen, *Powder River Campaigns,* 262.
[18] Lee diary, 4 September 1865 entry.
[19] Ibid.

along the River gradually lessened until we came to a portion which was destitute of timber, & everything else. In some places the Bottom widened out into an open plain, bounded by low & irregular Bluffs, most of which were bare. The whole route to day was destitute of grass, & the greater portion of [the] Bottom was entirely bare, presenting a barren surface of white clay & sand, except portions that was covered with a stuntified growth of sage brush & patches of Cactus."[20]

They marched fifteen miles and went into camp. "A messenger from Col. Sawyer's train of emigrants came into camp tonight with the news that his train had been attacked by the Indians, supposed to be the same ones that we had fought; that Capt. Cole, of the Sixth Michigan, and two of his men were killed; that the train was parked and the men doing their best to defend themselves."[21]

The camp—roughly thirty-five miles south of the Yellowstone River— would be their northernmost bivouac.

TUESDAY, 5 SEPTEMBER 1865

The Sawyers Expedition

"[Capt. James] Kellogg and 27 men being a mail party came in at sunrise," wrote Lewis H. Smith. "[T]wo men have gone to Connor for more men."[22] The third man in the original messenger party came back with Kellogg. Sawyers learned of Connor's position, far to the north on Tongue River, near the Yellowstone. Kellogg decided to wait for Connor's reinforcements before proceeding on to Fort Connor.[23]

Corwin M. Lee's journal entry reported suspicious behavior by Indians camped nearby:

Towards evening a party of Indians approached camp and were met by [John] Hardin. They brought back the Col.'s revolver, cap box, and knife, keeping the belt. Very anxious to trade for tobac[co] and caps, they invited Hardin down to their camp in the woods close by to get some buffalo meat. He started with them, but over heard one say, 'get him to camp and nepo (kill) him,' when he thought he had better make

---

[20] Miller diary, 4 September 1865 entry.
[21] Palmer's account, Hafen and Hafen, *Powder River Campaigns*, 140.
[22] Smith diary, 5 September 1865 entry, Doyle, *Journeys to the Land of Gold*, 377.
[23] Sawyers's official report, Hafen and Hafen, *Powder River Campaigns*, 262.

some excuse to return to camp although the others appeared to be opposed to any such a proceeding on their part. So he told them he would go back to our camp and get some fish for their chief and come back, but took care not to go out again.[24]

Connor's Command

General Connor did not react immediately to Sawyers's request for reinforcements. He delayed, awaiting the return of Capt. Levi Marshall and his company of fifty men who had been sent as a scouting party toward the Yellowstone River on 1 September to locate the other two commands. Connor now had to juggle his priorities even more, not only to relieve Sawyers but to locate the missing columns of Cole and Walker and to retain an adequate force to secure his supply train of about one hundred wagons.

The command did not move: "Lie in camp and wash clothes, rest and herd stock. Pawnees come in and report that Co. E [Captain Marshall's company] is down the river and will be here in another day. Rockets sent up as signals."[25]

The aforementioned rockets were intended to alert Cole and/or Walker of Connor's position. Lt. J. Willard Brown of the United States Signal Corps recalled:

In September, 1865, while serving as signal officer with Gen. P. E. Connor, on the Powder River Indian Expedition, a number of parachute rockets were sent up from a point on the Tongue River, twenty-five miles south of the Yellowstone, to learn the whereabouts of the right [Cole's] and centre [Walker's] columns of the expedition. The same was repeated at several camps on the return up the Tongue River, but without gaining reply from Lieutenant F. J. Amsden, who was serving with the right column. Afterwards, it was learned that the two columns were at the time on Powder River, where it was impossible to see the rockets on account of a high 'divide' between the Powder and Tongue Rivers.[26]

---

[24] Lee diary, 5 September 1865 entry.
[25] Hull, "Soldiering on the High Plains," 5 September 1865 entry.
[26] Brown, *Signal Corps*, 476. Lt. J. Willard Brown was in command of a fifteen-man detachment of the United States Signal Corps, assigned to the Powder River Indian Expedition. Palmer's report, Hafen and Hafen, *Powder River Campaigns*, 108.

Capt. Levi Marshall arrived in camp in the evening, having visited the Panther Mountain area designated by Connor as the rendezvous site. He reported no sign of Cole's command.[27]

The Lost Commands

Bivouacked near the mouth of Ash Creek on Powder River, Cole's force was attacked by a large party of at least one thousand Sioux warriors at dawn. After a long-range fight of about three hours, Cole broke camp and moved his command south.[28] Walker, who camped fifteen miles to the south, led a relief party north to assist Cole "after hearing the cannonading in the direction of Cole's camp."[29]

Fort Connor

Colonel Kidd decided that it was time to do something to relieve the boredom of garrison duty. He "concluded to start tomorrow with 20 or 25 men on a hunting expedition to Big Horn Mountains. Making my details cleaning up arms and getting ready today. Camp alarmed this evening by an escort with dispatches from Platte Bridge, who was at first mistaken for Indians."[30]

WEDNESDAY, 6 SEPTEMBER 1865

The Sawyers Expedition

This was a quiet day, as the Sawyers party remained corralled, waiting for relief from General Connor's command. Lewis H. Smith wrote: "fine day   Some Indians came and traded a little   stayed in corral waiting for Connor to send reinforcements   boys fishing in the creek and herding cattle[.]"[31]

---

[27] Palmer's account, Hafen and Hafen, *Powder River Campaigns,* 141. Lt. Fred Amsden, Signal Corps, U.S. Army, served as signal officer for Colonel Nelson Cole's Eastern Division of the Powder River Indian Expedition. *Civil War Soldiers and Sailors System.*

[28] Cole's official report of 10 February 1867, ibid., 76–78.

[29] Walker's official report, ibid., 97.

[30] Kidd diary, 5 September 1865 entry.

[31] Smith diary, 5 September 1865 entry, Doyle, *Journeys to the Land of Gold,* 377.

Connor's Command

The general reviewed his situation and explained his next moves in a letter, dated 6 September, to Capt. George F. Price, his acting assistant adjutant general at Fort Laramie:

> Col. Sawyers' wagon road party, escorted by 6th Michigan troops, was attacked on the 1st near the battle field of the 29th by Arapahoes. He had to corral, not having escort enough to go farther. He sent an express to me, which met the mail party. Capt. Kellogg, in command of the mail party wrote me that he would join Sawyers party, so I presume he is with it yet. I send this morning Capt. Brown with his own Company and the Omaha Scouts to the relief of Sawyer[s] with orders to escort him to the Big Horn. That leaves me with but 270 men in my command. Rather a small number to fight thousands of Indians and guard my larger train. Capt. Marshall with his Company has just returned from the Yellowstone and also scouts from all directions, but nothing is to be seen or heard of either of the other columns. I cannot account for their absence; they should have been here long before me. I fear that the men deserted so fast that they were compelled to turn back: if such is the fact you will send a strong and well mounted express to me immediately. I shall move up [south] the river about sixty miles to good grass (the country here is entirely destitute of grass) and again look for the other Columns, and remain in that vicinity until I hear from them.[32]

Capt. Albert Brown, with fifty men of Company L of the Second California Cavalry and eighty Omaha Indian scouts of Company A under Capt. Edwin R. Nash, was ordered to ride upriver—about ninety-five miles to the southwest—to relieve Sawyers's train and escort them out of danger. This did not set well with Nash:

> Having been with Capt Brown during the whole of the expedition this far & very satisfied that his energy would not satisfy no [one], I concluded to brave the wrath of the general [Connor] by applying to be relieved from Capt Brown or have some more energetic officer placed in charge. The general received my representation of Capt Brown with much more politeness than I expected but in the end remarked, 'Capt I would as soon you should have command of the escort as Capt Brown

---

[32]Connor letter to Captain Price, 6 September 1865, Grenville M. Dodge Papers. This letter, although dated 6 September, probably did not reach Fort Connor before 24 September, the date of Connor's return. There is no record of any dispatch riders to the fort prior to his arrival. Connor may have arrived at Fort Laramie simultaneously with the letter.

but I have reasons of my own for sending Capt Brown along in charge. And I assure you that Capt Brown has my most positive instructions to punish those Indians severely & I think you will find him different from what he has been on the trip heretofore.'[33]

Nash accepted General Connor's reassurance and the relief party, under Captain Brown and accompanied by seven supply wagons, headed north to relieve Sawyers's beleaguered train.

Connor's command "Broke Camp at 9 A.M. and traveled up the River 17 miles, and Camped where the grass was good & Timber the last on Tongue R."[34] Hull added: "Break track again and take the back track. Don't know what is to be done, only that we are going up the river."[35]

Fort Connor

Colonel Kidd described his hunting adventure: "I left camp at 10 A.M. with 20 men accompanied by Doc [Henry Johnson], [Lt. John T.] Gould, [Capt. Nelson C.] Thomas, and [Lt. Elias B.] Stone to hunt. Went up river. Discovered heavy smoke towards mountains. Make it out to be Indians. Marched 25 miles and saw no game. Camped on the river for the night in an old Indian camp and where have been burnt some wagons."[36] Captain Rockafellow, still bruised and battered from his spill during the buffalo hunt on 8 August, also reported on Kidd's hunting trip: "Colonel and about twenty men started on a hunt for grass & game. I cannot go as I am unable to ride without causing me much pain."[37]

Finding his missing commands and rescuing a civilian wagon train had become General Patrick Connor's major objectives—not what he had envisioned for his expedition during the hectic months of planning and preparation.

---

[33] Nash Diary, 6 September 1865 entry
[34] Miller diary, 6 September 1865 entry.
[35] Hull, "Soldiering on the High Plains," 6 September 1865 entry.
[36] Kidd diary, 6 September 1865 entry.
[37] Rockafellow diary, 6 September 1865 entry, Hafen and Hafen, *Powder River Campaigns*, 189.

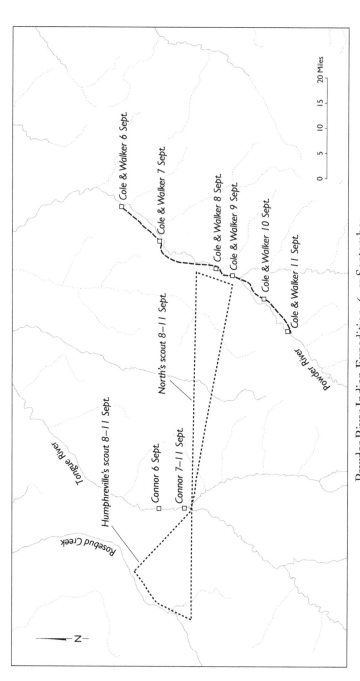

Powder River Indian Expedition, 6–11 September.

CHAPTER SEVENTEEN

7–11 September 1865

AN UNEXPECTED VISITOR

ITEMS FROM THE PLAINS
Major General Dodge is en route to Fort Kearney and Fort Laramie. He thinks the Indians can be kept in subjection with forces now at his command, although the number of disaffected red-skins on the Plains is estimated at 25,000.[1]

G en. Grenville M. Dodge left Fort Leavenworth during the first week of August for an inspection tour of his department. He was in Council Bluffs, Iowa, on 7 August, Fort Kearny on 15 August, Fort Mitchell on 28 August, and Fort Laramie on 29 August. Dodge, his staff, and escort of one hundred cavalrymen then left Fort Laramie and followed the well-traveled trail toward Fort Connor.[2]

THURSDAY, 7 SEPTEMBER 1865

Fort Connor

Colonel Kidd cut short his hunting trip and returned to the fort because of the close proximity of an Indian camp and the scarcity of game. Much to his surprise, he "Found General Dodge just arrived near my camp. Rec[eived] notice from him that he would visit the post tomorrow

---

[1] *Saint Louis Republican,* 2 September 1865.
[2] Varley, *Brigham and the Brigadier,* 254; *The War of Rebellion,* O.R., Series 1, Volume 48/2 [S#102], Dates on telegrams from Dodge to Pope confirm his presence at the locations listed.

and would then go up the river with small party."[3] Captain Rockafellow added, "He [Dodge] visits the fort in the morning when he is to receive proper salute. He marches 35 to 40 miles per day."[4]

Kidd, who frequently ordered dress parades during his trip to Fort Laramie, seemed to thrive on the pageantry of such an event. He probably spent the rest of the day preparing his men and the fort for Dodge's grand entry to Fort Connor in the morning.

The Sawyers Expedition

The weather turned colder as the men of the road-building party continued their wait in the wagon corral on the Tongue River bottomland. It was "cloudy and rainy in the afternoon   no Indian came to camp   too cold to venture out[.]"[5] C. M. Lee said, "still lying in camp waiting to hear from Connor and get a larger escort to go on with or be ordered back by him refusing to furnish any more of an escort."[6]

Connor's Command

The rescue of the Sawyers party and the search for the lost commands took priority over the original goals of the Powder River Indian Expedition. An air of uncertainty spread through the camp, and there were "Many rumors going around as to what we are going to do."[7] Connor moved his now-depleted command south a short distance and readied scouting parties to look for the Cole and Walker commands.

Miller described an early morning march: "Broke Camp at 1 A.M. and traveled a few [five] miles up the River and went into Camp at 10 A.M. where grass was good. On our return we have the advantage of knowing where the best grazing is, and avail ourselves of this benefit. The day being Cool & cloudy."[8]

---

[3] Kidd diary, 7 September 1865 entry.
[4] Rockafellow diary, 7 September 1865 entry, Hafen and Hafen, *Powder River Campaigns*, 190.
[5] Smith diary, 7 September 1865 entry, Doyle, *Journeys to the Land of Gold*, 377.
[6] Lee diary, 7 September 1865 entry.
[7] Hull, "Soldiering on the High Plains," 7 September 1865 entry.
[8] Miller diary, 7 September 1865 entry.

FRIDAY, 8 SEPTEMBER 1865

Fort Connor

General Dodge arrived at the fort at 10 A.M., initiating the military ceremony orchestrated by Colonel Kidd, who sent a cavalry "escort out to receive him [General Dodge] and we fired a salute of 13 guns. The Infantry turned out under arms. An escort to receive a Genl forms in two ranks facing inward & presenting saber. The Officer meets him before passing through and takes his position on left of Genl. The escort under [the] com[man]d of [a] Sergt. follow the rear of the Genls escort."[9] Dodge "was accompanied by Major McElroy, Capt Ford, Lt James and others of his staff, Gen Williamson, Mr Kasson M.C. [member of Congress] from Iowa. Mr Dodge the Genl's brother, all of whom remained to dinner, and enjoyed their visit."[10]

Colonel Kidd brought up the subject of the Sixth Michigan's mustering-out date. "I gave him [Dodge] a grand reception. He took dinner with me and Everything is arranged satisfactorily as far as the old men are concerned. We are to proceed in a few days to Leavenworth whence I suppose to Detroit before being mustered out. We shall probably not be mustered & dismounted till we get to Leavenworth."[11]

General Dodge and his party were interested to find out more about the Sawyers Expedition. Captain Williford, who commanded the infantry escort of the road-building party to Fort Connor, said, "it would be a good route if one half of the hills were inverted and dumped into the ravines."[12] Williford, certainly not a fan of James Sawyers after their adversarial relationship on the trail, proceeded to paint such a negative picture of the expedition that Dodge later wrote, "The wagon road expedition was a failure as far as making a road was concerned. It had a heavy train belonging to private parties, and while its real purpose seems to

---

[9]Rockafellow diary, 8 September 1865 entry, Hafen and Hafen, *Powder River Campaigns*, 190.
[10]Kidd diary, 8 September 1865 entry. Maj. Gen. James Alexander Williamson, an Iowa man, had been mustered out of the service in August 1865 and traveled with Dodge as a civilian. Both men had played important roles in Sherman's March through Georgia in 1864. *American Civil War Research Database.*   [11]Kidd letter to his father, 9 September 1865.
[12]Rockafellow diary, 8 September 1865 entry, Hafen and Hafen, *Powder River Campaigns*, 190.

have been to take the train through, and to that end its efforts were devoted, instead of making a road, building bridges, etc."[13] Williford received high praise from Dodge and was given credit for saving the party and taking them to Fort Connor. On Tongue River, James Sawyers's ears may have been burning.

The Sawyers Expedition

Unbeknownst to those involved in the after-dinner conversation at Fort Connor, the Sawyers party still waited for reinforcements in their wagon-made corral, ninety miles to the north.

Teamster C. M. Lee wrote: "Rained all night last night. About one o'clock in the night cattle stampeded in the corrill and ran from one side against the wagons on the other side, breaking the axle of one of them and causing it to fall to the ground, somewhat seriously frightening a couple of the boys who were asleep in it. Thinking it to be safer and better for the cattle they were turned out and driven into the brush. Rained all day and on the mountains it snows."[14] Lewis H. Smith added, "corral getting awfully muddy and uncomfortable[.]"[15]

Connor's Command

The weather remained cold and wet as scouting parties were sent out in two directions. Capt. Jacob Lee Humfreville, Company K, Eleventh Ohio, marched west with thirty men and guide Antoine Ladeau toward Rosebud Creek to reconnoiter that valley for Indians and any sign of the missing commands.[16] Capt. Frank North and fifty of his Pawnee scouts moved east toward Powder River with instructions from General Connor "to ascertain if possible the whereabouts of the missing columns which should have found me before this."[17]

Sgt. Lewis B. Hull wrote, "Expect the command will lie in camp until both parties are heard from. Build 'wicky up' and go to bed in the mud before dark for a wet sleep. Everything soaked[.]"[18]

---

[13] Dodge report to Lt. Col. J. M. Bell, 1 November 1865, ibid., 58.
[14] Lee diary, 8 September 1865 entry.
[15] Smith diary, 8 September 1865 entry, Doyle, *Journeys to the Land of Gold*, 377.
[16] Hull, "Soldiering on the High Plains," 8 September 1865 entry.
[17] Gen. Patrick E. Connor's official report of 4 October 1865, Grenville M. Dodge Papers.
[18] Hull, "Soldiering on the High Plains," 8 September 1865 entry.

SATURDAY, 9 SEPTEMBER 1865

Fort Connor

"Had a big storm from last night which continued all day today," Colonel Kidd recorded. "Powder River on the rampage. Ground around Fort heretofore a bed of dust is now mud. Gen Dodge party still encamped opposite. Went over this evening and had a good time. Gen leaves tomorrow."[19] Captain Rockafellow added, "The Maj & Inspector Genl [McElroy] visited fort this A.M. Did not require a formal inspection. He pronounced [Capt. W. H.] Tubbs B459647 superb."[20]

"It rained and snowed all Day," wrote Pvt. Sheldon Wight. "I hitched up my team and drawed a load of wood for the Col. and the rest of the day I shivered over a fire to keep warm."[21]

Colonel Kidd showed concern for the mail detail that he had dispatched to General Connor on 28 August: "Begin to be apprehensive about Kellogg who is now past due. Fear he may have been intercepted by Indians and perhaps killed."[22] Still unknown to those at Fort Connor, Captain Kellogg and the mail detail waited with the Sawyers train for reinforcements on Tongue River.

The Sawyers Expedition

"Rained all night and still raining," wrote Lee. "The mountains and all of the high hills around are covered with snow apparently from 3 to 6 inches deep."[23] Lewis H. Smith added, "but little doing except herding cattle   many of the boys going to the timber and making fires to keep warm   mud mud mud[.]"[24]

Sawyers and his men continued to await word from Connor, and grumbling and discontent became more commonplace. The cold, wet conditions made their precarious position progressively intolerable.

---

[19] Kidd diary, 9 September 1865 entry.
[20] Rockafellow diary, 9 September 1865 entry, Hafen and Hafen, *Powder River Campaigns*, 190. The B459647 must have been a government form dealing with commissary supplies, as Tubbs served as assistant commissary of subsistence officer for the expedition.
[21] Geyer, *Sheldon L. Wight*, 104.
[22] Kidd diary, 9 September 1865 entry.
[23] Lee diary, 9 September 1865 entry.
[24] Smith diary, 9 September 1865 entry, Doyle, *Journeys to the Land of Gold*, 377, 378.

Connor's Command

Waiting for word from his scouting parties, the general kept his column in camp. The weather made their lives miserable too: "Rained all night; camp almost flooded. Many moving out to higher ground. Go to bed for another wallow in the mud."[25]

The Missing Commands

On Powder River the weather had a deadly effect on the columns of Colonel Cole and Lieutenant Colonel Walker. Several miles below the mouth of the Little Powder River on 8 September, the commands, traveling together, had a five-hour moving fight with more than two thousand Sioux and Cheyenne warriors, with the conflict breaking off at dusk. Colonel Cole then chose a campsite on a barren prairie, unprotected from a winter-like storm that blew in. A blowing, freezing rain turned to sleet and snow and lasted through the night. On the morning of 9 September, an unimaginable scene unfolded: hundreds of their starving and worn-down horses and mules were dead or dying as a result of the storm. By the time they had moved to a protected area several miles upstream, over five hundred animals had been lost from the two commands. Cole then ordered the destruction of about one hundred of his wagons and the burning of much of their equipment.[26]

SUNDAY, 10 SEPTEMBER 1865

Fort Connor

The storm ended, and the weather turned clear and warmer. General Dodge and his party departed south for Fort Laramie. Rockafellow wrote, "The Big Horn Mountains and Ponkeen [Pumpkin] Buttes as also highest peaks of Powder River range are capped with snow and present a beautiful appearance in the sunlight."[27] Kidd, also impressed with the scenery, expounded, "This sight alone almost repays us for our unwanted

---

[25] Hull, "Soldiering on the High Plains," 9 September 1865 entry.

[26] Bennett diary, 8–9 September 1865 entry; Nelson Cole's official report, 10 February 1867 entry, Hafen and Hafen, *Powder River Campaigns*, 78–81.

[27] Rockafellow diary, 10 September 1865 entry, ibid., 191.

trip across the plains." He also became more concerned about his overdue mail detail: "Kellogg not yet in. Exceedingly anxious about him."[28]

The Sawyers Expedition

The mud in the wagon circle had become unbearable, so they "Moved corrill a couple hundred yards during the forenoon onto a good clean spot towards the river."[29] Lewis H. Smith added, "no news as yet from Connor   Cattle doing well but we get anxious for news   no Indians in sight all day[.]"[30]

Connor's Command

"Day Clear. Remained in Camp," Miller wrote. "Since last Thursday evening up to this morning we have had constant rain, & Tongue R. has risen so high that the crossings are difficult, & the road so muddy, that it is at present, almost impassable."[31] Sergeant Hull "Put all the blankets and clothing up to dry and [had] a square breakfast of bacon and steak. Orders against any shooting as we are getting close to Indians."[32]

Hull wrote that the command broke camp and marched five miles, while Miller said they remained in camp. Regardless of whose entry was correct, they were camped in the general vicinity of today's Ashland, Montana, on Tongue River.

The Missing Commands

On Powder River, the combined expeditions of Cole and Walker headed south. While crossing the river to the east side, a few miles above the confluence of the Little Powder River, they had a brief encounter with Sioux and Cheyenne warriors—the soldiers used their artillery effectively to keep them at bay. A few miles south, they passed through the site of a large abandoned Indian village, estimated by chief engineer Lyman Bennett at one thousand to fifteen hundred lodges. The struggling commands went into camp about five miles south of there.[33]

---

[28] Kidd diary, 10 September 1865 entry.
[29] Lee diary, 10 September 1865 entry.
[30] Smith diary, 10 September 1865 entry, Doyle, *Journeys to the Land of Gold*, 378.
[31] Miller diary, 10 September 1865 entry.
[32] Hull, "Soldiering on the High Plains," 10 September 1865 entry.
[33] Bennett diary, 10 September 1865 entry.

MONDAY, SEPTEMBER 11, 1865

The Sawyers Expedition

Still circled on the Tongue River, the men were becoming restless awaiting reinforcements or at least a message from General Connor. Lee summed up the day: "Cool morning but sunshiny. No word from Connor yet. The Col. [Sawyers] says that he will not offer to go ahead without hearing from him, but would go back first for if he should go ahead against the opinion of every man and any more trouble should happen to the men and train he would be blamed with it all, and he does not wish any more men killed if he can possibly prevent it."[34] The military escort's patience was probably wearing thin. "Capt [Don G.] Lovell agrees to wait til Thursday morning when we move in one direction or the other   No Indians seen today[.]"[35]

Nothing had been heard from Capt. Albert Brown and the relief party who left Connor's camp on 6 September—some seventy-five miles to the northeast.

Connor's Command

Moving their camp upriver a mile for better grass, the expedition anxiously awaited the return of the two scouting parties. At 4 P.M. Captain Humfreville returned with his party from their reconnaissance of the Rosebud Creek Valley, reporting no signs of Indians or the missing commands.

Miller, who apparently had an insider's relationship with General Connor, wrote:

Two hours later Capt. North & Scouts returned from Powder River, distant from this Camp 50 Miles. He struck a trail which led directly from Tongue R. to Powder R. & found a good road which abounded with fine grass. He reported as follows. On the evening of the third day after leaving Tongue R. He reached Powder R. where he found a late Camp which had been occupied since the recent heavy rains commenced, probably, the day previous. Upon examination, it proved to be the Camp of a Command, containing one or more Regiments. In the formation of the Camp, the horses were picketed in the form of a large

---

[34] Lee diary, 11 September 1865 entry.
[35] Smith diary, 11 September 1865 entry, Doyle, *Journeys to the Land of Gold*, 378.

hollow square, and about 240 lay dead in Camp, being all shot through the head, & the saddles Curry Combs Brushes & c. were evidently burnt, as the remains were to be seen in the ashes. The Camp was on the west side of the River, & the command moved up the bottom, with three Wagons abreast, leaving that number of plain road tracks, which, for a distance of two miles, were literally strewed with the Carcasses of Horses. Did not count them, but thinks there must have been altogether from five to Six hundred. Would have followed & overtaken the Command, but saw some Indians, & thinks he discovered a large Village a short Distance up the Bottoms, which induced him to return to Camp on Tongue R. which he reached in less than 24 hours, having traveled during the night.[36]

Miller's report of North's findings coincides very accurately with reports and diaries written by Colonel Cole and his chief engineer, Lyman G. Bennett. On the evening of the 10th, North and his party of Pawnee scouts discovered the 8 September campsite of Cole and Walker's commands on the west side of Powder River. After noting the high number of dead horses in this camp, they followed Cole's path for two miles, observing the trail of dead animals along the route to the next bivouac. This campsite—abandoned only hours before by the missing commands—no doubt contained still-smoldering fires from the destroyed wagons and equipment, as well as the carcasses of the dead animals. The "large village a short distance up the bottoms" would have to be the abandoned Indian camp that Cole's command had marched through earlier that day, a few miles south on the east bank.

Cole and Walker were camped only six and a half miles to the south, unbeknownst to North. North could only react to evidence of a terrible fight. As defended by his biographer, "Captain North felt that it was not safe for him to remain there with a force of only fifty men."[37] Connor concurred in his official report of the campaign: "The Indians were so numerous on this trail Capt North deemed it advisable to return, it being in his judgment folly to attempt to force a passage to Colonel Cole under the circumstances, with the small force at his disposal. Colonel Cole's trail was going up Powder River."[38] In hindsight judgment is easy, but

---

[36] Miller diary, 11 September 1865 entry.
[37] Grinnell, *Two Great Scouts*, 117.
[38] Gen. Patrick E. Connor's official report, 4 October 1865, Grenville M. Dodge Papers.

perhaps Captain North prematurely abandoned the search in the face of perceived heavy opposition.

The stalemate of Sawyers's party continued as they awaited the overdue reinforcements from Connor's command. Captain North and his Pawnee scouts had come very close to discovering the whereabouts of the eastern and center columns of the expedition but turned back. At least General Dodge's unexpected visit to Fort Connor had been a success.

CHAPTER EIGHTEEN

12–15 September 1865

CHARLIE'S RIDE

TUESDAY, 12 SEPTEMBER 1865

Blind to one another's movements and locations, the various elements of the Powder River Indian Expedition had very little idea of the where-abouts or activities of the other commands in the field. General Connor—finally aware that Cole's and Walker's missing columns were probably on Powder River—still had no knowledge of their exact position or their condition. Unaware of the existence of Fort Connor or that Connor's force was even in the field, the beleaguered commands of Colonel Cole and Lieutenant Colonel Walker trudged south toward Fort Laramie. At Fort Connor, Colonel Kidd—without knowledge of Connor's attack on the Arapaho village—worried about an overdue mail detail. In the middle of this confused situation sat the civilian party of James Sawyers and its small military escort, anxiously awaiting relief, or at least word from General Connor.

The Sawyers Expedition

The weather remained cool, and the men spent another uneventful day pondering their fate. A few Indians came to the wagon circle late in the day, assuring the road builders that they did not wish to fight but only to trade.

At supper time a rumor circulated through the camp that they would start for the Bighorn River in the morning, after which the military escort would leave them and return to Fort Connor. C. M. Lee wrote that

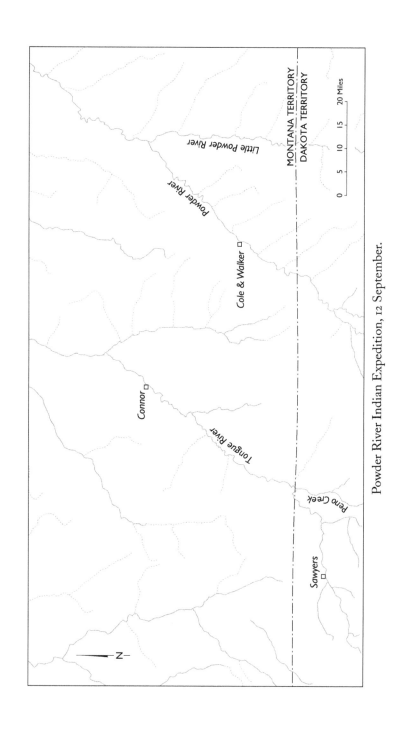

Powder River Indian Expedition, 12 September.

This report brought the matter which had been agitating the minds of the drivers for some time to a crisis, so after supper all hands repaired to where the Col. [Sawyers] was. He graciously ask[ed] if they wished to consult him and ask any questions. He was told that they did and wished to know what his intentions were. Answering in substance that he intended to go to the Big Horn, then if they thought it too dangerous to travel without an escort they corrill and fortify themselves and send to Virginia City for assistance. And if they thought they could travel at all he would have all of the wagons doubled up thus affording some 8 or 10 more extra men to carry guns and act as escort, that he did not himself apprehend any serious trouble, that last year Boseman traveled this route and was corrilled three times; and after explaining his [Bozeman's] intentions and business [to the Indians] was allowed to pass on his way. He thought we could do as well.

The teamsters were not about to buy into Sawyers's plan:

All this, of course, sounded very well and looks very plausible, but he was talking to men that knew him and had a summer experience with him and Indians, and with men that had to bear the brunt of all risk of life. So after some further conversation he was told decisively by their spokesman that he need not depend upon the drivers after the escorts left, for then they would leave. At the same time telling those whose sentiments he [the drivers' spokesman] was speaking to fall in line, at which 4/5 of the men stepped out without hesitation. The Col. rather taken down by this demonstration, and to make a show of his strength called on those who wished to go through at all events with him to step out and form another line. Then about a dozen fell in, opposed to some forty odd on the other side. This of course changed the program, so that the Capt. [Lovell] of the escort thought he might as well start back at once.[1]

James Sawyers, who confirmed this sequence of events in his official report, wrote, "No reinforcements appearing, I was constrained, to my regret, to announce that on the morrow we would retreat to Fort Connor."[2] Lewis H. Smith added, "Suppose we shall have to go to Laramie after all but hate to do so"[3]

---

[1] Lee diary, 12 September 1865 entry.
[2] Sawyers's official report, Hafen and Hafen, *Powder River Campaigns*, 263.
[3] Smith diary, 12 September 1865 entry, Doyle, *Journeys to the Land of Gold*, 378; Holman account, Hafen and Hafen, *Powder River Campaigns*, 337. Teamster Albert Holman wrote a somewhat different account of the meeting and confrontation. He seemed to have included

Connor's Command

General Connor wrote a message to Colonel Cole and/or Lieutenant Colonel Walker: "My scouts have just returned from Powder River, and report having seen a large number of horses shot and ordinance property destroyed at a camp of one or both of your columns on Powder River, sixty miles east of here. I send three scouts to tell you of my whereabouts and guide you by the best route to me or Fort Connor, on Powder River. You can place implicit confidence in the scouts and be directed by them in the route you will take. I hope and trust your condition is not as bad as I fear it is."[4]

After the scouts departed, Miller wrote, they "broke Camp & traveled up the bottom of T[ongue] R[iver]. 20 Miles." The three scouts sent out to locate the missing commands were a guide, Antoine Ladeau, and two Pawnees, one named Brannam and the other George Meyers, also known as Pop Corn.

Miller continued, "Owing to the recent heavy rains, the road the greater portion of the way was heavy. But, the grass improved. It was late when the Wagon Train got into Camp, & the stock was much fatigued. Some were shot—by the way."[5]

Fort Connor

For reasons unknown, Colonel Kidd discontinued his diary after 11 September. However, Captain Rockafellow continued to faithfully record in his daily journal, writing of the growing concern for the men still out on escort and mail duties: "No news from Capts Lovell or Kellogg and we are much alarmed for safety of Capt Kellogg and party which was the mail escort sent to Genl Connor's H'd Q'rs."[6]

---

the events of 3 September intermixed with 12 September. Holman's version had a newly elected leader running the Indian hostages out of camp. As there were no Arapaho hostages in camp on 12 September, Holman, whose account was published in 1924, appears to have been confused on his recollection of this event. The spokesman refered to by Lee and the newly elected leader of Holman's account are probably the same person, but both men fail to identify him.

[4]Connor letter to Cole and/or Walker, 11 September 1865, Hafen and Hafen, *Powder River Campaigns*, 49.

[5]Miller diary, 12 and 13 September 1865 entry.

[6]Rockafellow diary, 12 September 1865 entry, Hafen and Hafen, *Powder River Campaigns*, 191.

WEDNESDAY, 13 SEPTEMBER 1865

The Sawyers Expedition

The dawn brought cool weather and a heavy frost on the ground. Sawyers made one more attempt to convince the teamsters to go forward: "This morning the Colonel called the drivers together to see if they would go with one piece of artillery, but it made no material change in their sentiments. Then he was afraid they would desert the train before the stock and wagons could be got back to the Missouri River where they could be kept, but they assured him they would not do so. A good many Indians around this morning. Lieutenant Moon gave them nearly a barrel of crackers."[7]

"With heavy heart I moved the train back towards Fort Connor," wrote James Sawyers, "supposing that the object of the expedition had failed to be reached."[8] The party started on the back trail to Fort Connor at 9 A.M. After traveling twelve miles and going into camp, chief guide Ben Estes rode in and reported that soldiers were sighted riding toward them from the north. The riders turned out to be the advance party of the long-awaited relief force of Capt. Albert Brown. Everything changed, as Lee excitedly wrote, "Everyone was all excitement in a moment, and saw Virginia City in the future yet this fall after all our troubles. They proved to be a part of the escort sent by Connor, California troops and Winnebago Indians. The balances were behind and would not be up til tomorrow some time."[9]

Captain Brown had left Connor's camp, ninety-five miles to the northeast, on the morning of 6 September with a command of 140 men from Company L, Second California Cavalry, and Company A of the Omaha scouts, along with a train of seven supply wagons. Under ordinary weather conditions that trip should have taken about four or five days, but the violent storm had blown in on 8 September, and it continued to rain heavily until 10 September. The Tongue River—nearly impassable during that period because of high raging water—probably made passage in the

---

[7] Lee diary, 13 September 1865 entry.
[8] Sawyers's official report, Hafen and Hafen, *Powder River Campaigns,* 263.
[9] Lee diary, 13 September 1865 entry.

narrow canyon that they had to travel through almost impossible, hence the delay.[10] However, in his diary Captain Nash expressed his exasperation with Captain Brown and the slow progress: "You people in America may wonder how men out in this country can keep mounted & get a cavalry horse through at the rate of one mile per hour. I should myself have wondered yesterday but to night I have the privilege to say that I have seen the matter demonstrated & I know Capt Brown of the 2nd California Cavalry can do it."[11]

Because of the arrival of the relief force, however tardy, James Sawyers seemed to have the situation under control again, as the recalcitrant teamsters now agreed to reverse their course and head toward the Montana goldfields again. Emigrant Edward H. Edwards wrote, "If we move with out bad luck, I Expect that we will get through in three weeks. This morning we turn our faces westward again."[12]

Connor's Command

After traveling ten miles up the winding course of Tongue River, the expedition went into camp. Late in the afternoon, the three messengers that were dispatched the previous day to locate the missing commands came back to camp. They reported they had seen a group of about forty warriors, and that the Indians had "skidaddled" as soon as they saw them. Miller sarcastically wrote, "This trio of worthies imagined they had achieved a big thing, and deemed it advisable to return, and report the same to Genl. Connor."[13]

Fort Connor

That morning, "When we was a geting [*sic*] breakfast a Grisley [grizzly] Bear came up to the river Bank about 20 rod. I went and reported it to the Col."[14] Colonel Kidd and Captain Rockafellow rode out after the beast for a little sport. The captain described the action:

---

[10] Miller diary, 12 and 13 September 1865 entry. Miller's account of 9 September 1865 describes in detail the flood conditions of Tongue River during this period.

[11] Nash diary, 9 September 1865 entry.

[12] Edwards letter to his family, 15 September 1865.

[13] Miller diary, 13 September 1865 entry.

[14] Geyer, *Sheldon L. Wight*, 104.

We took up river accompanied by three Pawnees. Two miles up & near mouth of Dry Fork when in the bottom one of the Indians gave a yelp or two and we quickened our pace. Had not gone far before Col notified me 'Here he comes,' & sure enough the Col who was bare back & could not check his horse was going directly towards him [the bear]. I at once halted & dismounted and as the old fellow came bounding along gave him a shot which fortunately passed through his heart. He only went about twenty rods when one of the Indians fired & bear fell. I supposed of course his shot was the fatal shot, but on skinning him did not find any other holes except those which my shot made.[15]

That night Private Wight ate bear meat for dinner.[16]

THURSDAY, 14 SEPTEMBER 1865

The Sawyers Expedition

The remainder of Connor's relief force came into camp around noon, along with the supply wagons. Leaving little doubt about who now commanded the military escort, Lee wrote, "Captain Brown of the 2nd California Cavalry in command now. Ordered a list of all of the drivers ready for emergencies to detail from. The Dakota Cavalry are also ordered to go with us, much to their displeasure, with the piece of artillery. We will now have a very good escort, well mounted and armed, and one that is used to fighting Indians."[17]

The men from the Sixth Michigan Cavalry—Capt. Don Lovell's escort troops and Capt. James Kellogg's mail detail—headed south toward Fort Connor, as Brown took over the escort duties. Lovell and Kellogg, both of whom had been with the regiment since 1862, must have been elated at this turn of events, as this was the first step toward eventually heading home.[18] The mood of the men had to be very upbeat, as their long-awaited return to civilian life came closer to reality.

---

[15] Rockafellow diary, 12 September 1865 entry, Hafen and Hafen, *Powder River Campaigns*, 191, 192.

[16] Geyer, *Sheldon L. Wight*, 104.

[17] Lee diary, 14 September 1865 entry.

[18] Both Lovell and Kellogg joined the Sixth Michigan Cavalry on 13 October 1862, the day the regiment was formally mustered into the Union Army. *American Civil War Research Database.*

Connor's Command

General Connor added an endorsement to the envelope containing the letter addressed to Cole and/or Walker: "The scouts first sent with this were driven back by Indians and returned last evening. You should come over to this river immediately. Send word to me, at all hazards, of your condition on receipt of this. I will keep moving up this river at the rate of fifteen miles a day."

He then asked for volunteers to carry the message through the dangerous country to locate the missing commands. According to Cpl. Charles L. Thomas, "I was the only one to volunteer to go. My Capt. L. G. Marshall went to Headquarters with me. The General showed he was mutch disappointed when he saw I was the only one willing to go."[19]

Although years later Thomas received considerable recognition for his exploits, there is a question as to who and how many accompanied him on his ride that eventually found Cole. Connor, in his official report written on 4 October 1865, wrote, "I again sent out a Scout of two Ohio men and two Pawnee Indians."[20] Miller said, "Early this morning, before we left Camp, the Genl. sent off three messengers, two white Soldiers & one Pawnee, who volunteered from the ranks to go to Powder R. in search of other Com'ds."[21] Sergeant Hull agreed with Connor: "Two of Co. E and two Pawnees start up Powder river to hunt up lost command."[22] Sgt. P. W. Brown wrote years later, "Two members of our company volunteered to go provided they got a choice of mounts," making no mention of any Pawnee scouts.[23] No mention is made by Thomas of a companion, so that identity, if there was a second soldier, remains as one of the mysteries of the campaign.

Corporal Thomas, who was called Charlie by his family and friends, said that his horse had been wounded in the fight in the Arapaho village. Connor told him he could have any animal in camp for his mission, so

---

[19]C. L. Thomas letter to Walter M. Camp, 1920, Walter Mason Camp Collection. Recall that Corporal Thomas was the writer of a letter to his brother regarding his reaction to Lincoln's assassination in April. This letter was quoted in Chapter One herein, written while Thomas served at Deer Creek Station on the North Platte River.

[20]Connor's official report, submitted on 4 October 1865 to Major Barnes, Grenville Dodge Manuscript Collection.

[21]Miller diary, 14 September 1865 entry.

[22]Hull, "Soldiering on the High Plains," 14 September 1865 entry.

[23]Brown, *The National Tribune,* 9 June 1910.

Cpl. Charles L. Thomas, shown
proudly wearing his Medal of Honor.
Courtesy of Ron Tillotson.

Thomas then chose Lt. Oscar Jewett's fine gray horse, which Charlie
Thomas "was the finest horse I ever saw." Jewett objected and Connor
threatened to have him arrested. "When I [Thomas] went back to the
Genl for my instruction Capt. North & two Pawnee Indians were there.
The Genl said now Sargent I am not detailing you, you understand if you
undertake it you are to find Cole's command or Perish in the attempt."[24]
Two Pawnee scouts accompanied Thomas, riding out of camp about
7 A.M. embarking on their dangerous mission. The names of the scouts
accompanying him remain lost in history.[25]

Connor was very concerned about the well being of his subordinates'
commands and "the same evening sent Capt Marshall 11th Ohio Cavalry
with fifty men of his company and fifty Pawnee Scouts under Capt North
fearful that the former Scout [Thomas and the two Pawnees] would not

---

[24]C. L. Thomas letter to Walter M. Camp, 1920, Walter Mason Camp Collection.
[25]Thomas to Charles Curtis, 2 July 1894, regarding his application for the Medal of Honor,
Fort Laramie National Historic Site Reference Library. Although he referred to himself as
Sergeant Thomas, he was still a corporal. Thomas was not promoted to Sergeant until
1 March 1866. *American Civil War Research Database.*

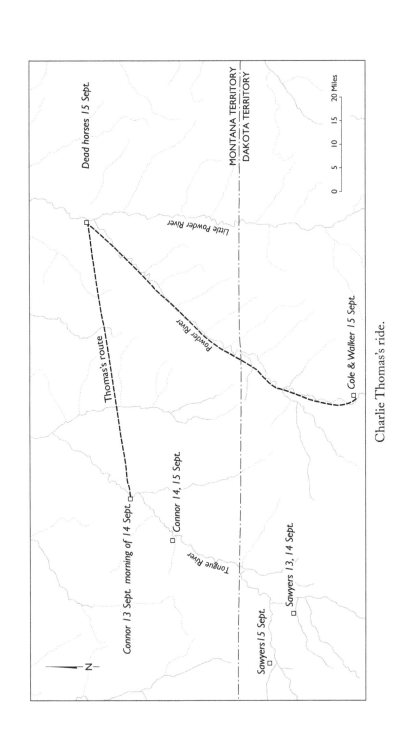

Charlie Thomas's ride.

reach Colonel Cole, and knowing him to be about out of provisions, with orders to cut their way through to him at all hazards and bring him to me, and not to return without finding him."[26]

Thomas's Ride

Cpl. Charles L. Thomas wrote of his daring ride in various correspondences many years later. Although there are discrepancies and some obvious inaccuracies in his accounts, his ride remains one of the most exciting endeavors of the Indian-wars period. The following account of his ride is a compilation of his descriptions of the action as he remembered them.

After departing Connor's camp, Thomas and his two Pawnee comrades headed somewhat east and a little north toward Powder River. Their first sighting of warriors came while following a well-timbered draw, as Thomas recalled:

> Here we found the carcus of an antelope, a fire burning with 6 or 8 spit sticks with meat on frying. We went through the timber to the south side. Saw 10 or 12 Indians riding east, too far away to shoot at. Not until between 2 & 3 o'clock did we have an encounter with them. At this time several appeared out of a deep gulsh [gulch] all laying flat on their horses. As soon as we fired a bunch of 40 or 50 rode out of the gulsh & attempted to rush us before we could relode our guns. We were armed with the Spencer rifles, had 8 loads in each gun. We shurley gave them a surprise. We dismounted several & killed several. If ever eny body ran it was the dismounted Indians, run, you don't know what running is. We got 3 or 4 of them at long distance & our long distance shots had mutch to do with our Suckses [success] in getting through.[27]

Late in the afternoon, the three scouts crossed the divide between the Tongue and Powder Rivers, and Charlie—who had consulted with Jim Bridger while still in camp—followed his advice: "He said when I started down on the Powder river side of the water shed to ride into a revien [ravine] if it was dry. 4 or 5 miles down it would most likely be dry all way to Powder river & without eny timber."[28] This was very sound advice, as riders on the ridgelines would be silhouetted against the sky. The small

---

[26]Gen. Patrick E. Connor's official report, 4 October 1865, Grenville M. Dodge Papers.
[27]Thomas letter to Walter M. Camp, 1920, Walter Mason Camp Collection.
[28]Ibid.

party continued toward Powder River throughout the night, and "When darkness fell we could observe small Indian camp-fires and had no trouble avoiding them."[29]

FRIDAY, 15 SEPTEMBER 1865

The Sawyers Expedition

The wagon train traveled twelve miles northwest and went into camp near the spot where they had remained circled for twelve days. C. M. Lee wrote: "As we got into the stream, the Winnebagoes brought in six prisoners, some of those that were around us before. They were very anxious to make a treaty. At sundown they were allowed to depart, saying they would meet us tomorrow for peace, with more of their men."[30]

Captain Nash, seemingly always the critic of Brown's actions, angrily wrote of the Arapaho prisoners: "I freely admit that I am entirely disgusted with Capt Brown's treatment of them. He is extremely friendly towards them & has even sent over an order to me to furnish some of my company rations to feed them. I returned the order saying that no Indian of the plains who was or had been hostile to the whites could have the pleasure of an ounce of my company rations while I was alive to command them. In this I was supported by both my lieutenants. I informed Capt Brown that he could consider me ready at any moment to hang or shoot the prisoners, but never to feed them."

When Brown ordered the release of the prisoners, the fiery Nash objected: "I have been to Capt Brown and protested & even threatened that the moment he let them loose I would let my men go for them. He is very angry & talks much about putting officers under arrest & c. He says the captives have promised to meet us tomorrow five miles further on the road with the whole band & then make a treaty. I then proposed that he keep 4 Indians as captives & let one go and bring in the band. But he refuses saying he believes the chiefs are sincere & will meet him as per agreement & that he wishes to get through as quietly as possible."[31]

---

[29] Beyer and Keydel, *Deeds of Valor,* 2:128.
[30] Lee diary, 15 September 1865 entry.
[31] Nash diary, 15 September 1865 entry.

Despite Nash's protestations the five or six Arapahos were released. Captain Brown ordered six of the civilian bullwhackers to stand guard duty, which caused considerable grumbling among them. However that soon passed and the men carried out their assignments.

Connor's Command

"Very quiet in camp. Have boiled elk for dinner," wrote quartermaster Sergeant Hull. "Very different from three years ago; then at Harper's Ferry among the Rebels. Now at Tongue river, far from anywhere."[32]

Thomas's Ride

Charlie's adventure continued: "I reached Powder River just at daybreak. At the mouth of the canyon, along which I and the Pawnees were riding, a horse appeared and immediately afterward an Indian came out from under the shelving rocks where he had been sleeping. He was less than ten feet from me as he raised up, threw his blanket off his shoulder and held his rifle in his left hand. I shot him dead."[33] Another warrior escaped by jumping down a fifteen foot embankment and disappeared into the brush.

Charlie and the two Pawnees rode to the river and discovered Cole's trail. While watering their horses, they heard Indian signal calls both up and down the river from them. At this point, they decided to ignore General Connor's instructions—to only move at night—and kept traveling following Cole's trail south, since "The Indians knew we were in the valley."[34]

"We pushed on unmolested by Indians," wrote Charlie, "until about 9 o'clock [A.M.], when we struck a small stream. The valley below was strewn with carcasses of horses and mules. The sight brought the cold sweat to my brows."[35] The trio had come upon the area of the missing commands' camps of 8 and 9 September, where the storm had killed worn-down and starving animals. This area is a few miles north of today's Broadus, Montana, on the west side of Powder River.

The three men then

---

[32] Hull, "Soldiering on the High Plains," 15 September 1865 entry.
[33] Beyer and Keydel, *Deeds of Valor,* 2:128.
[34] Thomas letter to Walter M. Camp, 1920, Walter Mason Camp Collection.
[35] Beyer and Keydel, *Deeds of Valor,* 2:128.

rode up the trail for A number off [sic] miles with out seeing eny Indians. About 10 o'clock came to a kind of a horse shoe bend in the valley . . . this bench was covered so thick with brush that they had to cut a road through. here we ran into 17 Indians, 5 of them became good Indians. after they got across the river they went east & we kept on up the trail. After a while they came back to the trail & others came from the table land & from the brush until they were too thick to count. When they prest us to clostly we would stop our horses & fire on them & invaerbaly drive them back & scater them. This running fight continued till about 4 o'clock when I saw at some distance up the trail a company formed acrost the trail. I thought it was a company of Cole's men. When I got close enough to distinguish them I saw they were Indians blocking the trail. Now they were to right & left, front & rear of us. I knew enough of Indians fighting never to retreat, it is all ways the retreater who is lost.[36]

Thomas and his Pawnee companions had no choice but to fight their way through. He ordered one of the Pawnees to cover their rear, while he and the other scout rode forward firing their repeaters at the blocking warriors. "Just at this time I was struck in the right leg with an arrow," Thomas wrote. "We broke thair line, some ran to the river & some towards the bluff. I had shot the one who stood on the trail. He had his horse fastened to his left arme with a hair larriet. That horse could not get away. I cut the horse loose from the Indian & led him along for a remount in case we needed one."

The Indian's horse turned out to be a cavalry mount that belonged to the Sixth Michigan Cavalry.[37] Thomas found the soldier's "letters and pictures in the saddle-pockets. There was also in one of the pockets a tintype picture of the Indian himself and $95 in United States notes."[38]

As the shadows lengthened, Thomas and the two Pawnees continued south on Cole's trail. "Just before Sundown I noticed about 100 yards from the trail some one lying behind a sage brush. I thought it was an Indian. I drew up my gun to shoot him. He threw up his arm & called

---

[36]Thomas letter to Walter M. Camp, 1920, Walter Mason Camp Collection.
[37]Ibid.
[38]Beyer and Keydel, *Deeds of Valor*, 2:130. Ron Tillotson of Hardin, Illinois, C. L. Thomas's great-great-grandson, has in his possession the original tintype, which has been passed down through the family with the understanding that it represents the Indian that Charlie shot, described above.

don't shoot. I am a white man." Pvt. John E. Hutson of Battery L, Second Missouri Light Artillery, had been unable to keep up with the column moving south and fell by the wayside.[39] Barefoot with feet full of prickly pear thorns and unable to walk any farther, he had laid down by the side of the trail, waiting for the Indians or starvation to put him out of his misery.[40] Charlie loaded Private Hutson on the spare horse and they rode on toward the missing commands' camp.

"About 9 o'clock we were fired on by Cole's outer picket. We returned thair fire thinking it was Indians," Thomas recalled. "Then we heard the bugle call to arms. No sound before or since has sounded so good to me." After convincing Cole's pickets that they were messengers from General Connor, Thomas, the two Pawnees, and the rescued Private Hutson rode into Cole's camp, a few miles south of today's Arvada, Wyoming.

Thomas delivered the message from General Connor to Colonel Cole and told him of the existence of Fort Connor. "After giving him the message & answering questions for him & other officers, I ask Cole why he shot so maney horses in one of his camps. He said when did you see that camp[?] Saw it this morning I said. You don't pretend to tell us you rode from thair to day. I crossed the river at least 3 or 4 miles below it this morning. His adj. said it was 84 miles to the camp where the greatest number of horses were kild [sic]."[41] The estimate of Cole's adjutant, probably Capt. Junius G. W. McMurray, was accurate—Charlie and his Pawnee comrades had traveled over eighty miles since reaching Powder River at dawn.[42]

Fort Laramie having been his goal, Colonel Cole now learned of the existence of Fort Connor—only 60 miles away—which shortened his distance by about 160 miles. His command had been out of rations for

---

[39] Thomas letter to Camp, 1920, Walter Mason Camp Collection. Thomas wrote that Hutson had been with a scouting party that had been attacked by warriors, and all were killed but him. There is no official record or diary that supports the incident. His other letters aren't specific as to why Hutson was out there.

[40] Bennett diary, 12–15 September 1865 entries. Many cavalrymen of Cole and Walker's commands were marching on foot, because of the large numbers of horses lost. Chief engineer Lyman G. Bennett wrote of many barefoot men walking, suffering badly from the long march through rough country.

[41] Thomas letter to Camp, 1920, Walter Mason Camp Collection.

[42] Cole's report of 7 February 1867, Hafen and Hafen, *Powder River Campaigns*, 91.

days and, after losing hundreds of their horses and mules, "more than 1/2 of the men were dismounted, that a great many of the men were with out shoes & many were suffering with disentary & other bowl [bowel] troubles, that they were killing horse & mules ever day for rations & cooking the meat with out salt or pepper. That the command was in a deplorable condition. That it was a question whether eny one would have lived to reach the Platt river."[43]

Thomas and his companions had been busy. They had covered 135 miles in thirty-nine hours without stopping, traveling through a rough and unmapped terrain inhabited by many Sioux and Cheyenne. En route they had several hot encounters with many warriors—Thomas "left Camp Connor with over 350 rounds of ammunition and had 17 shots left when I arrived at Colonel Cole's camp."[44] He said in one letter, "My old Spencer rifle was getting so hot I could not hold the barrel with my necked hand."[45] On top of this, they rescued Private Hutson, who surely would have perished had they not found him.

Thus ended one the most incredible accomplishments of the Indian-wars period. Certainly Thomas's many accounts of the adventure leave unanswered questions and discrepancies. He had a flair for the melodramatic and self-promotion in his writing, but one can not dispute the results.[46]

In 1894 Charles L. Thomas was awarded the Medal of Honor for his 1865 exploit. In recommending Thomas for the honor, his commanding officer, Capt. Levi G. Marshall, wrote, "The service of Sergeant Thomas was the most important of anything that ever occurred under my observation during the war, and required the most astonishing nerve and bravery."[47]

---

[43]Thomas letter to Camp, 1920, Walter Mason Camp Collection.

[44]Beyer and Keydel, *Deeds of Valor*, 2:130.

[45]Thomas to Charles Curtis, 2 July 1894, Fort Laramie National Historic Site Reference Library.

[46]Cole's first official report of the expedition to Connor, 25 September 1865, *The War of Rebellion*, O.R., Series 1, Volume 48/1 [S#101]. Cole wrote: "On the 15th a messenger and three men arrived with a dispatch from you." The third man could have been the rescued Private Hutson.

[47]Undated excerpt from the *Council Grove Republican* newspaper, pertaining to C. L. Thomas's Medal of Honor.

CHAPTER NINETEEN

16–20 September 1865

THE BEGINNING OF THE END

SATURDAY, 16 SEPTEMBER 1865

Cole's and Walker's Commands

The unexpected arrival of Corporal Thomas and the news of the close proximity of Fort Connor must have transformed the mood of the starving camp from one of hopeless desperation to guarded optimism. Word spread quickly through the ranks that relief was now only days away, not weeks—or the hundreds of miles to Fort Laramie. Trooper Ansel Steck, Company D, Twelfth Missouri Cavalry, recalled: "It was of far more importance to know that there was rations for the command 4 or 5 days march farther on."[1]

Colonel Cole provided Thomas and his party with an escort to return to General Connor, carrying the important news of the condition and location of the commands. He "sent him [Thomas] back with Lieutenant Jones, Second Missouri Light Artillery, and fifteen men mounted on my best horses to you [Connor], and continued my march to Fort Connor."[2] Thomas remembered much later that he didn't think that returning to Connor was such a good idea: "I told Cole if he would give me an escort I would return to Gen Connor & that was a fool thing to do. I was not

---

[1] Statement of Ansel Steck, 1 August 1894, certifying Thomas's mission in 1865, for application of the Medal of Honor, Fort Laramie National Historic Site Reference Library.

[2] Cole's first official report of the expedition to Connor, 25 September 1865, *The War of Rebellion*, O.R., Series 1, Volume 48/1 [S#101].

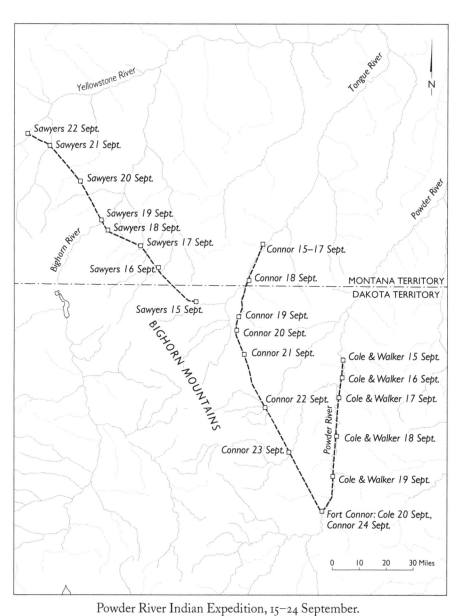

Yellowstone River

Tongue River

N

Sawyers 22 Sept.

Sawyers 21 Sept.

Sawyers 20 Sept.

Sawyers 19 Sept.

Sawyers 18 Sept.

Bighorn River

Sawyers 17 Sept.

Connor 15–17 Sept.

Powder River

Sawyers 16 Sept.

Connor 18 Sept.

MONTANA TERRITORY

DAKOTA TERRITORY

Sawyers 15 Sept.

BIGHORN MOUNTAINS

Connor 19 Sept.

Connor 20 Sept.

Connor 21 Sept.

Cole & Walker 15 Sept.

Cole & Walker 16 Sept.

Connor 22 Sept.

Cole & Walker 17 Sept.

Powder River

Cole & Walker 18 Sept.

Connor 23 Sept.

Cole & Walker 19 Sept.

Fort Connor: Cole 20 Sept.,
Connor 24 Sept.

0   10   20   30 Miles

Powder River Indian Expedition, 15–24 September.

ordered to report back to him, only to find Cole & direct him to the base of supplies. It was a risk no one is justified in taking."[3] Apparently Thomas misunderstood the importance of Connor knowing of the commands' location and condition, while Cole obviously understood the high priority of sending the messengers back, as confirmed by the escort provided.

While the messenger party headed northwest toward the general's camp, Cole and Walker marched their haggard commands south toward succor at Fort Connor.

The Sawyers Expedition

The road builders traveled northwest for nineteen miles, going into camp on the Little Bighorn River. C. M. Lee wrote:

> About sundown, the alarm of Indians was raised. Could see a lot of them coming down the stream full speed. Our Winnebagoes were on the move instantly, got their horses in, picketed the loose ones and mounted some bare back and without bridles, others with both on and rushed out whooping and yelling to meet those advancing, but they proved to be those that promised to meet us [Arapahos from the previous camp]. Fifty-two of them all together, very anxious to trade, one squaw looked like she might have been a white woman, or part white. The Capt. [Albert Brown] told them he was going through with the train and he didn't want to see them again until he came back. He also took the letter from Connor from them saying it was Black Bear's. When he came he might have it.[4]

Before parlaying with the Indians, Brown had trouble controlling the Winnebago scouts, who wanted to attack the approaching Arapahos. The scouts as well as the spectators back in camp had looked forward to a fight: "Our disappointment was also keen for we had hoped to have the privilege of witnessing from a safe distance a lively scrimmage between these two Indian tribes."[5]

Captain Nash of the Omaha scouts again fumed at what he perceived

---

[3]Thomas letter to Camp, 1920, Walter Mason Camp Collection.

[4]Lee diary, 16 September 1865 entry. Albert Holman, writing in his reminiscent account many years later, said they were approached by "a body of about four hundred Indians." Hafen and Hafen, *Powder River Campaigns,* 339.

[5]Holman account, Hafen and Hafen, *Powder River Campaigns,* 340.

as Captain Brown's lenient treatment of the Arapahos: "Capt Brown received them [Arapaho] with great profession of friendship and ordered that the soldiers should all return to their company camps and turn their horses out again to graze. This order, as far as my company was concerned, I loudly denounced & ordered my men to stand by their horses & not to ground an arm, but to be prepared for any event that might occur, for I was certain in my own mind that the Arappohoes were prepared to take any advantage of us that might happen in their favor."[6]

The Arapaho party camped about one mile away from Sawyers's camp. The Winnebago scouts stayed vigilant throughout the night.

Fort Connor

Much to the relief of those at the fort, at 11 A.M. Captains Kellogg and Lovell arrived with their men. Colonel Kidd and those at the fort learned of Connor's fight on Tongue River, Capt. Osmer Cole's death, and the Sawyers party's stalemate.[7] Colonel Kidd then prepared the men of the Sixth Michigan Cavalry for departure to Fort Laramie on the following day, turning over command of the fort to Captain Williford, whose Companies C and D of the Fifth U.S. Volunteers would now assume garrison duty.

Connor's Command

Captain Palmer wrote, "September 15 and 16 were spent in recuperating our stock, as we found the mules too weak to pull the wagons."[8]

Sergeant Hull described a hunting trip: "[Pvt. George W.] Freeman and [Pvt. Joshua] Grim go hunting, mounted on ponies. I start with them but get separated from them and run into a band of twelve or fifteen elk. Shoot several times, wounding one. One big buck with horns like a tree top. Grim and Freeman return at dark, having killed one deer and a buffalo. Had a fine roast and stew."[9]

---

[6]Nash diary, 16 September 1865 entry.
[7]Rockafellow diary, 15 September 1865, Hafen and Hafen, *Powder River Campaigns*, 192–93.
[8]Palmer's account, ibid., 144.
[9]Hull, "Soldiering on the High Plains," 16 September 1865 entry. Pvt. George W. Freeman was in Company K, Eleventh Ohio Cavalry, and Pvt. Joshua Grim was in Company K, Eleventh Ohio Cavalry. *American Civil War Research Database.*

SUNDAY, 17 SEPTEMBER 1865

The Sawyers Expedition

Lee commented on the expertise of the Winnebago scouts: "Our Indian escort proves first rate. They are continually on the alert."[10] The expedition traveled thirteen miles northwest and camped on Rotten Grass Creek, stopping early in the day "on account of breaking an axel [*sic*] on a wagon."[11]

Fort Connor

Pvt. Sheldon Wight wrote, "We got up at three Oclock and harnefsed our teems. the Regt. Sadeled [*sic*] up. we Started at Sunrise for Larmey [Laramie]."[12] Rockafellow expressed satisfaction: "'Homeward Bound' Started 6 A.M. from Fort Connor."[13] Colonel Kidd and the Sixth Michigan Cavalry left the fort, traveling southeast, following the Dry Fork of Powder River toward Fort Laramie. They marched about twenty-two miles, camping at Janise Springs, discovered and named on the buffalo hunt of 8 August for guide Nicholas Janise.

Connor's Command

Sergeant Hull wrote of one man's adventure: "Bolton got lost and came suddenly on an Indian camp of about thirty, and being unperceived, escaped and came back to camp.[14] Squad of Co. E came back and reported that they have struck trail of other command and had seen where they had eaten mules and horses. Saw signs of Indians in different places."[15] The command marched up Tongue River fourteen miles and went into camp.

---

[10] Lee diary, 17 September 1865 entry.

[11] Doyle, *Journeys to the Land of Gold,* 379; Smith diary, 17 August 1865 entry, ibid., 373,.

[12] Geyer, *Sheldon L. Wight,* 104.

[13] Rockafellow diary, 17 September entry, Hafen and Hafen, *Powder River Campaigns,* 193.

[14] Pvt. Charles L. A. Bolton was in Company K, Eleventh Ohio Cavalry. *American Civil War Research Database.*

[15] Hull, "Soldiering on the High Plains," 17 September 1865 entry. The squad of Company E was probably from the party led by Capt. Levi Marshall that Connor had sent out on 14 September.

MONDAY, 18 SEPTEMBER 1865

The Sawyers Expedition

No Indians were sighted as the train continued northwest toward the Bighorn River. "In coming down into the valley of the river," wrote C. M. Lee, "there is a very long and steep hill to descend. Had to rough lock the wagons with log chains. We put part of the teams behind the wagon to assist in [it] holding back. All got down safely."[16] They went into camp on a small tributary of the Bighorn River, probably War Man Creek.[17] While crossing that creek to the campsite, Lee continued: "the wagon driven by Nute Hollester was upset; the first for a long time."[18]

James Sawyers described this area as a "hunter's paradise," writing of an abundance of buffalo, antelope, elk, deer, and bear. "The hunters, during this day's march, killed three bears and a large quantity of other game."[19] Lee expressed his distaste for bear meat: "The scent of them is very offensive to me, so much that I cannot bear the meat at all, though some of the boys expressed a great liking for it."[20]

Connor's Command

"Break camp and March nearly all day. Suppose this will be our last camp on Tongue river," wrote Sergeant Hull, after traveling nineteen miles up the river. Thomas returned to the main column with the companions of his daring ride, as Hull continued: "The two Co. E boys and the two Pawnees met us on the march, having found Col. Cole's command and brought a squad of fourteen back."[21] Hull again referred to "two Co E boys," which leads one to believe that there was a second anonymous white rider with Charlie on the mission to locate Cole's command.

Capt. Henry Palmer added to the confusion as his account, written in 1887, had Thomas and the Pawnees arriving on the previous day with an escort of Indian scouts.[22] Thomas disputed Palmer's account in a 1920

---

[16] Lee diary, 18 September 1865 entry.
[17] Doyle, *Journeys to the Land of Gold*, 379.
[18] Lee diary, 18 September 1865 entry.
[19] Sawyers's official report, Hafen and Hafen, *Powder River Campaigns*, 265.
[20] Lee diary, 18 September 1865 entry.
[21] Hull, "Soldiering on the High Plains," 18 September 1865 entry.
[22] Palmer's account, Hafen and Hafen, *Powder River Campaigns*, 144–45.

letter to noted historian Walter M. Camp: "He is in error about the escort being Indians, they were white soldiers. Cole had no Indians with him."[23] Thomas is correct—Lieutenant Jones of the Second Missouri Cavalry and fifteen cavalrymen were the escort, as Cole did not have a company of Indian scouts with his command.

General Connor reacted to the news of the condition of the missing commands: "As it was I had but a few men with me, reduced by Scouts from the original number to 150 white Soldiers and 30 Pawnee Scouts with a train of one hundred (100) wagons, a herd of Beef cattle and captured stock to guard, not enough for any offensive measures and was thus forced reluctantly to return to Fort Connor intending to organize another Campaign from that point at once and continue offensive movements all winter or until such time as the Indians were well chastised."[24] Connor, at this point, was still unaware of the order from General Pope disbanding the District of the Plains and reassigning him to the District of Utah.

Cole's and Walker's Commands

The commands had marched eighteen miles south on Powder River. Just as they settled into camp, Capt. Levi Marshall and his party of fifty men from the Eleventh Ohio Cavalry and Capt. Frank North, with fifty of his Pawnee scouts, rode in. Chief engineer Lyman G. Bennett described the scene: "They had left the same day the four men who reached us a few days ago, but marching more slowly only reached us this evening. He found us all in a deplorable condition, half starved, ragged and worn down. His men were instantly beset by ours asking for bread and tobacco. Some of the men offered five dollars apiece for hard tack, but our new friends generously gave all their rations to our men which was hardly a taste around. Tobacco commanded fabulous prices but these men would not receive a cent."[25]

---

[23] Thomas letter to Camp, 1920, Walter Mason Camp Collection.

[24] Gen. Patrick E. Connor's official report of 4 October 1865, Grenville M. Dodge Papers.

[25] Bennett diary, 18 September 1865 entry. The reader will note that Bennett also refers to "four men" arriving as messengers from Connor. Bennett could be including the rescued Private Hutson, but all other witnesses who recorded their observations wrote of two white soldiers and one or two Pawnee scouts.

Historian George Bird Grinnell claimed that Frank North was the one to discover Cole

TUESDAY, 19 SEPTEMBER 1865

The Sawyers Expedition

The morning proved to be clear and warm and the wagons started early, traveling six miles to the Bozeman Trail ford on the Bighorn River. Lee described the crossing: "This is the largest stream we have crossed yet. Most places it will swim a team. We crossed over onto a small island, the water coming up to the hubs, then passed up the island a short distance and crossed the remaining portion of the stream. Here the water came almost to the wagon bed. Above or below the track it was still deeper and very swift. But all got across safely by having horsemen on each side to keep the cattle straight, except one of the emigrant wagons. His team swung down stream into deep water and came near drowning his family, but getting assistance promptly succeeded in getting out safely with a wet load."[26]

James Sawyers said that by 11 A.M. all the wagons were across except the military escort's seven supply wagons. The soldiers bivouacked on the south side of the river, while Sawyers's expedition camped on the north. Captain Brown's orders did not permit him to go farther than this point, since they "were considered nearly out of danger, [so] he detailed Sergeant James Youcham, with seven men, to proceed with us to Virginia City, and afterwards to report to him at Salt Lake City, while the balance of his command returned with him [Brown] to General Connor."[27] The campsite and the crossing were in the area where Fort C. F. Smith would be built in 1866, and is near today's town of Fort Smith, Montana, and the Yellowtail Dam.

---

and Walker's camp on 19 September and delivered the first message from Connor. Grinnell, *Two Great Scouts and Their Pawnee Battalion*, 118–20. It has already been well established in the previous chapter that Thomas and his companions arrived in Cole's camp on 15 September, carrying the message from Connor. North and his Pawnees actually arrived with Marshall on 18 September. Prior to his death in 1885, Frank North had collaborated on a manuscript with newspaperman Alfred Sorenson, dictating his experiences with the Pawnee scouts. This was published in serial form in the *Omaha Bee* shortly after Frank's death. The Sorenson account is virtually identical to Grinnell's and is obviously the source for his book. North must have been unaware of Thomas's role as a messenger to Cole, as no mention of Thomas is made in Grinnell's book or Sorenson's manuscript. Sorenson, "A Quarter of a Century on the Frontier."

[26] Lee diary, 19 September 1865 entry.

[27] Sawyers's official report, Hafen and Hafen, *Powder River Campaigns*, 265.

Connor's Command

After traveling north on Peno Creek and camping a few miles above their campsite of 27 August, Sergeant Hull reflected on a beautiful day: "Grass has grown nearly a foot in last three weeks. The day, scenery, atmosphere and all nature combine to form a picture that recalls the times three years ago when marching across Maryland. We were having a few of the comforts of civilization, altho marching hard. The leaves that three years ago were green are now a golden yellow, and our last view of Tongue river represents it as donning its autumnal robes. 18 miles."[28]

Cole's and Walker's Commands

Captains Marshall and North proceeded to Fort Connor with their men. Colonel Cole ordered all but 150 men—enough to guard their remaining wagons—to march ahead to Fort Connor, now only about twenty-five miles to the south. Walker probably went ahead with his Sixteenth Kansas Cavalry to Fort Connor, as he had no wagons, only a pack train.

On 16 September Cole had dispatched Lt. Fritz Schmitten to ride ahead to Fort Connor and obtain rations for his starving men.[29] Lyman Bennett described his return: "At 4 P.M. we met Lt Schmitten with 2 troupes and a wagon load of bread and a sack of coffee. In a moment the wagon was swarming with hungry men trying to get something to eat. A guard had all it could do to keep them away until the bread was issued. Many of the men have not tasted bread for two weeks and only a small amount of mule or horse meat. Their hunger was almost unsupportable and they were ready to commit any excess to get bread."[30]

At Fort Connor that evening, Captain North's Pawnee scouts celebrated their 29 August victory at Tongue River with a scalp dance.

WEDNESDAY, 20 SEPTEMBER 1865

The Sawyers Expedition

Captain Brown and his Second California Cavalry troopers, as well as Captain Nash's Omaha scout battalion, started south toward Fort Connor.

---

[28] Hull, "Soldiering on the High Plains," 19 September 1865 entry.

[29] Lt. Fritz Schmitten was a member of the Second Missouri Light Artillery. *Civil War Soldiers and Sailors System.*

[30] Bennett diary, 19 September 1865 entry.

It was a "Fine day; many buffaloes in sight; crossed one creek by bridging and another by fording; traveled eighteen miles over a country requiring considerable grading in places to make it passable, and camped on a creek leading into the Big Horn. Grass, water and wood poor at this camp."[31] They bivouacked on Little Woody Creek.[32]

Connor's Command

Sergeant Hull rode out with a company of the Eleventh Ohio accompanied by General Connor: "Go back on ridge of Tongue river and follow it up for several miles, looking for signs of Capt. Brown's command and for Arapahoes. Find Indians gone. Strike the Virginia City Road and follow it to other road and come in rear of train. Letters left in trees and one buried for Brown, ordering him to Ft. Connor."[33]

The train moved north, following Peno Creek for seven miles, and went into camp.

Cole's Command at Fort Connor

The wagons and the remainder of Cole's command marched twelve miles and went into camp five miles south of the fort. "The grass had been fed off with a range of five miles of the fort was the reason for camping here. We found newspapers as late as August 15th and devoured news from America with eagerness. We also found plenty of rations which had been brought down from the fort. Our troubles for the present are at an end and the boys can once more raise a whistle, a song, or a laugh; a thing not known for several days past."[34]

For all practical purposes, the Powder River Indian Expedition was over. General Connor's left column marched south toward the fort, still days away, but it was evident to all but Patrick Connor that nothing more would be accomplished this year.

---

[31] Sawyers's official report, Hafen and Hafen, *Powder River Campaigns*, 266.
[32] Doyle, *Journeys to the Land of Gold*, 379.
[33] Hull, "Soldiering on the High Plains," 20 September 1865 entry.
[34] Bennett diary, 20 September 1865 entry.

CHAPTER TWENTY

21 September–3 December 1865

A Trip Not To Be Envied

Connor's Command

Patrick Connor was not ready to abandon his mission. Still in a feisty mood, he expected to regroup the entire command at Fort Connor and embark on a fall and winter campaign. He believed that he could yet punish the warring tribes in their own territory and extract a lasting peace from them after sufficiently cowing them with his military force.

The column moved south at an almost leisurely pace for the next two days, ten miles on 21 September and only eight miles on the next day. The diaries of Captain Palmer and Sergeant Hull were dominated by hunting stories.

On 22 September Connor was dealt a fatal blow to his future plans: "Capt. Marshall and a detachment of his company came from Fort Connor with a letter to General Connor that he had been relieved of the command of the District of the Plains."[1] This, of course, was the condescending letter written by General Pope back on 24 August, informing Connor of his reassignment to the District of Utah.[2] As intense as Connor seemed to be, this had to be devastating news. Connor, no doubt chagrinned at this unexpected turn of events, later wrote, "I cannot but think that if the Campaign had been allowed to proceed as Major General Dodge and myself had arranged it and the troops then on the Plains

---

[1] Palmer's account, Hafen and Hafen, *Powder River Campaigns*, 148.
[2] Pope to Connor, 24 August 1865, *The War of Rebellion*, O.R., Series 1, Volume 48/2 [S#102].

be permitted to remain, all that was desired could have been accomplished by next spring at the least."[3]

The command quickened the pace over the next two days—traveling twenty miles and twenty-four miles respectively—arriving at Fort Connor late in the day on 24 September. Sergeant Hull wrote, "Train got behind and was out of sight almost all day. Gen. Connor gone to Fort Connor. We intended to camp a week eight miles from fort, but had no water, so whole outfit came to Powder river and camped on old camp ground of five weeks ago. Train not in till night."[4]

On the following day, orders were issued for the troops of the Powder River Indian Expedition to begin the march to Fort Laramie. General Connor met with Colonel Cole and members of staff and made arrangements for Connor's personal party of fifteen men to move out rapidly toward Fort Laramie in three ambulances on the next morning.

Capt. George W. Williford was ordered to stay as commander of Fort Connor, along with Companies C and D of the Fifth Infantry as garrison. Capt. Edwin Nash and the seventy men of Company A and Omaha scouts were assigned to remain for cavalry duty.[5]

At dawn on 26 September the fort was alive with activity—twenty-five hundred men of the expedition were in motion, beginning the trek towards Fort Laramie. Colonel Cole's command marched ten miles and then waited for the train of forty wagons promised to them by Connor to transport their most footsore and weary men to Fort Laramie.[6]

General Connor's party started late and as the three ambulances passed marching troops (on foot) from the Twelfth Missouri Cavalry, Lt. Charles H. Springer observed, "General Connor who was going to Fort Laramie in an ambulance passed us on the road, and as he saw some of our footmen barefooted he gave the boots from his own feet to our men."[7] Lyman G. Bennett, Cole's chief engineer who rode with Connor, con-

[3] Connor to Maj. J. W. Barnes, Official Report, 4 October 1865, Grenville M. Dodge Papers.
[4] Hull, "Soldiering on the High Plains," 24 September 1865 entry.
[5] Brown, *The Galvanized Yankees*, 134.
[6] Cole's report of 10 February 1867, Hafen and Hafen, *Powder River Campaigns and Sawyers Expedition*, 88.
[7] Springer, *Soldiering in Sioux Country*, 63, 26 September 1865 entry.

firmed the same scene: "Genl. Connor threw out an old pair of boots to one of the men, who was loud in his protestation of gratitude."[8]

On 28 September, Connor's party reached the North Platte River at Deer Creek Station, near today's Glenrock, Wyoming. Lyman Bennett described the telegraph station as "a small post with a rough log block house and quarters."[9] The party's passing of the station generated the following sensational news article:

> LATEST FROM THE POWDER RIVER
> MURDERERS—GEN. CONNOR HAS CLEANED OUT
> THE "FRIENDLIES," AND IS COMING TO LARAMIE
> We have been kindly furnished with the following received by telegraph yesterday P.M.
> "Gen Connor will be at Laramie in a few days; he is now at Deer Creek. He had four battles with the Indians—killed between four and five hundred. 500 Arapahoes are coming to Laramie to make a treaty."[10]

General Connor's advance party arrived at Fort Laramie on 30 September at 1 P.M. "The Genl. went to Mr. Bullock's first to see his wife & children. We were heartily welcomed by the officers of the post who thronged around us to learn of the Powder & Tongue expedition. The band serenaded and a fine dinner was provided for us weary and dirty sons of guns. Soap water and towels were the next resort and in a short time our dusty habiliments gave place to clean blue broadcloth and gilt buttons."[11]

The remainder of the expedition traveled at a slower pace. Sergeant Hull wrote on 1 October from a camp on the North Platte River: "Overtake and pass Cole's command encamped above Labonte's camp. Wagons till dark getting in; mules given out; all the stock tired. Hear that 11th Ohio and 16th Kansas are ordered to Leavenworth, but will not credit it yet; would be glad. It is a still, beautiful, moonshiny night; boys lying around talking and laughing, taking things easy."[12]

On 3 October they saw the "first white woman that we have seen in two months. Cross over the bluffs and camp below Star Ranche. Dead

---

[8] Bennett diary, 26 September 1865 entry.
[9] Ibid., 28 September 1865 entry.
[10] *Rocky Mountain Daily News (Denver)*, 29 September 1865.
[11] Bennett diary, 30 September 1865 entry.
[12] Hull, "Soldiering on the High Plains," 1 October 1865 entry.

body found near camp, man killed by Indians."[13] Only nine miles from Fort Laramie, this was a grim reminder that they were still in a dangerous country.

Finally, on 4 October, the majority of the men of the Powder River Indian Expedition arrived at Fort Laramie. "Again we pull up at Laramie after two months' absence, tramping," wrote Sergeant Hull, "have marched nearly 800 miles over all kinds of country."[14]

The St. Louis *Missouri Democrat*, unaware of orders ending the expedition, reported on 3 October: "It is thought, however, that the Sioux and Cheyennes are not half whipped, and that not less than 1,500 men should be stationed at Fort Connor and the campaign be continued in winter. Citizens are now fearful that the Sioux and Cheyennes will come back on the road and interfere with mail and telegraph."[15]

Thus the Powder River Indian Expedition came to a close. The high expectations of the architects of the campaign, Generals Pope, Dodge, and Connor, were not realized, and the taming of the northern plains was left unfinished. There would be assessment and recrimination as to why events happened or did not happen in the future, but for now, there was anticipation by many of the men in the ranks of going home after years of hard service in first a civil war and then a far-away wilderness campaign. With the exception of Companies C and D of the Fifth U.S. Volunteers and the company of the Omaha scouts who were left to man Fort Connor, all of the troops who had campaigned in the summer of 1865 headed home or to their next assignment.

The Sawyers Expedition

The Sawyers party continued northwest, arriving at the Yellowstone River on 22 September near the location of today's Billings, Montana. They now traveled in friendly Crow Indian territory. The caravan then marched uneventfully westward, following the Yellowstone River Valley.

An unusual event took place on 29 September near the mouth of Bridger Creek, about fifteen miles east of today's Big Timber, Montana. A fleet of thirty-six Mackinaw boats came into view, floating downriver

---

[13] Ibid., 3 October 1865 entry.
[14] Ibid., 4 October 1865 entry.
[15] *Missouri Democrat*, 3 October 1865.

from the west.[16] C. M. Lee wrote, "While watering at the river we were a little surprised to see a lot of mackanaw boats coming down the river loaded with men and a few women and children. They were no less surprised and alarmed when they discovered some of our men and took them for Indians, until they discovered the wagons on the bank, when they fired a salute of 40 or 50 guns in the air."[17] The boat travelers, estimated to be four or five hundred by Sawyers, were heading back to the States via the Yellowstone and Missouri Rivers, having been to the gold-fields in western Montana.[18] The boats pulled in and the two parties exchanged information and stories for about an hour. They had started downriver on 27 September from near the location of today's Livingston, Montana. Lee said they "expected to be at Omaha in 20 days, but I doubt it. At one o'clock they shoved out again."[19]

On 2 October the expedition crossed to the north side of the Yellow-stone at the Bozeman Trail ford, west of the mouth of the Boulder River. "The banks were dug down and well prepared for crossing, and the whole train crossed safely in an hour without serious trouble."[20] Lee described the crossing: "Just below the ford near the middle of the stream, the water is very deep. Care must be taken to keep out of it. Some teams were lost in it last year, I understand."[21]

The next day "Ruleaw [Hubert Rouleau], our guide, whom we hired on the Big Horn, who pretended to know all about the country, got lost, and we were obliged to retrace our steps for three miles in one place."[22] On the following day, the expedition crossed over to the west side of

---

[16]Doyle, *Journeys to the Land of Gold*, 368n54. J. Allen Hosmer, who wrote *A Trip to the States by Way of the Yellowstone and Missouri*, was with the party in the Mackinaw boats and described a meeting with the Sawyers party. A Mackinaw is "A scow-shaped boat used by fur traders around the Great Lakes and on the Missouri River, 40 or more feet long and 10 feet wide, controlled by a steersman and four oarsmen, with a very shallow draft, strictly for downstream travel." Winfred Blevins, *Dictionary of the American West* (Facts on File, Inc., 1993), 212.

[17]Lee diary, 29 September 1865 entry.

[18]Sawyers's official report, Hafen and Hafen, *Powder River Campaigns*, 268.

[19]Lee diary, 29 September 1865 entry.

[20]Sawyers's official report, Hafen and Hafen, *Powder River Campaigns*, 268.

[21]Lee diary, 2 October 1865 entry.

[22]Sawyers's official report, Hafen and Hafen, *Powder River Campaigns*, 269. Herbert Rouleau was one of Connor's original guides, who was assigned to escort duty for the Sawyers party. Sawyers hired him at the Bighorn River, but it soon became apparent that he knew little of the country west of there. Doyle, *Journeys to the Land of Gold*, 369, 763, 764.

Bozeman Pass, which divides the Yellowstone and Missouri River drainages, and went into camp. Lee gushed, "This is the most romantic camp we have had yet, completely enclosed by mountains."[23]

"The Col. [Sawyers] Charley Sayers [Sears] and Dick Rudd, one of the soldiers, started ahead this morning for Virginia City," wrote Lee on 5 October, "while the balance followed on with the train in charge of Judge [Lewis H.] Smith."[24] The train traveled five or six miles and entered the Gallatin Valley, encountering their first settlement since leaving the village of Niobrara, Nebraska Territory, on 13 June. Lee said they "began to find settlers scattered along the [Gallatin] river. . . . About noon, passed through Bozeman Town or East Gallatin, consisting of some half dozen buildings."[25] Lee checked out the local prices for important commodities and found "potatoes from 7 to 10 cents a pound, and whiskey 10 dollars a gallon."[26] After many sober days on a hard wilderness trail, not unexpectedly "boys got drunk tonight."[27]

From this point on to Virginia City, the trip turned out to be routine and without incident. On 11 October, while camped eight miles from their destination, Sawyers and Charlie Sears came out from Virginia City to join them. The next day, they "Came over the range between the Madison and Jefferson Rivers, and traveling eight miles came to Virginia City at 10 A.M."[28] After unloading the wagons at the warehouse of Higgins & Co., the train went into camp on "Stink Water Creek," several miles from town. Lewis Smith said, "Col. [Sawyers,] Charlie [Sears] and I stayed in town I invoiced goods all day and part of the night[.]"[29]

On the following day, Lee wrote, "Lay in camp, the colonel and the judge [Smith] preparing to discharge the men." On 14 October, "some 20 of the men were paid off and discharged, myself among the number."[30]

---

[23] Lee diary, 4 October 1865 entry.

[24] Lee diary, 5 October 1865 entry, Doyle, *Journeys to the Land of Gold*, 417. Sawyers continued writing his report as though he remained with the train. However, Lewis H. Smith confirms the sequence of events in his diary. Ibid., 381.

[25] Ibid., 417.

[26] Ibid.

[27] Ibid., 381.

[28] Sawyers's official report, Hafen and Hafen, *Powder River Campaigns*, 273.

[29] Smith diary, 12 October entry, Doyle, *Journeys to the Land of Gold*, 418n88. Today's Ruby River was called "Stinking Water" on maps of the era.

[30] Lee diary, 13 and 14 October 1865 entry.

"From this time [12 October] till the 24th," wrote Sawyers, "I was engaged in paying off the men and putting the outfit in good repair, recruiting the cattle, etc., preparatory to selling them. I finally placed the whole outfit in the hands of a commission merchant, who, being better posted than I could possibly be, was enabled to sell better, advantage for the government."[31] James Sawyers, along with his chief engineer Lewis H. Smith, then departed by stage to Sioux City, Iowa, via Salt Lake City.[32]

From Salt Lake City on 10 November, Sawyers wrote to his business associate, member of Congress, and sponsor of the bill that funded the expedition, A. W. Hubbard: "I had a long talk to day with Genl Connor about the Road. He was much pleased at all I told him of the Road from Ft Connor to Virginia City. But when I would talk of Running water [Niobrara River] White Earth River and the Sheyenne [Cheyenne] Country he said it would be Impossible to get a road through that country. I told him I had already made it and had drawn a heavy Freight train over it. Well he said it was too Sandy."[33]

Sawyers and Smith arrived in Sioux City on 3 December.

The Sawyers Expedition ended, but unlike the military, many of the men, such as Corwin M. Lee, Albert M. Holman, Samuel H. Cassady, and Edward H. Edwards, stayed in western Montana, having used the government funded expedition as a way to reach the goldfields. But theirs had not been an easy trip. Teamster Albert Holman summed up his feelings, and probably those of most of the men: "we went into camp for the last time, having been a weary six months in traversing this wild Indian country and traveling over 1,000 miles. It was a trip as not to be envied by anyone."[34]

---

[31] Sawyers's official report, Hafen and Hafen, *Powder River Campaigns,* 273.

[32] Doyle, *Journeys to the Land of Gold,* 357.

[33] Sawyers to Hubbard, 10 November 1865, Pearl Research Center, Sioux City Public Museum. See Appendix B for complete text of the letter.

[34] Holman account, Hafen and Hafen, *Powder River Campaigns,* 341, 342.

CHAPTER TWENTY-ONE

EXIT CONNOR

DENVER, October 1, 1865

Brig. Gen. P.E. Connor,
Fort Laramie:
   I congratulate you and thank you for the success you have met with. Please also extend my thanks to your command for their success and for all the fortitude they have shown under such trying circumstances and hardships.
           G.M. Dodge
                Major-General[1]

Despite Dodge's congratulatory note, Gen. Patrick Edward Connor, no doubt, felt as though he had had a rug pulled out from under him. However, being the professional soldier that he was, he moved on quickly and precisely. Connor departed Fort Laramie on 5 October, bound for Denver with his family and staff. Capt. Henry Palmer, who accompanied Connor, wrote:

> I completed my reports to the quartermaster and commissary departments, receiving the General's approval on all my papers and his thanks for service rendered; then accepted an invitation to a seat in an ambulance, riding with him to Denver, where we had been invited by the citizens to a reception in honor of General Connor. Left Fort Laramie with an escort of 20 men as far as Fort Collins; from that point pushed on to Denver without escort, arriving about October 15th. We were received with all the honors that could be bestowed, a grand feast was

---

[1]Dodge to Connor, 1 October 1865, *The War of Rebellion*, O.R., Series 1, Volume 48/2 [S#102].

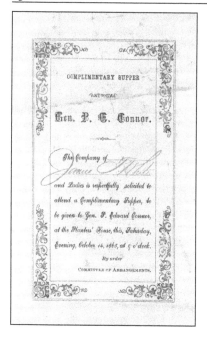

The invitation to Connor's Denver banquet. *Courtesy of the Denver Public Library, Western History Collection, X-738.*

prepared for us at the Planters Hotel, and the best people of Denver turned out en masse to the reception."[2]

Ovando J. Hollister, editor of the *Daily Mining Journal,* gave more details of the evening: "Gen. Connor and his staff came in on Thursday [12 October] and a complimentary supper was given him at the Planter's last evening [Saturday, 14 October]. . . . There was a military salute, music, toasts and responses, a dining hall tastily fitted up, tables well loaded, fair women, brave men, and sparkling wine. It was a spontaneous expression of the feeling of the town and Colorado toward one of the first of gentlemen and soldiers."[3]

The whirlwind tour continued. "The next day," recalled Palmer, "we were escorted by more than thirty carriages, filled with prominent citizens, to Central City, forty miles away in the mountains, where we were again received and toasted in the most hospitable manner."[4]

[2]Palmer's account, Hafen and Hafen, *Powder River Campaigns,* 150.
[3]Hollister's report of his interview with Connor, ibid., 371; invitation to Connor's dinner, Denver Public Library.
[4]Palmer's account, Hafen and Hafen, *Powder River Campaigns,* 150.

The general then took the stage with his family to Salt Lake City to resume his duties as commander of the District of Utah, at nearby Camp Douglas.[5] After arriving at their destination, another grand banquet was held in his honor on 26 October. The *Daily Union Vedette* reported, "It has seldom been our province to record a more heartfelt and enthusiastic reception than that which took place at Camp Douglas, Thursday, on the occasion of the return of the district commander, whose absence for six months has been attended by a series of military marches and successful engagements, with the red foe, who is the enemy of the white man." The champagne flowed freely, and at least twenty-two toasts were proposed.[6]

Adulation of Connor at this point seemed to be based upon his status as a man of action and the sensational early press releases that exaggerated the expedition's modest accomplishments. The general's reputation as an Indian fighter preceded him and the overstated claims in the newspaper accounts of many battles fought and hundreds of enemy casualties were evidently what the westerners wanted to hear and would react to. It would be many years before the full details of the campaign became general public knowledge.

Many historians have written that Connor never submitted an official report at the conclusion of the expedition; as such a document is not to be found in War Department records in the National Archives. A fire in the Commissary Building at Camp Douglas on 17 December 1865 destroyed most of his records of the campaign, and this is the reason generally given for the lack of a report.[7] However, Connor did, in fact, write a nine-page official report to Maj. J. W. Barnes, General Dodge's assistant adjutant general, on 4 October 1865, the day before he left Fort Laramie.[8] Author James F. Varley speculated that Dodge may have chosen not to forward Connor's report on to the War Department because of the highly critical statements in it about his subordinate commanders, Cole and Walker.[9]

[5] Madsen, *Glory Hunter,* 71, 72. Camp Douglas was established by Connor in late 1861. Overruling his men who wanted to name the new post after him, Connor named it after Stephen A. Douglas, the unsuccessful Democratic candidate for president in 1860. Douglas, who Connor admired, had died in the summer of 1861.

[6] *Daily Union Vedette,* 28 October 1865, Hafen and Hafen, *Powder River Campaigns,* 377.

[7] Madsen, *Glory Hunter,* 2.

[8] A copy of this document is in the Grenville Dodge Manuscript Collection in the archives of the Iowa State Historical Society (see Appendix A for the full text). Connor's official report, submitted on 4 October 1865 to Major Barnes, Grenville Dodge Manuscript Collection.

[9] Varley, *Brigham and the Brigadier,* 256.

Connor resumed active command of the Military District of Utah, whose main purpose was to keep the peace between the Mormons and the gentiles (non-Mormons) residing in the territory. Early in 1866, he traveled to Washington, D.C., to testify before a congressional committee investigating "The Condition of Utah." Scheduled to be mustered out of the volunteer army on 30 April, Brigadier General Connor was given the brevet (honorary) rank of major-general. Offered a commission as a colonel of the cavalry in the regular army, he turned it down to return to civilian life and expand his mining interests.

Returning to Utah, Connor spent the rest of his life pursuing the development of his mining properties in that territory and Nevada. Because of the potentially volatile situation in Utah between the Mormons and the gentiles, he moved his family back to California, settling them in a fine house in Redwood City in the late 1860s. Connor lived primarily in Utah and eastern Nevada managing his mining properties, occasionally finding time to visit his family in California. During this time, the Connors had two more sons born, Eugene in 1869 and Hillary in 1873, giving them four sons and a daughter.

Among the accomplishments credited to him are founding the town of Stockton, Utah, writing Utah's mining laws, establishing Utah's first daily newspaper (*The Union Vedette*), introducing commercial navigation upon the Great Salt Lake, and founding the gentile Liberal Party in Utah. Connor involved himself in politics in Utah and Nevada but never served in elected public office.[10]

Connor's wife, Johanna, died in July 1889 at age fifty-three in California. Patrick Connor did not attend the funeral, being in Washington, D.C. Newspaper accounts reported that he was ill with "inflammatory rheumatism" at the time of his wife's death.[11]

Although his mining ventures were initially successful, he eventually lost many of his best mines through over-extension of credit and poor business practices. During the last few years of Connor's life, he was relatively poor. The *Salt Lake Tribune* said of him, "In business he could never keep his details up with his enthusiasm, and he made a mistake when he left the army. He was not educated, he often erred in business

---

[10]Ibid., 156–62.
[11]Ibid., 259; *The San Mateo Times and Gazette*, 13 July 1889.

judgment, but when it came to country he was true as steel, and his judgment was as clear as a diamond."[12]

However, in his later years, Connor's business failures did not detract from his fiery, self-confident personality. In a letter to historian Grace Hebard, B. P. Oliver of San Francisco recalled: "I had, during his life-time, many discussions with Genl. Connor in regard to what I considered his barbarous orders to show no mercy to the Indians, but to the end of his life he maintained that the only good Indian was a dead one. General Connor must have been an ideal commander and fighter. He was cool and phlegmatic, absolutely without fear and nerves."[13]

Patrick Edward Connor died on 17 December 1891 at age seventy-one in Salt Lake City, after an illness of three weeks. He was put to rest in a burial plot in the post cemetery at Fort Douglas.[14]

In 1865 the San Francisco *Alta California* quoted Mark Twain: "I am waiting patiently to hear that they have ordered General Connor out to polish off those Indians, but the news never comes. He has shown that he knows how to fight the kind of Indians that God made, but I suppose the humanitarians want somebody to fight the Indians that J. Fenimore Cooper made. There is just where the mistake is. The Cooper Indians are dead—died with their creator. The kind that are left are of altogether a different breed, and cannot be successfully fought with poetry, and senti-ment, and soft soaps, and magnanimity."[15]

Westerners liked a man of action—one who got things done regardless of odds or obstacles—and Patrick Connor was just that sort of a man.

---

[12]Ibid., 274; *Salt Lake City Tribune*, 18 December 1891.
[13]B. P. Oliver to Grace Hebard, 3 February 1923, Box 9, Folder 15, Hebard Collection, Ameri-can Heritage Center, University of Wyoming.
[14]Madsen, *Glory Hunter*, 271.
[15]Ibid., 154; *Alta California*, 11 August 1865.

CHAPTER TWENTY-TWO

THE AFTERMATH

C hief Black Bear survived Connor's attack on his village on Tongue River. He may not have even been in the village, as one diarist reported that he had gone with some warriors to fight the Crow on the Bighorn River.[1] Next to Medicine Man, Black Bear was considered the most influential chief among the Northern Arapaho. While some young men joined the Sioux and Cheyenne in the Red Cloud War of 1866–68, the major Arapaho chiefs such as Medicine Man and Black Bear were working for a peaceful accommodation with the whites. Black Bear's name appears as one of the signers of the 1868 Fort Laramie Treaty.[2]

After the treaty signing, some Northern Arapaho men served as scouts for the army. The tribe concluded a peace treaty with their longtime enemy, the Shoshone, who had a reservation in Wyoming, in February 1870. The Arapaho—faced with a choice of moving to Indian Territory (Oklahoma) or to the Sioux Reservation on the Missouri River—negotiated for a Wyoming homeland. Arrangements were made by the army for the Northern Arapaho to temporarily live on the Shoshone Reservation, although this move was not welcomed by the Shoshone.

In March restless young Arapaho warriors began raiding, attacking a mining camp near Atlantic City on South Pass and at St. Mary's Station on the Sweetwater River. Eight whites were killed and considerable private property was taken. Local miners, after determining, in their eyes, the guilt of the Arapaho, formed a civilian militia of 275 men—75

---

[1] Nash diary, 30 August 1865 entry.
[2] Trenholm, *The Arapahoes, Our People,* 221; Loretta Fowler, *Arapahoe Politics, 1851–1978* (Lincoln: University of Nebraska Press, 1982), 44–45.

243

mounted men and 200 men on foot—under the leadership of "Captain" H. G. Nickerson.[3]

On 8 April 1870 Black Bear traveled with a small unarmed party headed to Camp Brown—near today's Lander, Wyoming—to trade. Near the mouth of the Little Popo Agie River, the mounted militia, led by a miner named Bill Smith, attacked the defenseless group, killing all fourteen adult males and two women. Black Bear's wife and child were captured, along with seven other children. Black Bear—whose village had been attacked by Connor's force less than five years earlier—thus came to a rather ignominious end. His death was listed as a murder in the Bureau of Indian Affairs records.[4]

After the killing of Black Bear, the Arapaho left the Shoshone Reservation and moved east, living in the vicinity of Fort Fetterman, Fort Robinson, and the Red Cloud Agency. Arapaho warriors served as scouts for General Crook during the Great Sioux War of 1876–77. They continued to lobby for a permanent reservation in Wyoming. In October 1877 a delegation of tribal chiefs—both Sioux and Arapaho—met with President Rutherford B. Hayes in Washington, D.C. As a result of that conference, the Northern Arapahoes were granted permanent status on the Shoshone Reservation in west-central Wyoming.[5]

Capt. George W. Williford and Companies C and D of the Fifth U.S. Infantry spent a lonely and cold winter at Fort Connor. George W. Johnson, one of the galvanized Yankees of D Company, wrote to friends back home: "Here we were detained, and are now the only garrison stationed on Powder River. Since we have been here, we have been busy in building quarters and making ourselves comfortable. The Indians have made several calls but never stay long enough for us to give them what

---

[3]Nickerson achieved the rank of captain in the Civil War on 4 March 1865 while serving with the 186th Ohio Infantry. He served as a civilian Indian agent in 1870, as his title of captain was strictly honorary at that time. *American Civil War Research Database.*

[4]Trenholm, *The Arapahoes, Our People,* 231–33; Fowler, *Arapahoe Politics,* 46–48. The Arapaho claimed that only eight men were killed, compared to the whites' claim of fourteen. Camp interview with Jacob Fry, envelope 36, file 15, box 4, Walter Mason Camp Papers, Lilly Library, Indiana University.

[5]Fowler, *Arapahoe Politics,* 48–66; Trenholm, *The Arapahoes,* 260–62.

they deserve, a sound drubbing. The weather is excessively cold here, snowing almost every other day. We are about one thousand miles from any white settlement."[6]

On 6 November 1865, Winnebagoes from Capt. Edwin Nash's Omaha scouts drove their horse herd out four miles from the fort to graze. Arapaho warriors attacked the party, killing one of the herders and making off with a few horses. The Winnebagoes then tightened their vigilance around the fort to a point where enemy warriors gave them a wide berth for the rest of their time there.

As the winter stormed on, the lack of vegetables in the men's diet caused an outbreak of scurvy. The cold and poorly ventilated quarters were conducive to other diseases such as consumption and typhoid fever, and at least four deaths resulted from those causes. Captain Williford became seriously ill and was moved by ambulance to Fort Caspar, where he died on 29 April 1866.

Desertions became a problem as the weather warmed, with more than fifteen men departing without leave in the early spring. Emigrant trains bound for Montana arrived and soldiers were assigned for escort duty through the dangerous country ahead. Rather than return to the fort, some of the men continued on toward the goldfields.

Captain Nash acted as post commander until mid-May, when his company was ordered to report to Fort Laramie to be mustered out. Lt. Daniel Dana then took over command of the fort. Finally, on 28 June the Eighteenth Infantry, led by Col. Henry B. Carrington, arrived at Fort Connor, since renamed Fort Reno, to relieve the Fifth Infantry. The two companies of men from the south finally left Powder River behind, departing for Fort Laramie on 6 July 1866.[7]

Col. James Harvey Kidd left Fort Connor on 17 September 1865 with the men of the Sixth Michigan. One week later, they arrived in the late

---

[6]Letter to Mrs. Elder from George W. Johnson, 18 December 1865, Fort Phil Kearny State Historic Site.

[7]Brown, *The Galvanized Yankees*, 134–36. Company A, Omaha scouts, was mustered out 16 July 1856. Companies C and D, Fifth U.S. Infantry, mustered out 11 October 1866.

A mature James Harvey Kidd.
*Courtesy of the Bentley Historical
Library, University of Michigan,
James Harvey Kidd Collection.*

morning at Fort Laramie.[8] After waiting until 7 October, orders were finally issued for the "old men" (those whose term expired prior to 1 February 1866) to proceed to Fort Leavenworth to be mustered out. Those of the Sixth Michigan whose term ended after the deadline were reassigned to the First Michigan Cavalry and were sent to Utah to serve under General Connor.[9]

On 24 October, Kidd, while at Fort Kearny, expressed his outrage in a letter to his father. "Indians are already at work on the road. The P.R. Expedition has been a fizzle only equaled by the way in which we are all humbugged in this country. My men who have some of them less than 8 months to serve have been sent to Utah, while troops who have 18 months to serve and have never done anything are on the road two days in my rear to be mustered-out."[10]

---

[8]Rockafellow diary, 24 September 1865 entry, Hafen and Hafen, *Powder River Campaigns,* 195.
[9]Major-General Frank Wheaton, 7 October 1865, Special Order Twelve, Whittenberg, *One of Custer's Wolverines,* 167–68.
[10]J. H. Kidd to father, 24 October 1865.

Kidd and his men rode into Fort Leavenworth in early November. Although his official mustering-out date was 7 November, the bureaucracy moved slowly and it was almost Christmas before Kidd finally arrived home in Ionia, Michigan, as a civilian.

In June 1866, J. H. Kidd was notified by the War Department of his promotion to brigadier general by brevet, retroactive to 15 June 1865—a belated recognition of his excellent wartime service.

He joined his family's business in early 1866 and also contributed written articles to a local newspaper about his wartime experiences. He purchased an interest in the *Ionia Sentinel* in 1870, later becoming sole owner, and remained in the newspaper business for the rest of his life.

A bachelor until 1871, Kidd married eighteen-year-old Florence S. McConnell of New York City on Christmas Day. They had a new home built in Ionia shortly after the wedding. Kidd and his wife Florence lived in that house for the rest of their lives together. Their only child, Frederick McConnell Kidd, was born in 1881.

In 1876 Kidd involved himself in the Michigan National Guard, in which he held various important positions until he retired in 1905. He was active in Michigan politics as a Republican. Urged to run for governor of Michigan in 1897, Kidd declined the challenge.

Kidd became well known for his writing and lectures on the Civil War experience. He gave the keynote address at the dedication of the monument to the Michigan Cavalry Brigade at the Gettysburg Battlefield in 1888. In 1907 the city of Monroe, Michigan, erected an equestrian statue in honor of its favorite son, George Armstrong Custer. Kidd's dedication speech so stirred Custer's widow, Libby, that she wrote to him, thanking him for his loyalty to her deceased husband.

James Harvey Kidd suffered a stroke in January 1913. He lingered on until 18 March, dying at age seventy-three. He is buried in Highland Cemetery in Ionia.[11]

Capt. Benjamin Franklin Rockafellow of the Sixth Michigan Cavalry, a close friend and confidant of Colonel Kidd, was among the unlucky whose enlistment expired after 1 February 1865. He "received orders to go

---

[11]Wittenberg, *One of Custer's Wolverines*, 173, 180.

B. F. Rockafellow in his later
years. *From* History of the
Arkansas Valley, Colorado
*(Chicago: O.L. Baskin & Co.,
1881).*

to Platte Bridge and relieve Lt. Col. H. H. Vinton of comd [command]
of line of Pacific Telegraph road, L[aramie] to South Pass."[12]

Rockafellow arrived at Platte Bridge Station (near today's Casper,
Wyoming) on 2 October, relieving Lieutenant-Colonel Vinton on the
next day. He later proudly wrote, "While in command no depredations were committed by Indians."[13] Rockafellow served in that capacity
through 10 February, then mustered out at Salt Lake City in March
1866.[14]

Once again a civilian, he traveled to Denver to join his father, who had
moved there in 1860. After trying their luck at mining for less than a year,
they sold their claim and moved to Canon City, Colorado Territory.
Rockafellow married Katherine M. (Kittie) King of Lyons, Michigan, in

---

[12] Rockafellow diary, 26 September 1865 entry, Hafen and Hafen, *Powder River Campaigns,* 196.
Lt. Col. Harvey H. Vinton, Sixth Michigan Cavalry, mustered out at Fort Leavenworth,
Kansas, on 24 November 1865. *American Civil War Research Database.*
[13] Hafen and Hafen, *Powder River Campaigns,* 197.
[14] *American Civil War Research Database.*

1867. Over the time of their marriage they had three children, two boys and a girl. He and his father engaged in farming and various business enterprises. In the early 1870s the younger Rockafellow operated a dry-goods store, and also acted as an agent for a stagecoach line. He was an active participant in bringing the first railroad to the area. A Pueblo, Colorado, newspaper in 1873 referred to him as "one of Canon City's enterprising merchants."[15] He was appointed postmaster in August 1869 and served in that capacity for ten years.[16]

With all of his activities, he still found time to develop one the finest fruit orchards in all of Colorado. In 1889 the *San Luis Valley Courier* wrote, "The largest orchard in the state is owned by Captain B. F. Rocka-fellow and is located about two miles east of Canon City. This orchard comprises sixty five acres of trees and vines, and almost every variety of fruit—the tropics excepted—known to the horticulturist is here to been. This orchard is young, the trees range from two to four years in age, but even in this young stage several thousand bushels of apples will be picked from it this year."[17]

Rockafellow served on the state board of agriculture for many years, which among its activities oversaw the operation of the Colorado Agri-cultural College (later to be renamed Colorado State University) at Fort Collins. He was president of the board in 1908.[18]

B. F. Rockafellow died peacefully at his home on 29 March 1926, from complications of pneumonia and old age (he was ninety). He is buried in the Greenwood Cemetery at Canon City.[19]

James Alexander Sawyers arrived back in Sioux City, Iowa, on 3 December 1865. Probably as a result of General Dodge's correspondence, he received a request to report in person to Washington, D.C, to the secre-tary of the interior. There were questions to be answered about his alleged

[15] *Colorado Daily Chieftain* (Pueblo), 3 September 1873.
[16] Hafen and Hafen, *Powder River Campaigns,* 153n2.
[17] *San Luis Valley Courier* (Alamosa, Colorado), 16 October 1889.
[18] *Fort Collins* (Colorado) *Courier,* 6 May 1908.
[19] B. F. Rockafellow Collection, MSS 530, File Folder 1, Colorado Historical Society; *Daily Record* (Canon City, Colorado), 29 March 1926.

James A. Sawyers. *Courtesy of
the Sioux City Public Museum,
Sioux City, Iowa.*

mismanagement and financial interests in the commercial portion of his
train. Sawyers immediately left for Washington, where he defended himself successfully and delivered his official report of the expedition.[20]

In 1866 Sawyers obtained approval from the Department of the Interior to retrace his 1865 route. General Grant would not provide a military escort for this second expedition, citing that it would spread his
frontier troops guarding the Overland Road too thin. Undaunted, Sawyers headed west with a party of fifty-seven men and a wagon train on
12 June. His workmen improved the road, built some primitive bridges,
and fought several skirmishes with Indian warriors.

They arrived at Fort Reno on 16 July. Four immigrant wagons joined
them there. Five days later they reached Little Piney Creek, where Col.
Henry B. Carrington had seven companies from the Eighteenth U.S.
Infantry working on the construction of Fort Phil Kearny. Carrington
could not spare any troops for an escort, but thirty-two more wagons with
sixty-one immigrants joined Sawyers's group for the trip to the goldfields.

---

[20] Doyle, *Journeys to the Land of Gold,* 357.

As they moved north, there were more Indian attacks and attempts to run off their stock, but the second Sawyers Expedition suffered no loss of life during these encounters. Sawyers was able to shorten the route by about one hundred miles over the previous year's trip. After arriving in Virginia City, the train was once again disbanded and the men were discharged and paid off.[21]

Although James Sawyers proved that his Niobrara road could be traveled, it was never used, as the army already had its hands full protecting the Platte River route. The ensuing Red Cloud War and the construction of the Union Pacific Railroad soon made Sawyers's Niobrara route, as well as the Bozeman Trail, obsolete.

James Sawyers returned to Sioux City and resumed his role as a prominent businessman. In 1867 Sawyers built and operated the first steam ferryboat, the *Undine*, used at Sioux City to cross the Missouri River.

Sawyers's first wife, Margaret, died in 1869. The following year he married Jennie E. Bell, a former schoolteacher. Sawyers had three children by his first marriage and two by his second.

After Custer's 1874 Black Hills Expedition, gold seekers were clamoring for the hills to be opened to mining exploration, even though it was Sioux Indian land deeded to them by the treaty of 1868. The military attempted to keep miners out of the Black Hills at first. A quote from *The Iowa Journal of History and Politics* described how a group of Sioux City entrepreneurs attempted to profit from the situation: "Certain capitalists of Sioux City were quick to perceive the opportunity to reap a harvest of gold by transporting freight and passengers to the Black Hills. The first transportation company to be organized was the Sioux City and Black Hills Transportation Company. At a meeting on March 10, 1875, James A. Sawyers was chosen president of the company." Members of the board included A. W. Hubbard, the congressman who had introduced the legislation for Sawyers's 1865 road-building expedition, and C. E. Hedges, the owner of the company that sent the commercial train with Sawyers's expedition and the older brother of Nat Hedges, who was slain by Indians on the trip.[22]

---

[21]Johnson, *The Bloody Bozeman*, 203–204; Coutant, *History of Wyoming and the Far West*, 2:467–68.

[22]Shambaugh, *The Iowa Journal of History and Politics*, 331.

Even though Gen. William T. Sherman had issued orders on 25 March to expel all intruders from the Indian lands, the company sent a wagon train toward the Black Hills a month later. After several weeks on the road, it was halted by the military, the members of the party were arrested, and their wagons and goods were either destroyed or confiscated. The Sioux City and Black Hills Transportation Company was forced to suspend operations.[23]

In 1878 Sawyers left Sioux City and moved to Leadville, Colorado, to look after his mining investments. He moved to Eugene, Oregon, in 1887, then on to Santa Cruz, California, in 1890, where he died in Santa Cruz on 27 March 1898. His body was returned to Sioux City, where he was buried in the Floyd Cemetery.[24]

Corwin M. Lee, one of Sawyers's teamsters, tried prospecting near Virginia City for about ten months and then moved on to Diamond City, near Helena, Montana Territory, in August 1866. With prior experience as a gunsmith, he established a business there utilizing that trade skill.

In March 1868, Lee moved to Musselshell, Montana Territory, and built a boarding house, also intending to run a gun shop out of it. His diary entries for that period indicate that business was slow.

The last diary entry for C. M. Lee was written on 19 April 1872. There is no record of his later life available. He died on 17 November 1886 at an unknown location.[25]

Albert Milton Holman, another one of Sawyers's teamsters, stayed in Montana for several years. He tried his hand at mining and then fell back on his earlier trade, printing, joining Helena Typographical Union Number 95. He returned to Sergeant Bluff, Iowa, in 1867 or 1868, and entered the family business with his father and older brother, dealing in stock and merchandising. The family also started a brick-manufacturing plant during this time, which turned out up to fifty thousand bricks per day.

---

[23]Ibid., 333–35.
[24]Biographical information from Sioux City Public Museum, Pearl Research Center.
[25]Doyle, *Journeys to the Land of Gold*, 385–86.

In 1872 Holman married Emma Webster, a marriage that produced three daughters and a son. He remained in Sergeant Bluff for the rest of his life as a successful businessman and a respected community leader.[26]

The Sawyers Expedition left a strong impression on Holman, and he relived his 1865 adventure as a "bull whacker" with the surveying party in his 1924 book, *Pioneering in the Northwest*.[27]

Albert Milton Holman died on 3 March 1933 and was buried in the Sergeant Bluff Cemetery.[28]

Pvt. John Colby Griggs, a galvanized Yankee, served with Company D, Fifth U.S. Volunteer Infantry, under Captain Williford at Fort Connor. He left with his company for Fort Laramie in July 1866. Griggs mustered out at Fort Kearny, Nebraska, on 11 October 1866.

After discharge Griggs settled on a farm in Hall County, Nebraska, with his wife, Lucyann, and two children. The family had four more children. In 1883 the Griggs family moved to a homestead in Cherry County, Nebraska. Tragedy struck the Griggs family in 1884 when Lucyann died. He remarried in 1886 to Cora Bradish, and the couple had four more children.

Griggs moved again in 1892, this time to Spearfish, South Dakota. His later years were spent in Rapid City, South Dakota, where he died on 14 December 1914. John Colby Griggs was buried in the Mountain View Cemetery in that city.[29]

Capt. Henry Emerson Palmer was mustered out of the service in November 1865 after returning from Denver. Offered a commission as a second lieutenant in the Second U.S. Cavalry in February 1866, Palmer chose instead to return to the West as a civilian entrepreneur. In March 1866 he left Kansas City, Missouri, with four wagon loads of trade goods.

---

[26] Biographical information from Sioux City Public Museum, Pearl Research Center.
[27] Albert M. Holman, *Pioneering in the Northwest, Niobrara–Virginia City Wagon Road* (Sioux City: Deitch and Lamar Company, 1924).
[28] Biographical information from Sioux City Public Museum, Pearl Research Center.
[29] Paul, "A Galvanized Yankee along the Niobrara," 156.

Henry E. Palmer in 1884.
Courtesy of the Nebraska State Historical Society, RG2411, PHO 4229b.

Arriving at Fort Laramie in May, his small train then headed northwest, following the Bozeman Trail. He was accompanied by several of the guides who had traveled with Connor the previous year.

Palmer attempted to establish a trading post at Clear Creek (near today's Buffalo, Wyoming) but was promptly run out by Cheyenne warriors. He then moved north to the Bighorn River, staying for a month at an Arapaho village. Fortunately, he had sent one of his wagons loaded with trade goods ahead to the goldfields of Montana, as the Arapaho eventually confiscated his remaining inventory and set him afoot. He walked the distance to Bozeman, Montana, over one hundred miles.

In 1867 Palmer turned up in Idaho as editor of the Salmon River *Idaho Mining News.* He also took part in local civic activities: as "chief of the vigilantes."

Palmer returned to Wisconsin in 1868 for a brief stay and then moved on to Plattsmouth, Nebraska. After working as a grain dealer, he turned to selling fire insurance in 1870. He finally found his calling and operated a successful insurance agency in the area for many years. He married Laura Z. Case in 1870, a marriage that produced a son and a daughter.

In 1889 Henry Palmer moved to Omaha and opened a fire and casualty insurance agency, with his son George as one of his partners. He was fire and police commissioner in 1896–97 and a park commissioner in 1898.[30] In 1904 President Theodore Roosevelt appointed Palmer as postmaster of Omaha and he served in that capacity until 1908. The town of Palmer, Merrick County, Nebraska, southeast of Columbus, is named for Henry E. Palmer.

The Omaha Daily News reported in its lead story on Monday, 3 April 1911, that "Henry E. Palmer, western pioneer, civil war veteran and former postmaster of Omaha, died suddenly Sunday morning [2 April] while sweeping the snow from the front porch of his home." Palmer was buried at Forest Lawn Cemetery in Omaha.[31]

Sgt. Lewis Byram Hull mustered out with his regiment, the Eleventh Ohio Cavalry, at Fort Leavenworth on 14 July 1866. He settled on a farm in southeast Kansas in Butler County, near the county seat of El Dorado.

Hull died on 9 May 1902, and the editor of the El Dorado *Walnut Valley Times,* Alvah Shelden, wrote in Hull's obituary: "In the death of Lewis B. Hull, Butler County lost one of her best and most intelligent citizens. He was an early settler in the county, and a bright student of her conditions and possibilities. He read much and worked much. He experimented much in fruit and other horticultural lines. He bred fine stock and was an intelligent farmer in a very high sense. He reared a large family and spared no pains in giving his children the advantages of high education. He was public spirited and charitable. The good he did was beyond estimate."[32]

Pvt. Sheldon L. Wight, having one year to go on his enlistment, transferred to K Company of the First Michigan Cavalry and spent the winter at Fort Bridger, in the southwest corner of today's Wyoming. He was mustered out of the service on 30 June 1866 after traveling to Detroit, Michigan.

---

[30]Coutant, *History of Wyoming,* 2:535–37.
[31]*The Omaha Daily News,* 3, 4, 5 April 1911.
[32]Hull, "Soldiering on the High Plains," n1.

After escaping safely from a hotel fire in Detroit, Wight returned home to his parents' farm in Benton Township, Michigan. He married Mary Ann Weaver on 18 November 1866. They were both nineteen years old. Shortly after the birth of his first son in 1867 (altogether they would have five children), the Wights moved to Hamilton Township, where Sheldon had purchased land. He worked at a variety of jobs to support his family while building up his farm. Wight involved himself in local government, serving as justice of the peace in 1870 and later serving as township treasurer and Township Clerk.

In later years, Sheldon Wight ran a thriving photographic studio in Elsie, Michigan. Apparently self-taught, he worked his photography business up until his death on 25 May 1919, succumbing to cancer. Sheldon L. Wight was buried in Riverside Cemetery in Elsie, Michigan.

Sgt. Charles (Charlie) Lawrence Thomas was discharged out of service with the Eleventh Ohio Cavalry at Fort Leavenworth on 14 July 1866. He returned home to Boudes Ferry Landing, Ohio, and married Emma Alice Sargent, a widow with two sons, on 4 April 1869 at Higginsport, Ohio. Charlie and Emma eventually expanded their family with three daughters and a son.

Thomas convinced his new brother-in-law, Leander Wilkes, that their future belonged in the West. The two of them traveled to Kansas by rail in October 1870 to stake out free government land available there. First traveling to Topeka, then Emporia, the brothers-in-law learned that good government land for homesteading was still available in northwest Morris County. Charlie and Leander traveled two days by mule team to the area and chose the land that Thomas eventually homesteaded. After filing their claims, the two returned to Ohio.

In March 1871 Thomas and his brother-in-law chartered a railroad car, loaded it with horses, farm implements, and household goods, and headed for Kansas and their new homesteads. Charlie's wife, Emma, her sister, Jennie Wilkes, and all of the children arrived at Parkerville, Morris County, Kansas, by train on 27 May 1871. They were all loaded, along with their luggage, onto a lumber wagon—with no springs, and the box was loaded with grass—and rode to their new home. Charlie had pur-

Charles L. Thomas and family members in 1898 while Charlie was
visiting in St. Joseph, Missouri. (*left to right*) Charles L. Thomas
(note that he is wearing his medal of honor); Nellie Thomas Goss
(one of Charlie's daughters); Nellie's children, Harley Landoline Goss
and Nina Alice Goss; Nannie Thomas Keller (Charlie's daughter) and
G. E. Keller (Nannie's husband). *Courtesy of Ron Tillotson.*

chased materials in Parkerville and built a fourteen-by-twenty-eight-
foot house prior to his family's arrival.

The first year in Kansas was hard, as Thomas and his family lost all of
their crops to a prairie fire in September, though fortunately saving the
house. In subsequent years, the hardships included swarms of voracious
grasshoppers that ate every growing plant in their path and a late winter
storm that literally buried the farm under deep drifts of snow, which
made feeding and keeping their farm animals alive a perilous chore. Low
prices for crops kept money hard to come by during those years.

Although some of his neighbors gave up their homesteads during this
time, Charlie displayed the same tenacity that he had shown on his
amazing ride in 1865 and through hard work and sacrifice kept his farm.

By the late 1870s and early 1880s crops were bountiful, prices for grain and corn were rising, and life got measurably better as Thomas began to prosper.

In January 1888 Thomas was installed as the first Post Commander of the Leander P. Wilkes Post No. 86, Grand Army of the Republic. There were eighteen charter members.[33]

In July 1894 Thomas wrote to his congressman, Charles Curtis, inquiring about the possibility of receiving the Medal of Honor for his 1865 ride to Cole.[34] Letters of recommendation also were written by his company commander, Capt. Levi G. Marshall, Capt. Henry E. Palmer, and at least two enlisted men, J. E. Brandon of the Second Missouri Light Artillery and Ansel Steck.[35] Thomas received the Medal of Honor on 18 August 1894.

In February 1913 Thomas sold his farm and retired, moving into a fine house in the nearby town of Dwight. In his later years Thomas received more honors. In June 1916 his name was entered on the Army and Navy Medal of Honor Roll. Commissioned brevet major of the Ohio National Guard, Thomas had his name recorded on a special Ohio State Roll of Honor in February 1921.

The secretary of war invited him to attend, as a guest of the government, the ceremony for the Unknown Soldier on Armistice Day, 11 November 1921. According to the reminiscences of his daughter Nellie Thomas Goss, Charlie did make the trip to Washington, D.C., and attended the ceremony along with other Medal of Honor recipients.[36]

In 1920 prominent historical researcher Walter M. Camp wrote to Charlie, inquiring about the details of the Powder River Indian Expedition and Thomas's role in it. They corresponded back and forth, and in the spring of 1921 Camp visited Charlie at his home in Dwight. Camp recalled: "I have seen the Serg. Thomas who went from Connor to Cole with two Pawnees and have had a long talk with him. He is a nice old man, 79 years old and accurate in his habit of speech. . . . Thomas has official documents which leave no doubt about what he did, and the

[33]Tillotson, "Prominent Events in the Life of Charles Lawrence Thomas."
[34]Thomas to Curtis, 2 July 1894, Fort Laramie Research Library.
[35]Undated excerpt from the *Council Grove Republican*. Statement of A. Steck, 1 August 1865, Fort Laramie Research Library.
[36]Tillotson, "Prominent Events in the Life of Charles Lawrence Thomas."

whole thing is very clear to me now. . . . Old Sergt. Thomas is very interesting and what he does not remember he does not try to tell."[37]

Charlie's wife Emma passed away on 27 September 1919. Charles Lawrence Thomas died on 24 February 1923, and was buried in the Dwight Cemetery. A passage in his memorial read: "He was loyal to his God and to his country. He knew no fear. His life was an open book. He was a gentle soul, unmixed with envy or hatred."[38]

---

[37]Camp to Dan Bowman, 31 May 1921, Bowman Manuscript Collection, Montana Historical Society.

[38]Tillotson, "Prominent Events in the Life of Charles Lawrence Thomas."

CHAPTER TWENTY-THREE

OBSERVATIONS AND CONCLUSIONS

Patrick Connor's war—the Powder River Indian Expedition of 1865—is generally judged as something less than a success when revisited by today's historians. Its stated goal of bringing a lasting peace to the northern plains was not achieved, as conflict continued sporadically for another dozen years. The campaign did bring temporary relief to the commercial routes to the south, as the warriors stayed in Powder River country to protect their families and villages as long as Connor was in the field. The Indians of Powder River country would never again feel as safe as they had prior to the summer of 1865, as Connor's was the first military expedition of this magnitude to invade their previously unchallenged stronghold.

So what went wrong with this plan that looked so good to generals who engineered the campaign in their offices hundreds of miles to the east? General Connor, in his official report of 4 October 1865, placed the blame on two factors: the lack of timely delivery of supplies intended for the expedition and the performance of his subordinate column commanders, Col. Nelson Cole and Lt. Col. Samuel Walker. Perhaps Connor was being a little simplistic, as the flawed planning of moving, supplying, and coordinating the large forces over this vast wilderness area has to be questioned.

One must remember that in the spring of 1865, the western theatre was a minor distraction in the larger picture of the Civil War. When the Powder River campaign was in the early planning stages, Generals Grant and Lee still faced off in a stalemate at Petersburg, Virginia, and General Sherman's victorious army marched through the South. The surrender of Lee at Appomattox in early April and the subsequent assassination of

President Lincoln kept attention focused on the East. Transitioning to a new president and mustering out the huge Union Volunteer Army of over a million men—reducing the expenses of maintaining that army—became the priorities by early summer.[1] Reconstruction of the South and a potential border conflict with Mexico also distracted the attention of the army and drained their resources during this hectic time. While all of these enormous events were taking center stage, Generals Pope, Dodge, and Connor were struggling to put together their Powder River expedition. It must have been like trying to paddle a canoe upstream in swift rapids.

There were several key areas that negatively affected this campaign from the beginning.

THE PLANNING

The original plans of March and April had a much greater chance of success. Recall that Brig. Gen. Alfred Sully was to lead twelve hundred men out of Fort Pierre on the Missouri River, traveling west to build a fort on Powder River and to cooperate with a column under Connor from Fort Laramie. Sully was the most experienced Indian fighter in the army at that time, with two years of campaigning against the northern Sioux in 1863 and 1864, following the Minnesota Sioux uprising of 1862. He scored major victories against these tribesmen at Whitestone Hill and Killdeer Mountain. His troops were seasoned veterans of warfare against the Plains Indians, having already operated in the arid country of northern Dakota Territory, a landscape similar to that of the planned campaign. Connor and Sully would have made an aggressive, dynamic team.

Nelson Cole, a competent artillery officer, had just had his regiment—the Second Missouri Light Artillery—converted to a cavalry unit, and his troops had never operated as such. His men were seasoned veterans, having fought in campaigns such as Vicksburg and Atlanta, but as artillery, not cavalry. Neither Cole nor his men had operated on the plains and were without experience in Indian warfare. When Sully and his cavalry were sent elsewhere, Cole and his men were not an equal replacement.

The decision to have Cole and his column march out of Omaha rather than Fort Pierre is a puzzling one. It took Cole six weeks and five hun-

---

[1] Nevins, *War for the Union,* 367.

dred miles of travel over a tough semi-mapped terrain to arrive at Bear
Butte with rapidly deteriorating animals. From Fort Pierre—only 152
miles from the same landmark and over good ground—they could have
easily reached Bear Butte in ten days, arriving with fresh horses and
mules. The men and supplies that were delivered to Omaha could have
been delivered to Fort Pierre by the same riverboats traveling up the
Missouri River. This decision probably did more to contribute to the
expedition's failure than any other factor. Cole probably could not have
purchased supplies at Fort Pierre, as he ultimately did at Omaha. However the pressure to be on the trail would not have been so severe with the
saved month and would have allowed more supplies to come through
normal channels.

Supplying the Campaign

The army's quartermaster system clearly could not meet the demands
of moving quickly to get the columns in motion. Connor wrote in his
official report, "I deem it proper for me to state that the Expedition was
organized and placed in the field without having received any of the
supplies intended for it by the (then) Dept-Commander [Dodge]. But in
order to make my campaign, I was compelled to direct store[s] and
supplies intended for other points to my Head Quarters, and was finally
compelled to take the field with a command poorly supplied with many
needed articles, and deficient in many parts of the rations."[2]

Plans called for the majority of the supplies, forage, and rations for the
campaign to be disbursed from Fort Laramie. The goods came mostly
from Fort Leavenworth (580 miles from Laramie), located on the Missouri River. Under ideal conditions, a train of freight wagons would take
five to six weeks to make the trip on the Overland Road. Heavy spring
rains slowed the traffic down even more, sometimes to a standstill. No
better alternative yet existed, as the transcontinental railroad had barely
begun construction and was years away from any usefulness. The slow,
tedious process of supplying the forts of the West and mounting a major
campaign such as the Powder River Expedition proved to be beyond the
army's capability at that time. The Indian raids along the Overland Road

---

[2]Connor's official report, submitted on 4 October 1865 to Major Barnes, Grenville Dodge
   Manuscript Collection.

also contributed to the delays, as civilian suppliers were often unwilling to move west without a military escort and the army would delay wagon trains until they were of sufficient size.

Connor's disparaging comments about the slow and unscrupulous civilian contractors during the final weeks of preparation clearly showed his frustration at the pace of the supply chain. It is no wonder that a man of action such as Connor would go outside the system to get things done, since the army's supply bureaucracy moved at its own snail's pace. General Dodge commented on the honesty of the civilian contractors in August: "It seems to me all the rascals in the west are combined to swindle [the] Government. My staff officers at Fort Leavenworth report great amount of swindling there and in Kansas."[3]

On 31 August, Cole sent a scouting party to the Panther Mountain area, designated by Connor as the rendezvous and supply depot for the eastern and center columns and found no trace of Connor. Based on this intelligence, Cole wondered if Connor was even in the field and made his subsequent movements on this finding. If Connor had been able to start his campaign just two weeks earlier, he would have had time to establish the supply base prior to the arrival of Cole's scout, as was expected from his written orders. But it didn't happen—Connor waited until 31 July, delaying for supplies. He started the campaign under-supplied and waited ten more days at Fort Connor for a train that finally arrived on 21 August and gave him sufficient stores to move north. Connor was at least fifty miles to the south when Cole's scouting party looked for him on 31 August. If Connor had been able to contact and re-supply the two columns at that point and had taken over full direction of the campaign, the results probably would have been much different.

COLE AND WALKER

History has not been kind to General Connor's two column commanders, Colonel Cole and Lieutenant Colonel Walker. Connor heaped much of the blame for the expedition's failures on his subordinates, even though he was late arriving at Panther Mountain, as previously noted. The term "incompetent" has been used to describe these two men, which is unfair, especially to Cole.

---

[3] Dodge telegram to Pope, 7 August 1865, Coutant, *History of Wyoming and the Far West*, 2:489.

Colonel Cole can be criticized for some of his decisions, such as the exposed campsite on 8 September, but his overall performance under extremely difficult conditions appears to be very acceptable. He kept loss of life from battle at a minimum (ten men out of fourteen hundred) after having skirmishes and fights with Sioux and Cheyenne warriors almost daily from 1 September to 10 September. He was cool under fire and used his artillery to the military's advantage, generally keeping the attackers at long range. Cole kept the command orderly and intact as they struggled south during their starving march up Powder River. "Unprepared" is a more accurate description of Cole's performance rather than "incompetent."

Unlike Cole, Walker had served in the western theatre of the war since 1861 and had experience in western Missouri and Kansas. His actions during the campaign at times seemed almost lackadaisical. His orders called for his command to act independently until the rendezvous at Panther Mountain. However, once he accidentally met Cole's command in northeastern Wyoming, Walker stayed in close proximity to Cole for the rest of the journey. While Cole sent a scouting party to Panther Mountain in search of Connor, Walker merely accepted the results of Cole's reconnaissance, making no attempt on his own to locate the general. With a more mobile command and without the encumbrance of wagons, Walker should have pushed on toward the Tongue in search of Connor, but instead chose to march with Cole up and down Powder River. Both commanders should have shown more initiative in attempting to find Connor's command.

Reluctant Indian Fighters

In his book, *One of Custer's Wolverines,* author Eric J. Wittenberg entitled his chapter on Kidd's Powder River experiences "Reluctant Indian Fighter."[4] There were many "reluctant Indian fighters" in the Powder River Indian Expedition. Colonel Kidd and the Sixth Michigan were not the exception; Kidd just documented his negative feelings better than most. General Pope wrote "that the volunteer organization sent to the plains from the east and from the Army of the Tennessee are in such a state of insubordination, and many of their officers are so much in sympathy with them, that they are next to useless for any service, and have by

---

[4]Wittenberg, *One of Custer's Wolverines,* 147.

their example infected the other troops now there to the extent of making them nearly inefficient."[5]

Mutinous troops wanting to go home became commonplace on the plains in 1865. Commanding officers all along the Overland Road complained about their troops rebelling. Several of Colonel Cole's companies refused to march in his column, both in Omaha and later on the trail. General Connor ordered cannons aimed at mutinous troops at Fort Kearny to gain their compliance. A portion of Lieutenant-Colonel Walker's Sixteenth Kansas rebelled just prior to leaving Fort Laramie as the center column of Connor's expedition. Two howitzers loaded with "grape and canister" convinced them to rethink their action and ride out with their regiment.

The overall effects on the expedition had to be very poor morale, although it is difficult to pinpoint specific examples of how it affected performance. In Cole's camp, disgruntled and mutinous soldiers caused their stock to stampede, hoping to abort the mission. The officers no doubt had to work much harder, knowing they were with men who did not want to be there. But when they had to fight, they did so, as basic survival instinct overcame bad attitude.

PADDLING UPSTREAM

With the end of the Civil War in April 1865, the government's priority became the reconstruction of the conquered South, discharging as quickly as possible the huge Union Volunteer Army and reducing the expenses associated with maintaining that force. At the same time the planners of the Powder River Expedition were attempting to build up troops, supplies, and the related expenses for the planned campaign.

These two opposing forces were bound to collide at some point. In June Major General Pope defended his actions to Lt. Gen. Ulysses S. Grant: "I will reduce cavalry as far as possible. . . . I think the Government will find it true economy to finish this Indian war this season so that it will stay finished. We have troops enough now on the plains to do it, and can do it now better than hereafter."[6]

In July secretary of war Edwin M. Stanton wired General Grant: "The Quartermaster-General has made a report this morning of requisitions

---

[5] Pope to Sawyer, 5 August 1865, *The War of Rebellion*, O.R., Series 1, Volume 47/2 [S#102].
[6] Pope to Grant, 19 June 1865, ibid.

from the department at Leavenworth indicating an expedition of magnitude and expense beyond the capacity of the appropriations to meet. The transportation estimates alone are $2,000,000 per month, and this exclusive of the cost of materials, &c. The Commissary Department also is in a state of alarm. I beg to direct your immediate attention to this subject, as I am not advised of the extent or necessity of the proposed operation."[7] Grant replied, "I know of no expedition, or the necessity for one, of the magnitude reported in your dispatch." He assured Stanton that he would look into it and "correct all extravagances."[8] That exchange took place on 28 July, while Connor was making final preparations and moving the various elements of Powder River Indian Expedition towards LaBonte Crossing on the North Platte River.

On 1 August, the day that Connor finally got his expedition in motion, General Pope, who now obviously had given in to the pressure from Grant and the War Department, sent Dodge a communiqué that opened, "I have telegraphed you several times in regard to a reduction of forces and expenditures in your command, and rely upon your reducing both as rapidly as possible." Pope went on to outline his plans to reduce forces to a minimum—to garrison the posts along the Overland Road and leave enough troops for escort duty. He then said, "The military expeditions now marching against the Indians cannot and should not be arrested until the campaign is terminated, which I confidently expect will be the case as early as October 1."[9] Pope had now, probably reluctantly, joined the downsizers and abandoned the campaign that he had initiated months earlier.

Dodge predictably protested, but the die had been cast. Secretary Stanton wired General Grant: "The president [Andrew Johnson] is much concerned about the Indian expedition. The Secretary of the Treasury declares his inability to meet an expenditure so large and unexpected, and not sanctioned by the Government. Have you any information to relieve the President's anxiety or to satisfy him as to the object and design of the expedition? Who planned it?"[10] Grant answered, "They have been planned under General Pope's direction, and I am not posted as to the

---

[7] Stanton to Grant, 28 July 1865, ibid.
[8] Grant to Stanton, 28 July 1865, ibid.
[9] Pope to Dodge, 1 August 1865, ibid.
[10] Stanton to Grant, 12 August 1865, ibid.

necessity of them. . . . I think all extraordinary requisitions should be disapproved."[11] On 21 August Stanton wired Grant: "No satisfactory information has been received in respect to the Indian expedition or measures taken to reduce its dimensions and expense."[12] On the following day Pope issued orders abolishing the District of the Plains and reassigning Connor to the District of Utah. The rug had now been pulled out from under Connor, Dodge, and their campaign.

One may ask how this turn of events affected an expedition that was already supplied and in the field beyond recall. General Connor returned to Fort Connor in late September with every intention of regrouping his men and returning north to chastise the warring tribes with a fall and winter campaign. General Dodge wrote, "If we cannot conquer them this summer and fall we must this winter; that is, I hold that now we have got after them we should not stop summer, fall, or winter until they are glad to sue for peace and behave themselves. I am confident we can strike some of them now, and in winter I know I can catch them all. They are now on the warpath and are not making any provisions for winter; are not hunting, planting, laying in meat, or in any way providing for the future as they usually do."[13]

Further campaigning by Connor was canceled and the army withdrew, leaving only a small garrison at Fort Connor. The warring tribes were emboldened and viewed this as a victory. The government then decided that it would be less expensive and more humane to negotiate treaties with the tribes rather than subdue them with military force.

General Dodge had described a strategy that would be used very effectively eleven years later by Col. Nelson A. Miles in the fall and winter of 1876 and into the spring of 1877. His year-round campaigning brought an end to the Great Sioux War of 1876, and the tribes of Powder River country either surrendered and moved to the reservations or fled to Canada.

Perhaps if Gen. Patrick Edward Connor had been allowed to complete his campaign in 1865, there may not have been a Fetterman disaster in the following year, and George Armstrong Custer might have died of old age.

---

[11] Grant to Stanton, 12 August 1865, ibid.
[12] Stanton to Grant, 21 August 1865, ibid.
[13] Dodge to Pope, 2 August 1865, ibid.

General Patrick E. Connor's Official Report of the Powder River Indian Expedition of 1865

Head Quarters Powder River Expedition[1]
Fort Laramie D.T. Oct 4th 1865

To
Major J. W. Barnes
Asst Adjt General
U.S. Forces Kansas and the Territories
Fort Leavenworth Kans

Sir:

I have the honor to submit the following report (and accompanying papers) of the Powder River Expedition. The organization of the Expedition was fully and minutely detailed to Major Genl Dodge in letters and telegrams from me during the months of May, June and July 1865. I also forwarded to him copies of my instructions to column Commanders under date of July 1865. For the Maps and Topography of the country traveled over, the Genl Com'dg is respectfully referred the report of Capt S. M. Robbins, Chief Engineer of District, who was detailed by the Dept Com'der for that duty. He has been ordered to Fort Leavenworth for purpose of completing the same. I deem it proper for me to state that the Expedition was organized and placed in the field without having received any of the supplies intended for it by the (then) Dept-Commander. But

---

[1] Grenville M. Dodge Papers, Vol. 145, File 3, Iowa State Historical Society, Des Moines, Iowa.

in order to make my campaign, I was compelled to direct store and supplies intended for other points to my Head Quarters, and was finally compelled to take the field with a Command poorly supplied with many needed articles, and deficient in many parts of the rations. I left Fort Laramie on the 30th of July 1865 and arrived at Powder River on the 11th August following where I established a Military Post and placed Colonel Kidd 6th Michigan Cavalry in Command. He named the Post Fort Connor. From that point I proceeded with the left column consisting of 250 white Soldiers, and 150 Indian Scouts with the supply train for the three columns along the base of Powder River and Big Horn Mountains to Pine Creek a tributary of Tongue River, where I arrived on the 23rd August 1865. Marched thence to Tongue River where I arrived on the 28th of same month. Observing a fresh trail crossing the road at this place, I sent out a detachment of Pawnee Scouts to ascertain the where-abouts of the Indians. The same evening I received a message from Capt North who was in Command of the detachment, informing me that he had found the Indian Village. I moved that night at 8 P.M. leaving a sufficient force to guard the train, and made a night march of forty (40) miles, reached the village at 7:30 A.M. of August 29, 1865 and immediately attacked it; routing and pursuing the Indians ten (10) miles. For the particulars of that battle I refer you to my official report of August 30th, 1865 only adding here that there in I reported thirty five (35) Indians killed. Subsequently the Indians acknowledged a loss of sixty three (63) warriors killed and a large number wounded. I destroyed all their lodges, winter stores, clothing, robes, etc. and captured five hundred (500) horses and mules. The loss on our side was an Omaha Scout killed and seven wounded as follows: Lieut Oscar Jewett my aid-de-camp and my three orderlies who were close to my person during the entire engagement. One (1) man of the Signal Corps and two men of the 11th Ohio Cavalry. I reached my camp at 2 A.M. of August 30th 1865 having marched over one hundred (100) miles, fought the battle and brought the captured stock back with me inside of thirty (30) hours. I also captured four squaws and seven children taking them with me to my camp where I released them next morning not wishing to be encumbered with them. The prisoners informed me that the Arapahoes (the tribe I had attacked) under the leadership of Black Bear and Medicine Man would they thought gladly make peace with the whites. I accordingly sent them word that I did not desire to kill them if they would behave themselves and be good Indians. I also sent them a letter for safe conduct to Fort Laramie in the event of their desiring to make a treaty with us.

I then resumed my march down Tongue River sending out scouting parties to ascertain the whereabouts of the right and center Columns. Continuing then until I was within forty (40) miles of the Yellow Stone at which point the grass became so scarce I halted and sent Capt Marshall 11th Ohio Cavalry with (50) men of his company to that river for the purpose of ascertaining if possible the whereabouts of the other commands concerning which I was now seriously annoyed. He returned without finding their trail or ascertaining anything about them in any way. It was evident they had not reached that stream or arrived at the designated place of rendezvous.

I immediately dispatched another detachment of fifty Pawnee Scouts under Capt North to Powder River to ascertain if possible the whereabouts of the missing Columns which should have found me before this date. On the 5th September I received a message from Colonel Sawyer of the Niobrara wagon Road Expedition stating that he had been attacked by Indians on Tongue River in the vicinity of the battle field of August 29th and did not have sufficient force to proceed. I sent Capt Brown's 2nd Cala Cavalry with his company and Capt Nash's company of Omaha Scouts to his assistance with orders to escort him to Big Horn river and then return to my Command. This reduced my force to two hundred and seventy men (270). On the 11th September Capt North returned from Powder River and reported having seen Colonel Cole's camp of a few days before with about three hundred (300) dead horses in it, they having been shot it is presumed by his order. The Indians were so numerous on this trail Capt North deemed it advisable to return, it being in his judgment folly to attempt to force a passage to Colonel Cole under the circumstances, with the small force at his disposal. Colonel Cole's trail was going up Powder River. I then moved up Tongue River a short distance to good grass and sent another scout 12th September which was driven in the next day. I again sent out a Scout (14th Sept) of two Ohio men and two Pawnee Indians and the same evening sent Capt Marshall 11th Ohio Cavalry with fifty men of his company and fifty Pawnee Scouts under Capt North fearful that the former Scout would not reach Colonel Cole, and knowing him to be about out of provisions, with orders to cut their way through to him at all hazards and bring him to me, and not to return without finding him. Three days after I received a message from Capt Marshall, stating that he had found Colonel Cole's right column and Lieut Colonel Walker 16th Kansas Cavalry with the center Column on Powder River within twenty five miles of Fort Connor marching south. I refer you to the report of Colonel Cole and Lt. Colonel Walker, copies of which are herewith enclosed for information concerning the condition of their columns.

I cannot regard these Column Commanders as having obeyed my instructions. Colonel Cole only sent out one Scout of one officer and fourteen men to ascertain my whereabouts, did not appear to make any effort to join me or reach the designated place of rendezvous. The Scout sent out by him reported that it reached Tongue River, and said that no indications of my presence could be discovered there, when I was at that very time marching down that stream and it was impossible to reach that river and not discover my trail which was large enough to attract attention almost as readily as a well beaten road. This scout, from all the information I could obtain only proceeded to Pumpkin Creek, a small stream between Powder River and Tongue Rivers. At the time Colonel Cole first commenced losing his stock he was within forty miles of me. Lt Colonel Walker made no effort to ascertain where I was or to reach the designated rendezvous, but satisfied himself with the single scout made by Colonel Cole. Had these Columns found me as was intended, I could have saved most of their horses, fed and partially equipped the men and made a Campaign of forty (40) days from the designated rendezvous, and I am fully satisfied that I could have succeeded in striking the village of the Sioux and Cheyenne fought by Col. Cole and Lt. Col. Walker and mentioned in their Report and by a well directed blow ended the war.

As it was I had but a few men with me, reduced by Scouts from the original number to 150 white Soldiers and 30 Pawnee Scouts with a train of one hundred (100) wagons, a herd of Beef cattle and captured stock to guard, not enough for any offensive measures and was thus forced reluctantly to return to Fort Connor intending to organize another Campaign from that point at once and continue offensive movements all winter or until such time as the Indians were well chastised.

Upon my arrival on 24th September I found orders assigning me to Command of District of Utah announcing new organizations of Districts and muster out of troops.

In obedience to these orders I at once proceeded to Fort Laramie with my command so that I could effect contemplated movements of troops to Salt Lake and Fort Leavenworth before the winter storms commenced. The Campaign may be briefly summed up as follows; Four pitched battles with the Sioux, Cheyennes and Arapahoes with a loss to them as near as can be ascertained of between four hundred and five hundred warriors, and a large number of wounded, the destruction of the Arapahoes Village and capture of five hundred horses and mules, with a loss of twenty four killed, wounded and missing. Of the Killed was Capt Cole 6th Michigan Cavalry. The Arapahoes sent word that they were coming to Fort Laramie to make a treaty. The Sioux and Cheyennes say they are going to Fort Randall for the same purpose, but I very much doubt whether any of them will keep their word. I think the Arapahoes have been well punished, but do not think the Sioux and Cheyennes have been. And I do not believe that any treaty effected with them, or any of the hostile tribes of the Plains this season will be productive of any lasting benefit. They may offer peace for the purpose of obtaining presents and a respite until they can prepare for a fresh outbreak. I again repeat of my firm conviction based upon my extended knowledge of Indian character that any peace made with these hostile Indians which is not first preceded by severe chastisement, such as will make them fear the power of the Government will only result in a renewal of hostilities and a repetition of the scenes of bloodshed and outrages which have retarded the interests of these territories during the past two years. I regret that my orders compelled me to abandon the Campaign before I had sufficiently finished the hostile Indians within my former Command so as to insure good conduct from them in future. I respectfully suggest in this connection as a necessary measure to keep the hostile Indians (who number at least 10,000 warriors) from the Mail and Telegraph roads, that a force of not less than one thousand men be stationed at Fort Connor and that expeditions be sent out during the winter in the directions of their Villages. This would naturally attract the attention of the warriors and hold them constantly within protecting distance of their families, and as a result prevent them from coming down to our lines of communications.

I also deem it proper to say that when I assumed Command of the District of the Plains, there were no supplies in it and but few troops and these were required to protect government property. Communications with the east were uncertain and extremely hazardous and the Indians had control of the country which was not in the immediate vicinity of the settlements and Military Posts. It affords me pleasure to state that now constant and regular communications is had with all portions of my former command, but at the same time I must fear that the withdrawals of so many troops from the Plains will destroy what has been gained as soon as these Indians are advised of it. I cannot but think that if the Campaign had been allowed to proceed as Major General Dodge and myself had arranged it and the troops then on the Plains be permitted to remain, all that was desired could have been accomplished by next spring at the least. The Arapahoes are the most troublesome Indians to deal with on the Plains. They have committed more depredations on the Mail and Telegraph roads than all the other tribes of Indians combined and while the government was feeding their old men, women and children at Fort Halleck and Camp Collins last winter and spring, their young men were out on stealing and murdering raids. When detected all fled north and were camped on Tongue River where I attacked them.

My Scouting parties sent out from time to time during the Expedition succeeded in killing twenty seven (27) Indians independent of the former battles fought. I respectfully recommend the establishment of a Post on the Little Missouri about due north of Bear Buttes and which can be supplied from Fort Pierre on the Missouri River. The distance from Fort Pierre to the proposed Post is two hundred (200) miles over good country for a wagon road.

Also another Post on Big Horn River near the mouth of Little Horn River. The Yellow Stone and Big Horn Rivers are navigable seven months of the year to the mouth of the Little Horn. This Post could be supplied by steamers. These Posts would be in the heart of the Indian country located where the Indians are compelled to go for their game and winter quarters and would thus afford every opportunity to the Government to hold them in check at all times.

The natural road from the Missouri River to Virginia City Montana will pass Fort Laramie and Fort Connor and the Post recommended on Big Horn, thus adding an additional importance to the Post recommended to be established at the later point.

> Very Respectfully
> Your Obedient Servant
> (sgd) P. Edw Connor
> Brig Genl USA
> Com'dg Powder River Expedition

An Informal Report on the Results of the Road-building Expedition

LETTER FROM JAMES A. SAWYERS TO CONGRESSMAN A. W. HUBBARD

Salt Lake City UT[1]
Nov 10th 1865

Hon A. W. Hubbard
Dear Sir

I arrived at this place a few days ago. I will have to wait 2 days longer to get a seat in the stage. I have paid off and discharged all the men except Judge Smith he is with me. In Virginia City I met Col McClain M.C. from Montana. he was glad to see me and very much pleased when I told him what I had done. I told him that I had brought over 36 wagons coupled together. made the road all the way good enough so that we did not have to uncouple them once all the way to pass over bad places. I took him to look at the wagons. he said he was surprised to see them look so well after being drawn over 1000 miles of new Road. he said it was a thing never done before taking a heavily loaded train over a new Road as far. he insisted that You and himself and I should be together before my Report should go before the Sec Interior. Yesterday I met him again at this place had quite a long talk with him. he says I must come straight to Washington and let You and him consult with me or me with you and him

---

[1]Sioux City Public Museum, Pearl Research Center, Sioux City, Iowa. Punctuation has been added to this letter for clarity.

before I make a report. I told him I had written to the Secretary of the Interior for permission to come to Washington to be answered at Sioux City. he said come anyhow so you may look for me about Christmas. I would much rather meet you at Sioux City but it was impossible for me to get through any sooner. I do hope to have a good portion of the appropriation left for another year. If you and others think best after looking at my report.

The fact is Judge I feel more interest in the Road to day than ever if possible. I find so much opposition to it. I had a long talk to day with Genl Connor about the Road. he was much pleased at all I told him of the Road from Ft Connor to Virginia City. But when I would talk of Running water [Niobrara River] White Earth River and the Sheyenne Country he said it would be Impossible to get a road through that country. I told him I had already made it and had drawn a heavy Freight train over it. well he said it was too Sandy. every one on this line will do all they can against the road. Would to God I had had an Escort so that I could have returned over the road and finished the whole thing up. I could have done so and not spent all the appropriation Either If I had had the soldiers. In going from Virginia City to Sioux City I traveled 1112 Miles, 1022 from Niobrara and 90 to Niobrara. In going home I will travel 1820: 410 Miles from this place to Virginia City, 1300 to Omaha. from Omaha to Sioux City 110 Miles. Making 708 Miles further this way than the way I came. these are facts and cannot be denied. that is what gets the Hounds there the advantage as the Niobrara Rout for grass wood and water are far superior to this rout, but the Interested parties on this line are rich and will make a strong fight. Ben Holladay is the Head of the concern. he charges for stage fare alone from Virginia City to Omaha 375 and 2 dollars per pound for all your baggage over 25 lbs. a stage Co could coin Money on the Niobrara Route at one third of that price. but Judge I must close. I will see you as soon as I can. I hope you have left me Instructions at Sioux City.

Respectfully Yours
James A Sawyers

McClain went by the way of California. the stage was so crowded he could not get on.

Bibliography

Manuscript Collections and Unpublished Material

Arapaho Tribe. Box 11, Folder 3. Grace Hebard Collection. American Heritage Center. University of Wyoming.

Bennett, Lyman G. Collection R274. Western Historical Manuscript Collection. University of Missouri–Rolla.

Bowman, Dan H. Manuscript Collection. Montana Historical Society.

Camp, Walter Mason. Papers, 1905–1925. MSS 57. L. Tom Perry Special Collections Library. Harold B. Lee Library. Brigham Young University.

——. Papers. Lilly Library. Indiana University.

Connor, P. E. Box 33, Folder 28. Grace Hebard Collection. American Heritage Center. University of Wyoming.

Dodge, Grenville M. Manuscript Collection. Iowa State Historical Society.

Edwards, Edward H. Letters, 1865–1867. Beinecke Rare Book and Manuscript Library. Yale University.

"Frank North, The White Chief of the Pawnees." Unpublished manuscript. File RG 2321. North Manuscript Collection. Nebraska State Historical Society. Lincoln, Nebraska.

Holman, A. M. Biographical Material. Sioux City Public Library.

——. Biographical Material. Pearl Research Center. Sioux City Public Museum.

Jarrot, Vital. Letter to D. N. Cooney, 5 October 1865. Reference Library. Fort Laramie National Historic Site.

Jewett Family Papers, 1861, 1867. Collection Number 87–11. Special Collections Department. University Library. University of Nevada–Reno.

Johnson, George W. Letter of 18 December 1865. Fort Phil Kearny State Historic Site. Banner, Wyoming.

Kidd, James H. Papers, 1861–1910. Bentley Historical Library. University of Michigan.

Lee, C. M. Diary. K. Ross Toole Archives. University of Montana.

[Miller diary.] Powder River Expedition. Microfilm roll #129. Notes from an unknown soldier who was a member of the expedition. Kansas State Historical Society. Topeka, Kansas.

Nash, Edwin R. Diary. MSS82570. Manuscript Division. Library of Congress.

North, Frank Joshua. Manuscript File. Collection Number RG 2321. Nebraska State Historical Society.

North, Luther H. Box 40, Folder 33. Grace Hebard Collection. American Heritage Center. University of Wyoming.

O'Brien, Nicholas J. Vertical File. Wyoming State Archives. Cheyenne, Wyoming.

——. Box 40, Folder 35. Grace Hebard Collection. American Heritage Center. University of Wyoming.

Peck, W. H., ed. Collection of reports from Powder River Expedition furnished by Sen. Fred J. Toman, February 1943. Carter County Museum. Ekalaka, Montana.

Rockafellow, B. F. Collection. MSS 530, File Folder #1. Colorado Historical Society.

Sawyers, J. A. Biographical Material. Sioux City Public Library. Sioux City, Iowa.

——. Letter A. W. Hubbard, 10 November 1865. Sioux City Public Museum. Pearl Research Center. Sioux City, Iowa.

Sorenson, Alfred. "A Quarter of a Century on the Frontier or The Adventures of Major Frank North, the 'White Chief of the Pawnees.'" Undated manuscript, circa 1885. MS448, Frank Joshua North Collection, Nebraska State Historical Society.

Thomas, Charles. Letter to his brother, 16 April 1865. Furnished by Ron Tillotson, Hardin, Illinois.

——. Letter to Charles Curtis, 2 July 1894. Reference Library. Fort Laramie National Historic Site.

Tillotson, Ron. "Prominent Events in the Life of Charles Lawrence Thomas." Unpublished paper by great-great-grandson of Thomas. Hardin, Illinois.

Tongue River Fight. Box 9, Folder 15. Grace Hebard Collection. American Heritage Center. University of Wyoming.

Wilcox, John. Letter to sister, 23 April 1865. Reference Library. Fort Laramie National Historic Site.

SECONDARY SOURCES

Adams, Charles. "Raiding a Hostile Village." National Tribune. 11 February 1898.

Becher, Ronald. Massacre along the Medicine Road. Caldwell, Id.: Caxton Press, 1999.

Benson, Joe. *The Traveler's Guide to the Pony Express Trail.* Helena, Mont.: Falcon Press, 1995.

Beyer, Walter F., and Oscar F. Keydel. *Deeds of Valor.* Vol. 2. Detroit: Perrien-Keydel Company, 1907.

Blevins, Winfred. *Dictionary of the American West.* New York: Facts on File, Inc., 1993.

Bray, Kingsley M. *Crazy Horse: A Lakota Life.* Norman: University of Oklahoma Press, 2006.

Brown, Dee. *Bury My Heart At Wounded Knee.* New York: Holt, Rinehart & Winston, 1970.

———. *Fort Phil Kearny: An American Saga.* Lincoln: University of Nebraska Press, 1962.

———. *The Galvanized Yankees.* Lincoln: University of Nebraska Press, 1986.

Brown, J. Willard. *Signal Corps, U.S.A., in the War of the Rebellion.* New York: Amo Press, 1974.

Bruce, Robert. *The Fighting Norths and Pawnee Scouts.* Lincoln: Nebraska State Historical Society, 1932.

———. "The Powder River Expedition of 1865." *United States Army Recruiting News*, 1 August, 1 and 15 September, 1 and 15 October 1928.

Burnett, F. G. "History of the Western Division of the Powder River Expedition." *Annals of Wyoming* 8, no. 3 (January 1932).

Campbell, Walter S. (Stanley Vestal). *Jim Bridger, Mountain Man.* Lincoln: University of Nebraska Press, 1970.

Clodfelter, Michael. *The Dakota War: The United States Versus the Sioux, 1862–1865.* Jefferson, N.C.: McFarland & Company, 1998.

Coutant, Dr. C. G. *History of Wyoming and the Far West.* Vol. 2. New York: Argonaut Press, Ltd., 1966.

Cozzens, Peter. *The Long War for the Northern Plains: Eyewitness to the Indian Wars, 1865–1890.* Mechanicsburg, Penn.: Stackpole Books, 2004.

David, Robert Beebe. *Finn Burnett, Frontiersman.* Mechanicsburg, Penn.: Stackpole Books, 2003.

Doyle, Susan Badger. *Journeys to the Land of Gold.* 2 vols. Helena: Montana Historical Society Press, 2000.

Essin, Emmitt M. *Shavetails & Bell Sharps: The History of the U.S. Army Mule.* Lincoln: University of Nebraska Press, 1997.

Fowler, Loretta. *Arapaho Politics, 1851–1978.* Lincoln: University of Nebraska Press, 1982.

Franzwa, Gregory M. *Maps of the Oregon Trail.* St. Louis: The Patrice Press, 1990.

Genoa, Nebraska, Historical Stars. Genoa, Nebr.: Genoa City Office, [n.d.].

Greene, Jerome A., and Douglas D. Scott. *Finding Sand Creek.* Norman: University of Oklahoma Press, 2004.

Geyer, Patricia Wight. *Sheldon L. Wight: His Story.* Charlotte, Mich.: Charlotte Lithograph, Inc., 1998.

Grinnell, George Bird. *The Fighting Cheyennes.* Norman: University of Oklahoma Press, 1955.

——. *Two Great Scouts and Their Pawnee Battalion.* Lincoln: University of Nebraska Press, 1973.

Hafen, LeRoy R., and Ann W. Hafen. *Powder River Campaigns and Sawyers Expedition of 1865.* Glendale, Calif.: The Arthur H. Clark Company, 1961.

Hafen, LeRoy R., and Francis Marion Young. *Fort Laramie and the Pageant of the West, 1834–1890.* Lincoln: University of Nebraska Press.

Halaas, David Fridtjof, and Andrew E. Masich. *Halfbreed.* Cambridge, Mass.: Da Capo Press, 2004.

Hampton, H. D. "The Powder River Expedition 1865." *Montana: The Magazine of Western History* 14, no. 4 (Autumn 1964).

History of the Arkansas Valley, Colorado. Chicago: G. L. Baskin and Company, Historical Publishers, 1884.

Holmes, Louis A. *Fort McPherson, Nebraska, Fort Cottonwood, Nebraska Territory.* Lincoln: Johnsen Press Company, 1963.

Humfreville, J. Lee. *Twenty Years Among Our Hostile Indians.* Mechanicsburg, Pennsylvania: Stackpole Books, 2002,

Hull, Myra B., ed. "Soldiering on the High Plains: The Diary of Lewis Byram Hull, 1864–1866," *Kansas Historical Quarterly* 7, no.1 (February 1938). Kansas State Historical Society.

Hyde, George E. *Life of George Bent.* Norman: University of Oklahoma Press, 1968.

——. *Red Cloud's Folk.* Norman: University of Oklahoma Press, 1937.

Hyde, William, and Howard L. Conrad, eds. *Encyclopedia of the History of Saint Louis.* New York: Southern Publishing Company, 1899.

Jacobsen, Jacques Noel, Jr. *Regulations and Notes for the Uniform of the Army of the United States, 1861.* Union City, Tenn.: Pioneer Press, 1990.

Johnson, Dorothy M. *The Bloody Bozeman.* New York: McGraw-Hill Book Company, 1971.

Johnston, Florence. "The Powder River Expedition," *Second Biennial Report of the State Historian of the State of Wyoming.* Period ending September 30, 1922.

Jones, Robert Huhn. *Guarding the Overland Trails: The Eleventh Ohio Cavalry in the Civil War.* Spokane, Wash.: The Arthur H. Clark Company, 2005.

Kautz, August V. *The 1865 Customs of Service for Non-commissioned Officers and Soldiers.* Mechanicsburg, Penn.: Stackpole Books, 2001.

Klokner, James B. *The Officer's Corp of Custer's Seventh Cavalry 1866–1876.* At-glen, Penn.: Shiffer Military History, 2007.

Knudsen, Dean. *An Eye for History: The Paintings of William Henry Jackson.* Gering, Nebr.: The Oregon Trail Museum Association, 1997.

Luebers, H. L. "William Bent's Family." *Colorado Magazine* (January 1936).

Longacre, Edward G. "Unwilling Frontiersmen." *Michigan History Magazine* 82, no. 4 (July/August 1998).

Madsen, Brigham D. *Glory Hunter: A Biography of Patrick Edward Connor.* Salt Lake City: University of Utah Press, 1990.

Mattes, Merrill J. *The Great Platte River Road.* Lincoln: University of Nebraska Press, 1987.

McDermott, John D. *Circle of Fire: The Indian War of 1865.* Mechanicsburg, Penn.: Stackpole Books, 2003.

Michno, Gregory F. *Encyclopedia of Indian Wars: Western Battles and Skirmishes, 1850–1890.* Missoula, Mont.: Mountain Press Publishing Company, 2003.

———. *Battle at Sand Creek: The Military Perspective.* El Segundo, Calif.: Upton and Sons, Publishers, 2004.

Murray, Robert A. *Military Posts in the Powder River Country of Wyoming, 1865–1894.* Buffalo, Wyo.: The Office, 1968.

———. *The Army Moves West.* Fort Collins, Colo.: Old Army Press, 1981.

Nevins, Allan. *War for the Union, 1864–1865.* Vol. 4. New York: Charles Scribner, 1971.

Paul, R. Eli, ed. "A Galvanized Yankee along the Niobrara River." *Nebraska History Quarterly Magazine* 70, no. 2 (Summer 1989).

Rogers, Fred B. *Soldiers of the Overland.* San Francisco: The Grabhorn Press, 1938.

Scott, Douglas D. *Custer's Heroes: The Little Bighorn Medals of Honor.* Wake Forest, N.C.: AST Press, 2007.

Service, Alex. *The Life and Letters of Caspar W. Collins.* Casper, Wyo.: City of Casper, 2000.

Shambaugh, Benjamin F., ed. *The Iowa Journal of History and Politics.* Vol. 20. Des Moines: The State Historical Society of Iowa, 1922.

Smith, J. Gregg. "Powder River Expedition." *True West Magazine* (April 1967).

Springer, Charles M. *Soldiering in Sioux Country, 1865.* Edited by Benjamin Franklin Cooling III. San Diego: Frontier Heritage Press, 1971.

Steffen, Randy. *The Horse Soldier, 1776–1943.* Vol. 2. Norman: University of Oklahoma Press, 1978.

Stevens, Walter B. *Saint Louis: The Fourth City.* St. Louis: S.J. Clark Publishing, 1889.

Sully, Langdon. *No Tears for the General: The Life of Alfred Sully, 1821–1879.* Palo Alto, Calif.: American West Publishing Company, 1975.

Trenholm, Virginia Cole. *The Arapahoes, Our People.* Norman: University of Oklahoma Press, 1970.

Thomas, Dean S. *Cannons: An Introduction to Civil War Artillery.* Gettysburg, Penn.: Thomas Publications, 1985.

Unrau, William E., ed. *Tending the Talking Wire.* Salt Lake City: University of Utah Press, 1979.

Utley, Robert M. *Frontiersmen in Blue: The United States Army and the Indian, 1848–1865.* Lincoln: University of Nebraska Press, 1967.

———. *The Lance and the Shield: The Life and Times of Sitting Bull.* New York: Henry Holt and Co. Inc., 1993.

Varley, James F. *Brigham and the Brigadier.* Tucson, Ariz.: Westernlore Press, 1989.

Wagner, David E. *Powder River Odyssey: Nelson Cole's Western Campaign of 1865.* Norman: The Arthur H. Clark Company, 2009.

Ware, Eugene F. *The Indian War of 1864.* New York: St. Martin's Press, 1960.

Wittenberg, Eric J. *One of Custer's Wolverines.* Kent, Ohio: Kent State University Press, 2000.

Wright, James. *No More Gallant a Deed.* St. Paul: Minnesota Historical Society, 2001.

INTERNET SOURCES

Civil War Soldiers and Sailors System. National Park Service. http://www.civilwar.nps.gov/cwss.

ELECTRONIC RESOURCES

American Civil War Research Database. CD-ROM. Historical Data Systems, Inc., 2002.

Topo USA. CD-ROM. Version 5.0. DeLorme, 2004.

The War of the Rebellion: A Compilation of the Official Records of the Union and Confederate Armies. CD-ROM. The Guild Press of Indiana, Inc., 1997.

Index